How To Stop Sinning

Any Type Of Sin

by Alan Ballou

Jedidiah Speak

Copyright ©2013 Alan P. Ballou

Acknowledgments

Praise God! All of the glory and honor belongs to my Lord Jesus Christ. Amen. I am absolutely nothing without the Lord my God, and I am so grateful for His grace, love, mercy, patience, kindness, and gifts that He has poured out upon His people. May the Lord be blessed forever. Praise God, hallelujah!

I am very thankful for my wife Lucie, who is by my side everywhere we minister to God's people, and has dropped everything to help me write this book. She has worked harder than I have in editing the unreadable early drafts. If you, the reader, could view my rough drafts, you would know that the Lord has given my wife a special gift. I thank the Lord for her, and may the Lord continue to enable us to help others through His Word.

CONTENTS

3. THROUGH LOVE   66

FORWARD

I lived a very difficult life during my teenage years, but I am not going to blame it on anything but my own ignorance and sinfulness. While living in foster homes, I was forced to attend church services, but I didn't understand anything at that time except that I was running from God.

I don't remember anything that was preached, but I can tell you that there was some yelling in my direction. I knew who he was talking to, but I wasn't going to stand up in front of the whole church.

As soon as I got to a place to where I wasn't forced to attend church services, I stopped attending, and soon afterwards I dropped out of high school as well. My destruction continued as I kept running from God.

At age seventeen, I was homeless after being kicked out of a shelter for disobedience. A little old lady allowed me to sleep in an abandoned part of her shot gun house, and a godly lady named Miss Mosley sent me two sandwiches everyday. May the Lord bless them tremendously. No one really knew my situation because I was too embarrassed to tell anyone.

I was a total misfit and I hated the world to the point that I wished I had never been born. My destruction continued and so I joined the Marines to keep from freezing to death and to stay out of jail. Ruin and misery continued to mark my path and I became a drunk among other things, to silence my conscience.

At age nineteen, I was in Beaufort, South Carolina at a little country store in the middle of nowhere. A Pentecostal woman pulled up and parked while I was in the store. She was clearly looking for someone from the moment she parked. She walked into the store as if she knew exactly where she was going, and who she was going to see.

Once she saw me, she never looked away. I changed aisles and she turned in order to meet me head on. I had never seen her before and I was a thousand miles away from anyone who knew me, but she started telling me my life story. She was full of fire.

I thought that God had sent her, but at that time, I didn't want any part of it. It scared me so badly that I walked out as she continued talking to me. After that I became worse than I had ever been. From that day, until I was age twenty-four, my life was a blur. I was a miserable drunk and hated everybody and everything.

I straightened up a little and at age twenty-seven. I found a church where the pastor didn't yell and nobody challenged me or inquired about what I believed. I still didn't know the first thing about the Bible, but at this church I didn't have to know anything. Finally, I felt good in church, but I knew something was missing.

To me, church was something I did in order to fit in with people who were going to Heaven some day. However, there wasn't any difference in the way I lived. I was still caught up in sins. I didn't get drunk as much, but I still had to drink in order to deal with everyday life. Even when I tried my best to do what was right, I still did wrong.

In the early nineties, after making a mess of everything I had touched for the past thirty years or so, I was at a breaking point. I didn't know what to do or what to say, but I knelt down and in my own broken words I asked God to forgive me, to save me, and to show me what to do. Praise God! That same day I had no desire to do the things I used to do. In fact, the only thing I wanted to do was read the Bible.

God saved me and changed me. He placed His Word in my heart and made me a different person. It didn't happen overnight, since there were still areas of my life that I did not want to give up right away, but finally it happened. Praise God, halleluiah. The Lord has changed me.

Now I want to help as many people as possible. My mission is to make disciples of Jesus Christ. I serve Christians, who contact me from all over the world, in matters concerning deliverance and healing, free of charge.

I began to hear the verses in my conscience. As people were speaking, the verses either confirmed or rejected what was being said. Praise God. I started teaching Sunday School, even though I had never attended before, but I knew that it was what God wanted me to do.

Back as far as elementary school, every time a teacher would call on me in class, or even look in my direction, I would start crying. I used to have a fear of crowds unless I was drinking. Now I have no fear teaching the Word of God as long as the verses are flowing in my conscience. If the Lord is with me, I can teach, but if He is not with me, I'm a duck out of water. He has turned my weakness into a strength. Praise God.

Today I never take notes or focus on what I will be saying before I teach. I rely on the Holy Spirit to reveal to me what needs to be taught. The only time I know for sure what I am teaching beforehand, is when I am teaching at a healing or deliverance seminar. Praise the Lord!

For the past nineteen years, the Lord has allowed me to teach weekly classes in my community at different denominations, homeless shelters, and church functions. Praise God. The Lord has allowed me to help and teach His people from all over the world in matters concerning sin and healing through the internet. Wherever the Lord opens a door for me, I willingly conduct healing and deliverance seminars.

This book is written to help people like me, who want to stop committing sins that lead to death. I want to help everyone, but especially people who may have made a mess of their life and don't know how to turn things around.

How do we find the help we need in a circle of people who somehow seem to not have a problem with sins that lead to death? It's difficult to find someone to talk to who can answer questions with the truth, and who will not use our information inappropriately; gossipers. I want to give people the tools that I used to escape sins that lead to death, and I want to help them along the way if they have questions or concerns.

God loves all of us (John 3:16) and Jesus Christ died for the sins of the whole world (1 John 2:1-2). God wants everyone to be saved (1 Timothy 2:4), and all to come to repentance (2 Peter 3:9). Therefore, I want to help all people. Praise God.

You will see results, since God's Word cannot fail. I want you to be totally set free from sins that lead to death without having to battle a whole lifetime. If you have to struggle with the same sins year after year, then you are not free.

As you read this book, I want you to test what I am saying. Double check the scriptures in order to make sure that your beliefs are in line with what is actually written in the Bible.

One of the biggest mistakes I have found is that many Christians do not believe the very Bible they carry every week. Deception slips in when we do not know the whole truth for ourselves (Ephesians 4:13-14). We should use the Bible to verify, test, and approve what we think we know, and everything we hear (1 Thessalonians 5:21, 2 Corinthians 10:3-5). Those who are mature use the Word of God constantly (Hebrews 5:11).

I'm simply asking that you check the verses that I have mentioned since the power of God is in the Word of God (Romans 1:16). My desire is that you allow that power to judge your views. Allow it to change you. This entire book is an attempt to do just that.

I have listed as many verses as I legally can in this book. The maximum is five hundred verses from one Bible. I have taught different classes in different denominations using the New King James Version, the New International Version, and the Amplified Bible. My favorite is the NKJV, but I believe the NIV (1984) is good for people who are just starting out, and the Amplified Bible is great for studying.

Please look the verses up in your Bible, but I know from experience that what I am going to show you in this book will work with the verses I have given you. If you have a question, or if I can be of service to you, free of charge, please contact me. I am a servant. May the Lord bless you. www.howtostopsinning.com

1. THE QUESTION

THE BLOOD
OBEY THE DOCTRINE
THE CHALLENGE
ANSWER THE QUESTION
NEVER SPEAK AGAINST SCRIPTURE
THE QUESTION

1

THE QUESTION

✿✿✿

Can Christians stop sinning? I usually accept questions openly while I am teaching, but I didn't want to answer that question at the very beginning of my deliverance seminar to a room full of alcoholics, drug addicts, sex offenders, and the like. Many of them had been trying to break their addictions far longer than I had been saved, and I could sense they were eager to prove that no one could stop sinning.

I don't consider "if we can stop sinning" to be a difficult question because the answer is clearly written in scripture. However, in order to reach people who have accepted and believed something that is not in the Bible, we have to break it to them gently to keep them from walking out before they hear the evidence (2 Timothy 2:24-26).

Israel was on fire for God, but their zeal for God was not based on what was actually written (Romans 10:1-2). If we are not careful we can wind up in a similar situation being filled with all types of deceptive philosophy (Colossians 2:8). We have to test everything and hold on to the good (2 Thessalonians 5:21, Acts 17:11).

As believers, none of our beliefs should be against what is actually written in our Bible (2 Corinthians 10:3-5, 1 Corinthians 4:6-7, Proverbs 30:6). That in itself should be a red flag in our mind. Check the verses.

THE BLOOD

Can Christians stop sinning? The Bible does not say that we cannot stop sinning. However, it does say that we were born under the power of sin (Romans 3:9, 7:14, Galatians 3:22), but the blood of Jesus Christ delivers Christians from the dominion (power) of darkness (Colossians 1:13, Revelation 1:5). Please check that truth with some of my favorite versions of the Bible below.

Colossians 1:13
13 He has delivered us from the power of darkness and conveyed us into the kingdom of the Son of His love, NKJV

Colossians 1:13
13 For he has rescued us from the dominion of darkness and brought us into the kingdom of the Son he loves, NIV

Colossians 1:13
13 [The Father] has delivered and drawn us to Himself out of the control and the dominion of darkness and has transferred us into the kingdom of the Son of His love, AMP

Revelation 1:5
...To Him who loved us and washed us from our sins in His own blood, NKJV

Revelation 1:5
...To him who loves us and has freed us from our sins by his blood, NIV

Revelation 1:5
...To Him Who ever loves us and has once [for all] loosed

and freed us from our sins by His own blood, AMP

Jesus Christ has delivered those who are in His Kingdom from the power of darkness (Colossians 1:13 above). According to Ephesians 2:4-6, when we were saved we were seated with Christ in His Kingdom. Therefore, being born under the power of sin doesn't mean that we remain that way after accepting Jesus Christ as Lord, or that we cannot stop sinning. Praise God.

This is also evident in the testimony of new converts. Many people are suddenly freed from sins that lead to death when they first become Christians. I'm sure that you have heard life-changing testimonies from people who have recently accepted Jesus as Lord. However, most of them find themselves caught up in sin again a few years later.

OBEY THE DOCTRINE

Even after being delivered from the power of darkness, we could still be a slave to sin or given over to our sinful nature (2 Peter 2:19, Romans 6:14-16). In these cases sin can still control us to where the evil we don't want to do, we will be forced to continue doing (Romans 7:18-20). However, this does not have to be a permanent condition, since the remedies are written in the Bible alongside the conditions. We have clear instructions to follow in order not to be a victim of sin's control as mentioned in Romans 6:17-18 below.

Romans 6:17-18
17 But God be thanked that though you were slaves of sin, yet you obeyed from the heart that form of doctrine to which you were delivered. 18 And having been set free from sin, you became slaves of righteousness. NKJV

Romans 6:17-18
17 But thanks be to God that, though you used to be slaves to sin, you wholeheartedly obeyed the form of teaching to which you were entrusted. 18 You have been set free from sin and have become slaves to righteousness. NIV

Romans 6:17-18
17 But thank God, though you were once slaves of sin, you have become obedient with all your heart to the standard of teaching in which you were instructed and to which you were committed. 18 And having been set free from sin, you have become the servants of righteousness (of conformity to the divine will in thought, purpose, and action). AMP

In certain situations, we call the effects of being a slave to sin an addiction, but if we wholeheartedly obey the instructions, we will be set free from the control of sin according to those verses. With such a doctrine written to guide Christians into being set free from the control of sin, the only reason we would have to continue in sin is if we didn't know the truth (lack of knowledge), we didn't believe the truth (unbelief), or if we did not want to obey that doctrine (rebellion).

We are set free from the dominion of darkness through the blood of Jesus, and there is a way that Christians can be set free from being a slave to sin according to Romans 6:17-18 above. Therefore, can Christians stop sinning?

Some would argue that there are sins of omission to which I would say, "show me the verse and I will believe it." James 4:17 says that anyone who knows the good he should be doing and doesn't do it commits sin, but not everyone knows what they should be doing. Sins of omission, for those under the new agreement (New Testament), apply to those who know the good they ought to be doing.

There are many different things that the Bible calls sin and we will cover them later, but the bottom line is that Christians can be set free from the power of sin, and set free from sin's control according to what is written in the Bible. Let me ask you again. Can Christians stop sinning?

THE CHALLENGE

If we were set free from the power of sin, and set free from being a slave to sin in accordance with Romans 6:17-18 above, then sin itself would no longer be able to make us commit sins. In that position we would have to be tempted into sinning, and then choose to sin in order to continue in it. That's where all Christians should be in their walk of

18

faith according to 1 Corinthians 10:13 below.

1 Corinthians 10:13
13 No temptation has overtaken you except such as is common to man; but God is faithful, who will not allow you to be tempted beyond what you are able, but with the temptation will also make the way of escape, that you may be able to bear it. NKJV

1 Corinthians 10:13
13 No temptation has seized you except what is common to man. And God is faithful; he will not let you be tempted beyond what you can bear. But when you are tempted, he will also provide a way out so that you can stand up under it. NIV

God will not allow us to be tempted into sinning beyond what we are able to stand up under, according to that verse. What does that tell you about sin? If nothing can force us to sin, we would have to choose to sin instead of choosing God's way out. Think about that. If we were in a position where we could not be tempted beyond what we could bear, then we would have to choose to sin in order to sin.

We might be ignorant of this whole process and not know to look for God's way out, but we would still have to choose to yield to the temptation in order to commit sin in that situation. Therefore, once we learn the doctrine that delivers us from sin, the question becomes if we want to stop sinning. Consequently, the challenge is being able to convince Christians to put child-like faith in what the Bible says, and to destroy any beliefs that are against what is written (2 Corinthians 10:3-5, Luke 18:17).

ANSWER THE QUESTION

What does the Bible say, and how do you read it? That was my answer to the question as to whether or not I believed Christians could stop sinning. "If it is in your Bible, I will accept it and believe it," I added, "but if it is not in there, I will not accept it." I was taking a chance that he didn't have some strange new Bible that I had not heard about.

I didn't answer him directly because I wanted the answer to come from the Bible he trusted. That way, it would not be a question of what I believed or which Bible I used, but did he believe his Bible?

Besides that, I believe that if I had answered the question directly he probably would have stormed out in protest, taking as many followers as he could with him because they believed what he was saying (Ephesians 4:13-14). I call that face value. Many put all of their trust in a person rather than checking everything with scripture, which is what we should be doing (1 Thessalonians 5:21, 2 Corinthians 10:3-5, Acts 17:11).

He quickly accepted my challenge in front of everybody, smiling, as if he was going to prove his case, but shock was soon to be his expression; as well as everybody else's in the room who had believed that Christians could not stop sinning. Many of us have excuses we have learned to rely on that sound like verses when it comes to justifying sin, but finding an actual verse or passage of scripture that backs up that belief is impossible.

"All have sinned and fallen short" declared one, and "The good we want to do we cannot carry it out" said another. It was as if everyone in the room had been taught what to say before the deliverance seminar had even begun, but not any of the partial verses they were quoting were in the context they were written in.

The leader of the rebellion then shouted, "If any man saith he is without sin he is a liar." I answered him first. I said, "What that verse actually says is that if we claim to be without sin we deceive ourselves and the truth is not in us." It does not say "if we claim we can stop sinning," like you are interpreting it to be (1 John 1:8).

Yes, we have all sinned, but the Bible does not say that Christians cannot stop sinning, but the exact opposite. There are things we can do in order to never stumble or fall again according to 2 Peter 1:10 below. Is that in your Bible?

2 Peter 1:10
10 Therefore, brethren, be even more diligent to make your call and election sure, for if you do these things you will never stumble. NKJV

2 Peter 1:10
10 Therefore, my brothers, be all the more eager to make your calling and election sure. For if you do these things, you will never fall. NIV

Wouldn't you say that's a long way from "we always fall short" which is how some people interpret Romans 3:23? We have all fallen short, but that doesn't mean that we have to continue falling short, since there is something we can do that will guarantee that we will never fall again (2 Peter 1:10 above).

In fact, the Bible is very clear when it comes to continuing in sin after being delivered from darkness through the blood of Jesus, and knowing the truth.

Hebrews 10:26-27
26 For if we sin willfully after we have received the knowledge of the truth, there no longer remains a sacrifice for sins, 27 but a certain fearful expectation of judgment, and fiery indignation which will devour the adversaries. NKJV

Hebrews 10:26-27
26 If we deliberately keep on sinning after we have received the knowledge of the truth, no sacrifice for sins is left, 27 but only a fearful expectation of judgment and of raging fire that will consume the enemies of God. NIV

Is it ok to continue in sin after we have received the knowledge of the truth? Since we have been delivered from darkness through the blood of Jesus, given a doctrine to follow that will set us free from sin's control, and put into a position where we cannot be tempted beyond what we can bear, what would be our reason to willfully continue sinning? Obviously there is something that we have missed if we think that it is ok to continue in sin.

Therefore, take a good look at one of the verses that people have learned to use as an excuse to continue in sin; 1 John 1:8 below. Let's also read 1 John 2:1, 3:4-10, and 5:18 which are all contained in the same letter. Read them out loud a few times to decide for yourself if you accept and believe the written Word of God, or if you have come to believe something that is against what is written.

1 John 1:8-2:1
8 If we say that we have no sin, we deceive ourselves, and the truth is not in us. 9 If we confess our sins, He is faithful and just to forgive us our sins and to cleanse us from all unrighteousness. 10 If we say that we have not sinned, we make Him a liar, and His word is not in us. 2:1 My little children, these things I write to you, so that you may not sin. And if anyone sins, we have an Advocate with the Father, Jesus Christ the righteous. NKJV

1 John 1:8-2:1
8 If we claim to be without sin, we deceive ourselves and the truth is not in us. 9 If we confess our sins, he is faithful and just and will forgive us our sins and purify us from all unrighteousness. 10 If we claim we have not sinned, we make him out to be a liar and his word has no place in our lives. 2:1 My dear children, I write this to you so that you will not sin. But if anybody does sin, we have one who speaks to the Father in our defense — Jesus Christ, the Righteous One. NIV

If we say that we have no sin or if we say that we have not sinned we are deceived and liars. However, that does not say that we cannot stop sinning. In fact, within the next few verses John tells us that the reason he wrote his letter was so that we would "not sin" (verse 2:1 above). Imagine that.

How can John write us for the purpose of not sinning, and at the same time imply that we cannot stop sinning? He is not saying that we cannot stop sinning, but that all of us "have" sinned and "have" fallen short (Romans 3:23).

Yes, I have sinned, but by the blood of Jesus Christ and the doctrine that delivers us and sets us free from sin, I have stopped committing sins that lead to death and I want to teach you how to do the same, according to what is actually written in the Bible. Praise God, hallelujah!

There are sins that lead to death and sins that do not lead to death (1 John 5:16-17). We will cover this in detail later, but read Galatians 5:19-21, 1 Corinthians 6:9-10 , and Ephesians 5:3-5 for a list of sins that will keep us out of the Kingdom of God if we do not stop them.

A few verses before 1 John 1:8, John tells us that if we walk in darkness we do not have fellowship with the Father (1 John 1:5-7). Therefore, he couldn't possibly be saying that we cannot come out of darkness, and besides, we have been called out of darkness (1 Peter 2:9). Check those verses. If you are not convinced yet, please allow the rest of John's letter to explain itself.

1 John 3:4-10
4 Whoever commits sin also commits lawlessness, and sin is lawlessness. 5 And you know that He was manifested to take away our sins, and in Him there is no sin. 6 Whoever abides in Him does not sin. Whoever sins has neither seen Him nor known Him. 7 Little children, let no one deceive you. He who practices righteousness is righteous, just as He is righteous. 8 He who sins is of the devil, for the devil has sinned from the beginning. For this purpose the Son of God was manifested, that He might destroy the works of the devil. 9 Whoever has been born of God does not sin, for His seed remains in him; and he cannot sin, because he has been born of God. 10 In this the children of God and the children of the devil are manifest: Whoever does not practice righteousness is not of God, nor is he who does not love his brother. NKJV

1 John 3:4-10
4 Everyone who sins breaks the law; in fact, sin is lawlessness. 5 But you know that he appeared so that he might take away our sins. And in him is no sin. 6 No one who lives in him keeps on sinning. No one who continues to

23

sin has either seen him or known him. 7 Dear children, do not let anyone lead you astray. He who does what is right is righteous, just as he is righteous. 8 He who does what is sinful is of the devil, because the devil has been sinning from the beginning. The reason the Son of God appeared was to destroy the devil's work. 9 No one who is born of God will continue to sin, because God's seed remains in him; he cannot go on sinning, because he has been born of God. 10 This is how we know who the children of God are and who the children of the devil are: Anyone who does not do what is right is not a child of God; nor is anyone who does not love his brother. NIV

The verses above should erase any doubt in your mind that Christians can and should stop sinning, unless you do not believe, or you are blinded by Satan (2 Corinthians 4:3-4). In this case, ask God the Father in the name of our Lord Jesus Christ to enable you to come to Jesus (John 6:44, 60-69), or forgive you for speaking against the truth, respectfully. After that, try reading the verses over and over again, out loud, until your eyes are opened and you can see them.

Undoubtedly, the Apostle John is not telling us that we cannot stop sinning, on the first page of his letter, and that we can stop sinning on the second, third and fifth pages of his letter (1 John 5:18). Therefore, anyone who quotes 1 John 1:8-10 in such a way as to imply that we cannot stop sinning is blind and does not have the truth living in them. We cannot interpret any verse in such a way that our interpretation will violate other verses in the same letter, or in different letters.

Clearly, Christians can stop sinning and should stop if they have been born of God. Take a look at what John wrote on the fifth page of his letter and imagine that you were sitting there at the first reading of it.

1 John 5:18
18 We know that whoever is born of God does not sin; but he who has been born of God keeps himself, and the wicked one does not touch him. NKJV

1 John 5:18
18 We know that anyone born of God does not continue to sin; the one who was born of God keeps him safe, and the evil one cannot harm him. NIV

After hearing verses from page two, three, and five of John's letter, would you have to wonder if he meant that we cannot stop sinning on the first page of his letter? The person "born of God" does not continue in sin. Is that crystal clear? Can Christians stop sinning?

NEVER SPEAK AGAINST SCRIPTURE

Anyone in any position in any church can be as blind as a bat when it comes to Kingdom teaching (Matthew 13:19, Ephesians 4:17-19). Many do not know that by simply speaking against the faith, we can fall away from the faith (1 Timothy 6:20-21).

Never speak against the Word of God and know that those who do, simply do not have the verses they speak against living in them. They may have been able to see them at one time, but they have been taken from them because of the deceptive philosophy they came to accept and proclaim (Mark 4:24-25, 1 Timothy 6:20-21, 2 Corinthians 4:13).

We can easily be tricked into believing something that isn't in line with the truth when we do not know it for ourselves (Ephesians 4:13-14). Once we believe a lie and proclaim it, then it becomes truth for us, but we are not free (1 Timothy 6:20-21). Only the truth sets us free (John 8:31-36, 17:17).

Within the righteousness that comes by faith, there are things that we should say as well as things we should never say (Romans 10:6-8). Never speak against what is written and never say amen (let it be so) to anything that is not in line with what is written.

Read these verses carefully, and you will see that saying Jesus is Lord is only the beginning. People who are righteous, made right in God's eyes by faith, say certain things and refuse to speak certain things.

Romans 10:5-10
5 For Moses writes about the righteousness which is of the

*law, "The man who does those things shall live by them."
6 But the righteousness of faith speaks in this way, "Do
not say in your heart, 'Who will ascend into heaven?'"
(that is, to bring Christ down from above) 7 or, "'Who will
descend into the abyss?'" (that is, to bring Christ up from
the dead). 8 But what does it say? "The word is near you,
in your mouth and in your heart" (that is, the word of faith
which we preach): 9 that if you confess with your mouth
the Lord Jesus and believe in your heart that God has
raised Him from the dead, you will be saved. 10 For with
the heart one believes unto righteousness, and with the
mouth confession is made unto salvation. NKJV*

*Romans 10:5-10
5 Moses describes in this way the righteousness that is
by the law: "The man who does these things will live by
them." 6 But the righteousness that is by faith says: "Do
not say in your heart, 'Who will ascend into heaven?'"
(that is, to bring Christ down) 7 "or 'Who will descend into
the deep?'" (that is, to bring Christ up from the dead). 8
But what does it say? "The word is near you; it is in your
mouth and in your heart," that is, the word of faith we
are proclaiming: 9 That if you confess with your mouth,
"Jesus is Lord," and believe in your heart that God raised
him from the dead, you will be saved. 10 For it is with your
heart that you believe and are justified, and it is with your
mouth that you confess and are saved. NIV*

Notice that at first the Apostle Paul describes the righteousness which comes through observing the Law (the Laws of Moses). Whoever does the works of the Law shall live by them (verse 5 above).

If anyone could obey the whole Law they would be declared righteous (Romans 2:13).The problem with that is that nobody can obey the whole Law (Romans 3:19). Therefore, no one will be declared righteous by observing it, but righteousness is still a requirement to enter the Kingdom of Heaven (Matthew 5:20).

Through the Gospel a different way of obtaining righteousness is revealed, which comes through faith in Jesus Christ to all who believe (Romans 1:16-17, 3:21-22). This is why we seek God's Kingdom and God's righteousness first after we are saved into the Kingdom of Christ (Matthew 6:33, Ephesians 2:6-8). Check the verses.

Knowing that no one will be declared righteous by observing the Laws of Moses (Romans 3:19), makes us able to understand the term "but now" in Romans 3:21. Now a new way of righteousness that comes through faith is revealed in the Gospel (Romans 3:21-23, 1:16-17). It has always been there, since the people of old lived by faith (Hebrews chapter 11), but the Gospel makes it known (reveals it).

This new way of righteousness includes saying certain things and not saying certain things according to verses 6-8 above, but it does not include any of the works of the Law (apart from, Romans 3:21-22). Therefore, we should always be careful to speak in line with the faith (2 Corinthians 4:13), in order that the righteousness that is imputed to us may be fulfilled (James 2:20-24). We will cover this in more detail later. For now know that we cannot speak against scripture and be righteous by faith (Romans 10:5-10 above).

Saying amen to false doctrine is the same as saying it yourself. When is it safe to say amen? After someone reads the Bible word for word say amen. If they interpret the verses they have just read, do not say anything unless you know the truth for yourself. After you know the truth for yourself, then it will be very obvious who does not know it by their fruit, which includes the words they speak (Matthew 12:33-37, Romans 10:6-8, Ephesians 4:13).

Surely something is way off when someone uses a verse out of John's letter as their evidence to say that we cannot stop sinning. It's called blindness. They really can't see the rest of the letter and so in their eyes they are not trying to deceive people.

It's not that they are evil people since anyone can be blind in certain areas (1 Corinthians 10:12, Galatians 6:3-4), but listening to them use 1 John 1:8 as an excuse is like using a bed sheet to cover up a Boeing 747, and saying, "See, there's no plane there."

Whatever part of the Bible they speak against is simply one area of deception. No one can speak against what they believe unless they

27

are deceived, or they deliberately decide to lie in order to protect their denominational beliefs; the fear of men (John 12:42-43).

THE QUESTION

So let me ask you a question. Can Christians stop sinning? After reading the verses, the leader of the group finally said, "Theoretically speaking I guess we can." Praise God! "Theoretically speaking we can" is a very long way from "no we can't!" That stronghold in his thinking was broken by the Word of God because he is a believer (2 Corinthians 10:3-5, Hebrews 4:12). The power of God is in the Word of God (Romans 1:16).

It doesn't matter if we don't understand it now. Don't speak against what the Holy Spirit wrote. We don't fully understand how God raised Jesus from the dead, and yet as Christians we believe what is written, and do not question it.

Don't worry about understanding everything right now. Accept and believe what is written (Proverbs 3:5). Understanding will come as we obey the precepts (Psalm 111:10, 119:98-105).

Jesus will open our understanding once we have walked with Him, just as He did with the twelve (Luke 24:45, 1 John 5:20). Judging by what is written in Luke 24:45, that should take less than a second.

After reading the verses out of 1 John, about ninety-percent of the people at the meeting agreed that we could stop sinning with a confirming, yes! The remaining were either blinded by Satan (2 Corinthians 4:3-4), or they refused to admit their beliefs because of their particular religion or denomination (John 12:42-43).

John 12:42-43
42 Nevertheless even among the rulers many believed in Him, but because of the Pharisees they did not confess Him, lest they should be put out of the synagogue; 43 for they loved the praise of men more than the praise of God. NKJV

John 12:42-43
42 Yet at the same time many even among the leaders believed in him. But because of the Pharisees they would

not confess their faith for fear they would be put out of the synagogue; 43 for they loved praise from men more than praise from God. NIV

However, they could no longer speak against the truth and fool those who now knew it (Ephesians 4:13-14). They were free, and so are you if you believe the verses I have shown you. Praise God, hallelujah!

I want to help you reach a place where no one can trick you, or prevent you from receiving what God has promised us according to what is actually written in the Bible. However, you must believe what is written in your Bible. You must allow the Word of God to judge your attitudes and thoughts (Hebrews 4:12). The Word itself works by itself inside those who believe it (2 Thessalonians 2:13).

I am a believer. My denomination is Christian, and I believe everything that is in the Bible. If we do not believe our own Bible, how can we convince others to believe? Imagine that.

My name is Alan P. Ballou. I am a servant. Lord willing, I am available for questions and ministering (help). As long as the Lord allows me to live, I will continue to serve the body of Christ free of charge. If you have questions, or need help with what I have explained in this book, please contact me through my website www.howtostopsinning.com.

2. By Faith

Continue in your faith
Refusing to change
The Word brings health
Faith is
Use the promises
Obedience through faith
Close your eyes
Spirit of faith
New attitude
Believe
We have an obligation
To the point of retaining it
Hold to the teachings
Take a stand
Kingdom

2

BY FAITH

ೞಲಡಿ

All Christians were given a measure of faith (Romans 12:3). However, I don't think that many of us realize that we can have dead faith (James 2:14-19), or weak faith (Romans 14:1), and not know it.

We can fall away until we shipwreck our faith (1 Timothy 1:18-20), or shrink back from faith until we reach destruction, all the while thinking the devil is on our back (Hebrews 10:36-39). On the other hand, we may have great faith, and not know how to use it (Acts 14:8-10).

We were given the gift of faith, or "the measure of faith," as some people call it, when we accepted Jesus as Lord. However, this is not the only "amount" of faith we will have (Ephesians 2:8, John 6:44).

After accepting Jesus as Lord, we are supposed to pursue faith (1 Timothy 6:11), grow our faith (2 Thessalonians 1:3), increase our faith (2 Corinthians 10:15, Luke 17:5), and abound in faith (2 Corinthians 8:7). Faith also comes by hearing the Word of God (Romans 10:17). Therefore, without question all of us should have more faith than the amount we were given to start with. Sadly that isn't always the case.

In this chapter, I want to make sure that you are continuing in your faith, and that you know how to apply faith with what God has promised us concerning being set free from sin. Although we are going to focus on stopping sin, these principles work in every area of our life because the whole Christian life is lived by faith (Romans 1:16-17).

CONTINUE IN YOUR FAITH

Everyone that was saved through Jesus Christ is required to continue in their faith in order to remain holy in His sight, without blemish, and free from accusation (Colossians 1:21-23, Romans 11:22). Even the worst sinner, who is an enemy of God because of his mindset (Romans 8:5-8), is made holy through Christ's sacrifice, and continues to be holy "if" he continues in his faith.

Colossians 1:21-23
21 And you, who once were alienated and enemies in your mind by wicked works, yet now He has reconciled 22 in the body of His flesh through death, to present you holy, and blameless, and above reproach in His sight 23 if indeed you continue in the faith, grounded and steadfast, and are not moved away from the hope of the gospel which you heard. NKJV

Colossians 1:21-23
21 Once you were alienated from God and were enemies in your minds because of your evil behavior. 22 But now he has reconciled you by Christ's physical body through death to present you holy in his sight, without blemish and free from accusation 23 if you continue in your faith, established and firm, not moved from the hope held out in the gospel. NIV

We do not live by philosophy, but by the Word of God, and His Word says that we are holy, blameless, and above reproach in His sight, if we continue in our faith (Deuteronomy 8:3, Matthew 4:4). The word "if" in verse 23 above sets up a little known condition. If we do not continue in our faith, we do not remain in the same condition we were in when we first came to the Lord.

We have to continue in God's kindness or face being cut off (Romans 11:22). Haven't you noticed that many people stop committing various sins when they accept Jesus as Lord because His blood sets them free from the power of darkness (Colossians 1:12-13), but a few years later they are caught up in the same sins? Nobody explained to them that they needed to continue in their faith.

It is our responsibility to pursue faith through hearing the Word, and to accept what it says without rejecting it. Whoever continues in the Word remains in this process. Whoever does not continue in it no longer follows the Lord and is in danger of being cut off (John 6:53-63, 1 John 2:24, John 15:1-6). Check the verses.

Read Hebrews 10:36-39 below and notice what happens to the Christian who shrinks back from living by faith.

Hebrews 10:36-39
36 For you have need of endurance, so that after you have done the will of God, you may receive the promise: 37 "For yet a little while, And He who is coming will come and will not tarry. 38 Now the just shall live by faith; But if anyone draws back, My soul has no pleasure in him." 39 But we are not of those who draw back to perdition, but of those who believe to the saving of the soul. NKJV

Hebrews 10:36-39
36 You need to persevere so that when you have done the will of God, you will receive what he has promised. 37 For in just a very little while, "He who is coming will come and will not delay. 38 But my righteous one will live by faith. And if he shrinks back, I will not be pleased with him." 39 But we are not of those who shrink back and are destroyed, but of those who believe and are saved. NIV

According to those verses, we have to continue living by faith or we will shrink back to destruction. This one teaching alone will resolve a great number of problems among those who came to the Lord more than four years ago, but are now caught up in the same sins they were involved in before they came (Luke 13:6-9, 2 Peter 2:20-21). The tendency is to be "saved" again, and again, but simple repentance is the answer (1 John 1:9).

What kind of faith do you have, and have you continued growing your faith by hearing the Word of God since you accepted Jesus as Lord (Colossians 1:21-23)? The instructions say to check yourself to see if you are within the faith (2 Corinthians 13:5). Test yourself. If you have not continued in faith since you came to the Lord, then ask the Lord to forgive you and start over today (1 John 1:9).

REFUSING TO CHANGE

Repentance is a change of mind that leads to a change in behavior. When we harden our heart (refuse to change), we don't necessarily stop attending church, singing in the choir, or even preaching, but we stop repenting of sins that are directly against what is written, to the point of blindness (Hebrews 6:4-8, Ephesians 4:17-19).

Ephesians 4:17-19
17 This I say, therefore, and testify in the Lord, that you should no longer walk as the rest of the Gentiles walk, in the futility of their mind, 18 having their understanding darkened, being alienated from the life of God, because of the ignorance that is in them, because of the blindness of their heart; 19 who, being past feeling, have given themselves over to lewdness, to work all uncleanness with greediness. NKJV

Ephesians 4:17-19
17 So I tell you this, and insist on it in the Lord, that you must no longer live as the Gentiles do, in the futility of their thinking. 18 They are darkened in their understanding and separated from the life of God because of the ignorance that is in them due to the hardening of their

34

hearts. 19 Having lost all sensitivity, they have given themselves over to sensuality so as to indulge in every kind of impurity, with a continual lust for more. NIV

The New Testament tells us how to live and insists on us changing. We don't want to be told how to live, and so we stop reading our Bible, or avoid certain passages of scripture. Hardening our heart (refusing to change), or having a blind heart because we put the Word down altogether, is against God's will for our life (Romans 12:1-2, James 1:21). That's like saying, "Jesus, I want you to be my Lord and save me from God's wrath, but I don't want you to tell me what to do."

We don't want to hear the verses that identify darkness, because we are still living in it (John 3:19-21). This is why some people only read stories out of the Old Testament and avoid the New Testament where Kingdom teaching is found (Luke 16:16, John 1:17).

Notice that it is our thinking that becomes useless (futile, verse 17 above). When we stop renewing our mind with the truth, which allows the Word to sanctify us (John 17:17), then we are no longer in the process of being transformed (Romans 12:1-2).

Being transformed is the first sacrifice we should give to God for what He has done for us. This is the first thing we should focus on after being saved into the Kingdom of Christ, even before serving. We cannot test and approve what the will of God is for our life until we are transformed (verse 2 below).

Romans 12:1-2
1 I beseech you therefore, brethren, by the mercies of God, that you present your bodies a living sacrifice, holy, acceptable to God, which is your reasonable service. 2 And do not be conformed to this world, but be transformed by the renewing of your mind, that you may prove what is that good and acceptable and perfect will of God. NKJV

Romans 12:1-2
1 Therefore, I urge you, brothers, in view of God's mercy, to offer your bodies as living sacrifices, holy and pleasing

to God this is your spiritual act of worship. 2 Do not conform any longer to the pattern of this world, but be transformed by the renewing of your mind. Then you will be able to test and approve what God's will is his good, pleasing and perfect will. NIV

We don't change or clean up before we come, but after we come, and this process includes renewing our minds with the truth. Now that we are saved, we should stop living like the people of this world (do not be conformed to this world), and be transformed into a new person by renewing our mind with the truth (Romans 12:1-2 above). The Word is truth (John 17:17).

According to Colossians 1:21-23 (mentioned earlier in this chapter), we were enemies in our mind before we came to the Lord. We come as we are, but if we do not allow the Word to change us after we come, our understanding will be darkened, we will be separated from the life of God, and Kingdom teaching will be taken from us (Mark 4:24-25, Matthew 13:18-23).

THE WORD BRINGS HEALTH

The Lord has allowed me to minister to many Christians who thought they were waiting on God to heal them, when in all reality they were separated from the life of God because they had put the Word down, or had stopped allowing the Word to transform them. They stepped away from the process. A simple prayer of repentance and a commitment to reading the Word of God out loud from the New Testament, and allowing it to change them was all that was needed to heal them. Praise God, halleluiah.

If you are not continuing in your faith by seeking God's Kingdom and His righteousness first place in your life, then you are not in the process of becoming a new creation (Matthew 6:33). Those who belong to Christ are in the process of allowing the Word to change who they are to the point of killing their sinful nature (Galatians 5:24-25). Through Jesus, Who is the Word (John 1:14), they are dying to sins, and living for what is right (righteousness). By His stripes they are being healed (1 Peter 2:24). Check the verses.

If you have an illness, you should try this first. Read a minimum of

36

eight chapters a day from the New Testament. Read it out loud so that you can hear it in your ears. If you are at home or out of work, read two or three times that amount. Repent of anything that comes to mind as you go, which will allow what you hear to mold you into the likeness of Christ (Hebrews 4:12, Romans 8:29).

As I have mentioned, Kingdom teaching is found in the New Testament (Luke 16:16), as well as God's new way of righteousness (Romans 3:21-26). Therefore, if you are not reading (hearing Romans 10:17) the New Testament like there is no tomorrow, then this is one of the reasons for sin and destruction in your life. I am confident that this teaching alone will heal millions; glory be to God almighty.

People who do not learn how to mix faith with every promise in the Bible, and even the Gospel itself, do not receive what is promised (Hebrews 4:2 below).

Hebrews 4:2
2 For indeed the gospel was preached to us as well as to them; but the word which they heard did not profit them, not being mixed with faith in those who heard it. NKJV

Hebrews 4:2
2 For we also have had the gospel preached to us, just as they did; but the message they heard was of no value to them, because those who heard did not combine it with faith. NIV

We may know much about our new agreement with God through our Lord Jesus Christ, but unless we combine faith with that knowledge, the Word will be of no value to us. I'm sure this identifies the problem for millions who attend church services today without experiencing results from the promises they quote.

Only real faith in a promise, guarantees the results of that promise. The promises I will show you in this chapter and throughout this book, require the type of faith I am describing here. We need to learn it and put it into practice so that we will not be waiting for results in vain.

FAITH IS

We have to believe in order to have faith, but faith is not belief. Faith is our assured hope in the unseen evidence (Hebrews 11:1 below). If you did not believe that Christians could stop sinning before reading this book, then you couldn't possibly have put faith in the promises that I will show you in order to stop sinning.

Hebrews 11:1
1 Now faith is the substance of things hoped for, the evidence of things not seen. NKJV

Hebrews 11:1
1 Now faith is being sure of what we hope for and certain of what we do not see. NIV

Hebrews 11:1
1 Now faith is the assurance (the confirmation, the title deed) of the things [we] hope for, being the proof of things [we] do not see and the conviction of their reality [faith perceiving as real fact what is not revealed to the senses]. AMP

Our explanation of what faith is should sound similar to the verses above. Real faith includes our assured hope, the substance of our hope, or the reason for our hope combined with the evidence of a promise written in the Word of God.

We could say that faith believes with certainty that what God has promised will come true, in accordance with the written evidence of scripture. However, we cannot put faith in a promise (evidence) that we do not know, or that we do not believe.

Later in this chapter, I'm going to show you some promises that work directly against sin. You will have to apply this type of faith to them. Listen to what I am telling you, since it is not just a matter of knowing what is written, but mixing faith with it.

I know many people who have heard these verses, but did not apply faith to them, and now they need someone to teach them all over again

(Hebrews 5:11-13). Therefore, as you hear the verses, first learn them, and then believe them, and then refuse to speak against them so that they will remain in you (Matthew 13:19-23).

USE THE PROMISES

God has already given us everything we would ever need for this life and it comes through our knowledge of Him, through using what He promised (2 Peter 1:3-4).

2 Peter 1:3-4
3 as His divine power has given to us all things that pertain to life and godliness, through the knowledge of Him who called us by glory and virtue, 4 by which have been given to us exceedingly great and precious promises, that through these you may be partakers of the divine nature, having escaped the corruption that is in the world through lust. NKJV

2 Peter 1:3-4
3 His divine power has given us everything we need for life and godliness through our knowledge of him who called us by his own glory and goodness. 4 Through these he has given us his very great and precious promises, so that through them you may participate in the divine nature and escape the corruption in the world caused by evil desires. NIV

Grasp and hold on to what that says. We participate in the divine nature through the promises. We have to use the promises that are written in the Bible in order to receive what we need for this life, including escaping the corruption that is in the world (verse 4 above).

How are we going to stop sinning? We're going to use some promises, written in the Bible, that pertain to being set free from sin and controlling our body. We are going to focus on accomplishing our part of the promise, and consequently, God is going to do His part.

That sounds simple doesn't it? That is simple, but if you do not learn it, believe it, and refuse to speak against it, then it will not be living in you when you need it. Let me give you an example of this. Be honest with yourself in order for this to work.

Take a piece of paper, start at the top of the page and write down the number of years you have been a Christian. The bigger the number the more sheets of paper you will need, but start with one. Everything you have ever needed for this life comes through a promise written in your Bible (2 Peter 1:3-4 above). Now, without looking, make a list of the promises you have been living by since you accepted Jesus as Lord.

The number of promises you write down is the number of promises that are living in you, and will be in your thinking when you need them. No one is going to remind you to live by faith while you are in line at the grocery store, or in traffic on the way home. Instead of waiting on Sunday morning to repent of your behavior during the week, now you are going to take the promises with you, allowing them to change who you are (transformed).

Every time I have done this exercise in a seminar, almost every piece of paper is blank. If we do not live by the promises, then we will not receive what is promised. The entire Christian life is lived by faith from start to finish (Romans 1:17).

If you wrote a few promises down, then the next step is to look them up to see if they match what is written. Are there any conditions, and do the promises you wrote down apply to you? This is usually a wakeup call for those who participate in it.

For the most part, we're not continuing in our faith, or offering our body as a living sacrifice, or allowing the Bible to tell us how to live (hardened heart). Therefore, we are separated from the life of God, and our understanding is darkened (Ephesians 4:17-19).

Your list should have a few of these verses on it. If we confess our sins He is faithful and just to forgive us of our sins and cleanse us from all unrighteousness (1 John 1:9). You shall know the truth, and the truth shall set you free (John 8:31-36). If we exalt ourselves we will be humbled, but if we humble ourselves we will be exalted (Matthew 23:12). If we forgive others when they sin against us, we will be forgiven, but if we do not forgive others, then we will not be forgiven (Matthew 6:14-15).

If we seek first the Kingdom of God and His righteousness, all the things we worry about will be handed to us (Matthew 6:33). If we are ashamed of Him, He will be ashamed of us when He comes (Luke 9:26). We all stumble in many ways, but if a man is never at fault at what he says, he is a perfect man able to control his whole body (James 3:2).

Those are instructions with conditions, or faith based promises. Every promise in the New Testament has a condition. If we do this, then that is going to happen. Real faith always makes us do our part in order to receive the things that we hope for (James 2:14-24). In other words, we are sure that if we do our part, God is going to do His part of the promise.

How are we going to stop sinning? We are going to stop sinning by putting faith in God's promises similar to James 3:2. There are many more promises in this chapter and throughout this book. However, knowing that the Bible says that we can stop sinning is one thing, but achieving it with lasting results can only be done by faith. We must know how to use faith with our knowledge.

James 3:2
2 For we all stumble in many things. If anyone does not stumble in word, he is a perfect man, able also to bridle the whole body. NKJV

James 3:2
2 We all stumble in many ways. If anyone is never at fault in what he says, he is a perfect man, able to keep his whole body in check. NIV

If we are never at fault in what we say, we will be able to control our whole body. Can a person with an addiction or a sin problem use that promise? That's a promise all of us can use; control our whole body. There are probably millions of self-help items sold every month which are designed to aid in controlling the body to grow muscle, lose weight, and so on, but faith is free and it works every time.

In order to gain control over our body by faith, we would have to tame our tongue. In order to tame our tongue by faith we would have to change our heart, and the only way to do that is to continually store the Word of God in it (Matthew 12:33-37), to the point of forcing it to remain in us (Romans 1:28-32, Matthew 13:18-23, John 15:7). Imagine that. Two promises from the Word of God can replace millions of man-made remedies.

Do you believe James 3:2? Will you learn it, and the other verses I have mentioned? Do you think you will ever speak against it in casual conversation? Your friends will. Are you going to take a stand and not be ashamed of the Word, or will you shrink back? You might want to read this book again in a few months just in case you shrink back.

OBEDIENCE THROUGH FAITH

Another example of how faith works is what Noah did when God told him about the flood (Genesis 6:13-22, Hebrews 11:7). Noah believed the information that God gave him. Therefore, Noah's faith caused him to obey God in building the Ark in order to receive what was promised; save his family.

Hebrews 11:7
7 By faith Noah, being divinely warned of things not yet seen, moved with godly fear, prepared an ark for the saving of his household, by which he condemned the world and became heir of the righteousness which is according to faith. NKJV

Hebrews 11:7
7 By faith Noah, when warned about things not yet seen, in holy fear built an ark to save his family. By his faith he condemned the world and became heir of the righteousness that comes by faith. NIV

As you can tell by that verse, Noah didn't just haphazardly build a boat. He was warned about a coming flood that would destroy everyone not on the boat, and so he built it to save his family. In the same way, our faith in Jesus makes us prepare for the future.

For example, faith in Jesus will make us mention Him to other people, because Jesus said that whoever was ashamed of Him and His Word, He would be ashamed of them at His coming (Luke 9:26). If we believe what Jesus said, then we would put faith in that verse and mention His name and His Word before others. In this way obedience comes from faith.

Noah believed God and so he put faith in what God said. He built the Ark in accordance with the instructions God gave him. In the same way, only those who believe Jesus put faith in Him, and only those who put faith in Him, follow His instructions. Obedience comes from faith (Romans 1:5, 1 Peter 1:2). Read the Words of Jesus below out loud.

Luke 6:46-49
46 "But why do you call Me 'Lord, Lord,' and not do the things which I say? 47 Whoever comes to Me, and hears My sayings and does them, I will show you whom he is like: 48 He is like a man building a house, who dug deep and laid the foundation on the rock. And when the flood arose, the stream beat vehemently against that house, and could not shake it, for it was founded on the rock. 49 But he who heard and did nothing is like a man who built a house on the earth without a foundation, against which the stream beat vehemently; and immediately it fell. And the ruin of that house was great." NKJV

Luke 6:46-49
46 "Why do you call me, 'Lord, Lord,' and do not do what I say? 47 I will show you what he is like who comes to me and hears my words and puts them into practice. 48 He is like a man building a house, who dug down deep and laid the foundation on rock. When a flood came, the torrent struck that house but could not shake it, because it was well built. 49 But the one who hears my words and does not put them into practice is like a man who built a house on the ground without a foundation. The moment the torrent struck that house, it collapsed and its destruction was complete." NIV

Jesus said, "Why do you call Me Lord and do not do what I say?" That's a good question. The flood or the trouble is coming whether we prepare for it or not.

In this world we will have trouble, but only those who hear the Word and put it into practice will remain standing afterwards (John 16:33). We can pray more, sing louder, jump higher, or whatever else, but the only way for the house to remain standing once the trouble comes is to put the Word into practice before trouble hits.

Some churches are in the business of rescuing people from trouble without giving them the remedy. That means they will need rescuing over and over again. I don't have a problem helping people who are willing to listen to the instructions. Those who hear God's Word, belong to God, and those who do not belong to God do not hear His Word (John 8:47).

I really don't think we realize what we do when we declare Jesus as our Lord and believe that God raised Him from the dead. It's not just a statement. We focus on being saved, but we need to rethink what we have declared if the "Parable of the Servants" or the "Ten Minas," as it is called in some Bibles, is true (Luke 19:11-27). Jesus Christ declares that those servants who did not want Him to be Lord over them would pay with their life. Check it!

CLOSE YOUR EYES

Faith is unseen. Therefore, when we consider using a promise from the Bible such as 2 Peter 1:10, which says "if we do these things we will never fall," we don't have to look around to see how other Christians are doing with it. Faith is not based on our neighbor's progress.

In fact, it makes no difference what we see, or how long anyone has tried because faith is not dependent on what we can see or have experienced. Faith is based on our hope combined with the unseen evidence (Hebrews 11:1). That is what we will learn to live by and not by what we can see with our eyes (2 Corinthians 5:7).

2 Corinthians 5:7
7 For we walk by faith, not by sight. NKJV

2 Corinthians 5:7
7 We live by faith, not by sight. NIV

All we need to do to apply our faith is to know and believe the written instructions of any promise found in the Bible. If the instructions say we can do something, be something, or have something, then we can accomplish it through faith, point, blank, period. Even if everyone who has ever tried has failed since the Apostle Paul's days, genuine faith cannot fail because God's Word does not return void (Isaiah 55:10-11).

People with weak faith only live by a few promises. Weak faith is an indicator that a person has not renewed their mind with the truth.

They don't necessarily reject the truth, but they don't know what to believe yet, and so they put faith in whatever they hear until it fails. Then they try the next new thing. If this describes you, then know that you will be tossed here and there by every wind of doctrine until you learn the truth for yourself (Ephesians 4:13-14).

You will not be able to fully understand the mature things, until you allow the elementary teachings to change you (1 Corinthians 3:1-3, Hebrews 5:11-14). Be determined to learn to live by faith right now. Then allow your faith to show you what to do.

A person with shipwrecked faith has rejected parts of the truth instead of allowing it to change them (Hebrews 3:16-19). These people are usually filled with philosophy and man-made reasons as to why it is okay to ignore certain parts of scripture and they speak against the faith (1 Timothy 1:18-20, Colossians 2:4-8). You can be sure that their understanding is darkened (Ephesians 4:17-19 above).

When someone refuses to allow the truth to change them, they harden their heart by refusing to change (Ephesians 4:17-18). After this is done over a long period of time, they can lose all sensitivity to the promptings of the Spirit (Romans 7:6), and be given over to sensuality, which is the pleasure of the senses (Ephesians 4:19).

Therefore, they become blind to the truth, and church for them becomes a place where they go to please the flesh. The seat has to be right, the lighting, the color of the carpet, and so on. They go to be served, instead of serving.

This is a recipe that attracts false teachers (Ephesians 4:13-14). If you are not learning to live by faith, then you are not learning to live the Christian life which is lived by faith from start to finish (Romans 1:16-17).

SPIRIT OF FAITH

Many try to stop sinning but fail, and consequently that becomes their testimony. When you hear people saying things like "I tried that for thirty years and couldn't do it," ask them which one of God's promises failed?

When people say things like that, they are testifying that they tried it God's way, and it did not work. Therefore, by their words they call God's Word a lie. Do not sit and listen to a testimony like that or say amen to it. Tell them that you are going to receive what is promised in your Bible by faith.

Most people do not realize it when they say something that is against what is written in the Bible because they do not know what is in the Bible. God's people are destroyed for lack of knowledge (Hosea 4:6). That's why they live in destruction.

The Spirit of faith always speaks in line with the written evidence. (2 Corinthians 4:13). If the Holy Spirit is the one leading you to speak, then you are speaking in line with what is written in the Bible, point, blank, period.

2 Corinthians 4:13
13 And since we have the same spirit of faith, according to what is written, "I believed and therefore I spoke," we also believe and therefore speak NKJV

2 Corinthians 4:13
13 It is written: "I believed; therefore I have spoken." With that same spirit of faith we also believe and therefore speak NIV

When a deceiving spirit is leading a person, they will speak with deceptive philosophy, heresies, and great swelling words of emptiness (1 Timothy 4:1-2, 2 Peter 2:1-3, 18). By their fruits you will recognize them (Matthew 12:33-37, 7:15-20). Usually their eyes are full of adultery and so they never stop sinning (2 Peter 2:14).

Those who speak against the evidence written in scripture cannot possibly be living by faith in that area of their life (Romans 10:6-8). People who are righteous by faith, always speak according to what is written and never against it.

Early one morning I was doing some electrical work directly in front of a crack house. A huge three hundred pound drug dealer had just gone back inside after offering me some crack cocaine, when a one hundred and twenty pound female sheriff's deputy arrived to serve him with a warrant. My eyebrows raised, my head tilted down so that I could see over my safety glasses, and my mouth swung open, as she knocked on the door.

I visualized her trying to place him in handcuffs, which placed me in a state of alarm. I didn't want to be the one who was going to have to try to pull him off her. So I said, "You're going to need some help." She turned around and replied, "The Lord is my helper, I will not be afraid of what man can do to me" (Hebrews 13:6). Praise God, halleluiah! She spoke her faith and that is what she received. I was embarrassed by what I had said because I knew the exact verse she quoted (Hebrews 13:6), and I thought, "how foolish of me to speak against the faith."

Without realizing it, I had tried to put fear in her. My flesh painted a picture, and since I feared that I would have to be the one to help her, I spoke. I would have done much better by just keeping my mouth shut, or by asking her if I could assist her in any way (Ephesians 4:29).

Minutes later she was loading him into her patrol car in handcuffs. Obviously, she didn't need me since the Lord was on her side, and the Lord showed me through her how to speak my faith in everyday situations.

It wasn't that I didn't know what was written in the Bible, but I did not use my faith in everyday situations. God wants to supply the water, the bread, the protection, a good nights sleep, and everything else we need (Matthew 4:4, Deuteronomy 8:3). He wants us to live by faith at all times, and not just when we need Him for something we can't do.

Let that sink in. God wants us to live by faith and not to put confidence in what we can do in the flesh (Philippians 3:3). He wants us to seek Him with everything we have, and then allow Him to supply us with the things we worry about (Matthew 6:25-34). Those who are right (righteous) in God's eyes live by faith (Romans 1:16-17) and speak their faith (Romans 10:6-8, 2 Corinthians 4:13).

NEW ATTITUDE

If your attitude had been in line with what is written in the Bible,

47

then nobody would have been able to make you believe that Christians could not stop sinning. In fact, your attitude would be just like what your Bible says concerning any subject because you would be allowing Jesus the living Word to judge your attitudes and thoughts (Hebrews 4:12, John 1:14, 6:63).

Hebrews 4:12
12 For the word of God is living and powerful, and sharper than any two-edged sword, piercing even to the division of soul and spirit, and of joints and marrow, and is a discerner of the thoughts and intents of the heart. NKJV

Hebrews 4:12
12 For the word of God is living and active. Sharper than any double-edged sword, it penetrates even to dividing soul and spirit, joints and marrow; it judges the thoughts and attitudes of the heart. NIV

Think about this. If what we believe does not match what is written, then who needs to change? I have known entire groups of Christians that have drifted so far away from the truth that they couldn't read certain books out of their Bible since it did not match with what they had come to believe. They were totally unwilling to allow the Word of God to judge their attitudes and thoughts, and I'm convinced that this is happening everywhere.

People who reject the truth, do not realize that the same Spirit that gives life to the body is also the Word that they reject (Romans 8, John 6:63). The danger in this is losing all sensitivity to the point of totally rejecting any scripture. They will get to where they cannot stand to listen to scripture. Listening to the Word of God to the point of holding on to it brings life and health to a person's body (Proverbs 4:20-22).

Those who do not allow the Word of God to change them, do not answer God's calling to be transformed (Romans 12:1-2). God doesn't listen to their call for help, since they ignore His call (Zechariah 7:11-13, Proverbs 1:22-33). Check the verses. This is the reason for millions of problems in the church today.

Lord willing, that doesn't describe you, but let that be a sign to you. The Holy Spirit wrote the Bible and He is the Word (2 Peter 1:20-21, John 6:63). Therefore, if someone is Spirit-filled and Spirit-led how can they reject the Word and speak against it? It cannot happen, and if it does you can be sure that they are following a deceiving spirit (1 Timothy 4:-1-2).

We need to be reprogrammed, or transformed (changed into different people) through the knowledge of the truth which is what is written in our Bible so that we will be able to test and approve what God's will is (Romans 12:1-2, John 17:17). At that point, our attitudes would be in line with what is written and not necessarily similar to what seems to be right.

BELIEVE

You have to believe what the Bible says since you cannot receive anything from the Lord if you do not believe (James 1:5-8). I'm certain that ignorance of this one spiritual principle is the reason millions of well-meaning people are waiting in vain for results.

James 1:5-8
5 If any of you lacks wisdom, let him ask of God, who gives to all liberally and without reproach, and it will be given to him. 6 But let him ask in faith, with no doubting, for he who doubts is like a wave of the sea driven and tossed by the wind. 7 For let not that man suppose that he will receive anything from the Lord; 8 he is a double-minded man, unstable in all his ways. NKJV

James 1:5-8
5 If any of you lacks wisdom, he should ask God, who gives generously to all without finding fault, and it will be given to him. 6 But when he asks, he must believe and not doubt, because he who doubts is like a wave of the sea, blown and tossed by the wind. 7 That man should not think he will receive anything from the Lord; 8 he is a double-minded man, unstable in all he does. NIV

That passage of scripture begins with receiving wisdom from God, but within it we learn a spiritual truth that works whether we know it or not. No one can receive anything from the Lord if he doubts that the Lord is able to do what He has promised.

All things are possible for those who believe (Mark 9:23), but if we do not believe, we do not have to worry about receiving anything from the Lord. Belief is a condition that cannot be ignored.

Many are saved, but few continue to follow Jesus because they do not believe some of His teachings (John 6:60-69). Check those verses because that is the reason millions of people stray from the truth today.

After reading chapter one of this book, if you do not believe that Christians can stop sinning, then you will not be able to stop. It's just that simple. No one can receive what they do not believe. Please go back and start this book over from the beginning. Find every verse I have mentioned in your Bible and read it out loud. Ask yourself if you are a believer or if you said a sinner's prayer for fire insurance, in order to avoid the lake of fire?

A sinner's prayer is not fire insurance. It's the beginning of a life-changing process. Believing Jesus is fire insurance (John 3:16). We're not sent out to have people repeat a sinner's prayer, but to make disciples of Jesus, which would require baptizing them, and teaching them to obey Jesus (Matthew 28:19-20).

If you have started in that process, but have fallen away, or if you don't know for sure if you believe, ask God the Father to enable you to come to Jesus (John 6:44), and receive His Word (John 6:60-69). Proclaim Jesus as the Lord of your life and believe in your heart that God raised Him from the dead in the same way that He will raise you, if you die with Jesus (Romans 6:5, 10:6-13).

The people who are right in God's eyes believe, and they believe to the point of being fully persuaded that God has the power to do what He has promised (Romans 4:20-25). If you do not believe that the promises God has made will come true, then you cannot be righteous in accordance with the definition found in the verses below.

Romans 4:20-24
20 He did not waver at the promise of God through unbelief, but was strengthened in faith, giving glory

50

to God, 21 and being fully convinced that what He had promised He was also able to perform. 22 And therefore "it was accounted to him for righteousness." 23 Now it was not written for his sake alone that it was imputed to him, 24 but also for us. It shall be imputed to us who believe in Him who raised up Jesus our Lord from the dead. NKJV

Romans 4:20-24
20 Yet he did not waver through unbelief regarding the promise of God, but was strengthened in his faith and gave glory to God, 21 being fully persuaded that God had power to do what he had promised. 22 This is why "it was credited to him as righteousness." 23 The words "it was credited to him" were written not for him alone, 24 but also for us, to whom God will credit righteousness for us who believe in him who raised Jesus our Lord from the dead. NIV

If God spoke it, the righteous believe it, point, blank, period. Just as the verses say, "this is why it was credited to him as righteousness." Now, how do you believe? Do you pick and choose the verses you like and ignore what you don't want to hear? That's pretty common because many only want to hear the "goody-goody" verses which is a sign that the scripture will not be fulfilled concerning them (James 2:20-24, 2 Timothy 4:3-4).

How can we believe John 3:16 and ignore John 1:14 that says Jesus is the Word made flesh, or John 6:63 that says the Word is Spirit and gives life, or John 17:17 that says we are sanctified by the truth which is the Word? Can we really pick and choose the parts of what Jesus said that we want to believe and ignore what's left? That would be like rejecting parts of Jesus Himself because He is the Word (John 1:14, 14:6).

Jesus doesn't condemn us. Praise God, Halleluiah! However, Jesus said that the very Word that we reject would condemn us on the last day (John 12:46-48 below).

51

John 12:46-48
46 I have come as a light into the world, that whoever believes in Me should not abide in darkness. 47 And if anyone hears My words and does not believe, I do not judge him; for I did not come to judge the world but to save the world. 48 He who rejects Me, and does not receive My words, has that which judges him — the word that I have spoken will judge him in the last day. NKJV

John 12:46-48
46 I have come into the world as a light, so that no one who believes in me should stay in darkness. 47 "As for the person who hears my words but does not keep them, I do not judge him. For I did not come to judge the world, but to save it. 48 There is a judge for the one who rejects me and does not accept my words; that very word which I spoke will condemn him at the last day. NIV

The very Word we reject will condemn us when? I have not heard the trumpets yet. Praise the Lord there is still time to change.

WE HAVE AN OBLIGATION

As we hear the truth our obligation is to live by it, and those who live by it come into the light (John 3:18-21). Faith comes by hearing the Word (Romans 10:17). When we allow Jesus in, Who is the Word made flesh (John 1:14), then we allow Him to change us from the inside out.

This process is called "the sanctifying work of the Spirit, through belief in the truth" (2 Thessalonians 2:13-15, Romans 8:12-14). To be sanctified is to be made holy, and Jesus has perfected forever, those who are being made holy (Hebrews 10:14).

Hebrews 10:14
14 For by one offering He has perfected forever those who are being sanctified. NKJV

52

Hebrews 10:14
14 because by one sacrifice he has made perfect forever those who are being made holy. NIV

If you are being sanctified by the Spirit, through the truth which is the Word (John 17:17), then you are holy (Colossians 1:21-23). In the beginning was the Word, and the Word was God and with God. (John 1:1). Then the Word became flesh in the form of our Lord and Savior Jesus Christ (John 1:14). The Spirit is also the Word (John 6:63, Romans 8:12-14).

That same Word announced the gospel in advance to Abraham (Galatians 3:8). How can that be you might ask? It's because the Word itself is alive and active (Hebrews 4:12) and works inside those who believe it (1 Thessalonians 2:13). To reject the Word, is to reject life.

Allowing what is written in our Bible to change us describes our obligation as Christians (Romans 8:12-14 below). Those who do not allow the change die. On the other hand, Jesus has perfected forever those who are being sanctified in this way (Hebrews 10:14, John 17:17).

Romans 8:12-14
12 Therefore, brethren, we are debtors — not to the flesh, to live according to the flesh. 13 For if you live according to the flesh you will die; but if by the Spirit you put to death the deeds of the body, you will live. 14 For as many as are led by the Spirit of God, these are sons of God. NKJV

Romans 8:12-14
12 Therefore, brothers, we have an obligation — but it is not to the sinful nature, to live according to it. 13 For if you live according to the sinful nature, you will die; but if by the Spirit you put to death the misdeeds of the body, you will live, 14 because those who are led by the Spirit of God are sons of God. NIV

By the Spirit we put to death the misdeeds of the body (verse 13 above). The Word of God, which is Spirit (John 6:63), will work all by itself if we continually put it in us and believe it (1 Thessalonians 2:13). Those who believe are eager to have the Word of God remain in them (James 1:21).

James 1:21
21 Therefore lay aside all filthiness and overflow of wickedness, and receive with meekness the implanted word, which is able to save your souls. NKJV

James 1:21
21 Therefore, get rid of all moral filth and the evil that is so prevalent and humbly accept the word planted in you, which can save you. NIV

Doesn't that sound like, "you shall know the truth and the truth shall set you free" (John 8:32), and "I have hidden Your Word in my heart so that I might not sin against You" (Psalm 119:11)? The truth, which is the Word itself, shall set you free (John 17:17, 8:32). Think about that.

That's why it is so important to preach the Word (2 Timothy 4:1-4). The Word itself already contains the power to save (Romans 1:16), the power to provide (Matthew 6:33), the power to heal (Psalm 107:17-20), the power to deliver from sin (John 8:31-36, Romans 1:28-32), and the power to give us anything needed for this life (2 Peter 1:3-4). Amen. Glory, halleluiah!

To the point of retaining it

Read the following verses below and see if you can count the number of sins that would cease to exist in a Christian's life if they just retained the knowledge of God found in the Bible. In other words, many sins will discontinue automatically (through faith in Romans 1:28-32 below) if we read the Word of God to the point of knowing the truth (retaining it).

Romans 1:28-32
28 And even as they did not like to retain God in their knowledge, God gave them over to a debased mind, to

*do those things which are not fitting; 29 being filled
with all unrighteousness, sexual immorality, wickedness,
covetousness, maliciousness; full of envy, murder,
strife, deceit, evil-mindedness; they are whisperers,
30 backbiters, haters of God, violent, proud, boasters,
inventors of evil things, disobedient to parents, 31
undiscerning, untrustworthy, unloving, unforgiving,
unmerciful; 32 who, knowing the righteous judgment of
God, that those who practice such things are deserving of
death, not only do the same but also approve of those who
practice them. NKJV*

Romans 1:28-32
*28 Furthermore, since they did not think it worthwhile
to retain the knowledge of God, he gave them over to a
depraved mind, to do what ought not to be done. 29 They
have become filled with every kind of wickedness, evil,
greed and depravity. They are full of envy, murder, strife,
deceit and malice. They are gossips, 30 slanderers, God-
haters, insolent, arrogant and boastful; they invent ways
of doing evil; they disobey their parents; 31 they are
senseless, faithless, heartless, ruthless. 32 Although they
know God's righteous decree that those who do such things
deserve death, they not only continue to do these very
things but also approve of those who practice them. NIV*

Show me someone who is willing to read the New Testament out loud (faith comes by hearing the Word) like it is the most important thing they have ever done, and I will show you someone who is on the path to totally eliminating that whole list of sins in their life (listed above).

Imagine that. Just by reading the Word of God to the point of retaining it, or making it live in us, hundreds of sins cease automatically.

How do you put faith in that promise? If your assured hope is in stopping sin in your life, then the evidence says you need to retain the Word of God (Romans 1:28-32 above). First of all, if you do not believe that promise, you will not obtain the results (James 1:5-8). If you are a believer, then you will need to retain the Word of God, and be careful not to speak against what is promised (Romans 10:6-8, 1 Timothy 6:20-21). That is how you would mix your faith with that promise. Just do it!

HOLD TO THE TEACHINGS

Anyone or anything that prevents you from hearing the Word of God straight out of your Bible to the point of knowing it, is against you, point, blank, period. Identify whatever or whoever is hindering you from being sanctified by the truth, and put a halt to it. You may have to deny yourself because it might be you (Matthew 16:24, 10:38).

People who do not know the truth in this area of the Christian life, willingly speak against retaining the knowledge of God. However, holding to the teachings is a condition that every Christian should be aware of. Notice the word "if" in 1 Corinthians 15:1-2 below.

1 Corinthians 15:1-2
1 Moreover, brethren, I declare to you the gospel which I preached to you, which also you received and in which you stand, 2 by which also you are saved, if you hold fast that word which I preached to you unless you believed in vain. NKJV

1 Corinthians 15:1-2
1 Now, brothers, I want to remind you of the gospel I preached to you, which you received and on which you have taken your stand. 2 By this gospel you are saved, if you hold firmly to the word I preached to you. Otherwise, you have believed in vain. NIV

Did you see the condition? Does that passage say, "saved if?" Were you tricked into believing that the Bible agrees with the "once saved, always saved" movement? The use of the word "if" after the word "saved" means that "saved" is conditional. That one verse should tell you that once saved always saved is a man-made doctrine.

That is why many Christians cannot see those verses; they accept and believe something that is directly against them. Once we accept and believe something that is directly against the truth, we are no longer allowing the truth to transform us.

How important is holding on to the Word according to 1 Corinthians 15:1-2 above? The Word that we are holding on to was God, was with God, became flesh in the form of Jesus Christ, and is Spirit (John 1:1-14, 6:63). That same Word that we are instructed to hold on to, is the same Word that can set us free from sin. Read the verses below a few times and see.

John 8:31-37
31 Then Jesus said to those Jews who believed Him, "If you abide in My word, you are My disciples indeed. 32 And you shall know the truth, and the truth shall make you free." 33 They answered Him, "We are Abraham's descendants, and have never been in bondage to anyone. How can You say, 'You will be made free'?" 34 Jesus answered them, "Most assuredly, I say to you, whoever commits sin is a slave of sin. 35 And a slave does not abide in the house forever, but a son abides forever. 36 Therefore if the Son makes you free, you shall be free indeed. 37 "I know that you are Abraham's descendants, but you seek to kill Me, because My word has no place in you. NKJV

John 8:31-37
31 To the Jews who had believed him, Jesus said, "If you hold to my teaching, you are really my disciples. 32 Then you will know the truth, and the truth will set you free." 33 They answered him, "We are Abraham's descendants and have never been slaves of anyone. How can you say that we shall be set free?" 34 Jesus replied, "I tell you the truth, everyone who sins is a slave to sin. 35 Now a slave has no permanent place in the family, but a son belongs to it forever. 36 So if the Son sets you free, you will be free indeed. 37 I know you are Abraham's descendants. Yet you are ready to kill me, because you have no room for my word. NIV

Jesus said that they were ready to kill Him because they had no room for His Word in them (verse 37 above). Imagine that. They were ready to sin because they had no room for His Word in them.

God is working in believers through His Word (1 Thessalonians 2:13). If we continue in our faith (Colossians 1:21-23), we will grow up in our salvation (1 Peter 2:2), and we will eventually know the truth, and it will set us free from sin (John 8:31-36).

Show me someone who is growing in the Word to the point of retaining it, and I will show you someone who is growing spiritually. Fleshly things give birth to more flesh, but spiritual things grow us up spiritually (John 3:6, 1 Peter 2:2).

Show me someone who does not read their Bible to the point of knowing it and I will show you someone who remains in sin (Romans 1:28-32). You may not be able to visibly see their sins, but they are there (1 Timothy 5:24).

Jesus said that everyone who sins is a slave of sin, and a slave does not abide (remain) in the family forever (John 8: 34-35 above). In other words, those who continue in sin may be in the family now, but they do not have a permanent place in the family. We have to strive, or make every effort to enter the narrow gate (Luke 13:23-28).

Luke 13:23-28
23 Then one said to Him, "Lord, are there few who are saved?" And He said to them, 24 "Strive to enter through the narrow gate, for many, I say to you, will seek to enter and will not be able. 25 When once the Master of the house has risen up and shut the door, and you begin to stand outside and knock at the door, saying, 'Lord, Lord, open for us,' and He will answer and say to you, 'I do not know you, where you are from,' 26 then you will begin to say, 'We ate and drank in Your presence, and You taught in our streets.' 27 But He will say, 'I tell you I do not know you, where you are from. Depart from Me, all you workers of iniquity.' 28 There will be weeping and gnashing of teeth, when you see Abraham and Isaac and Jacob and all

the prophets in the kingdom of God, and yourselves thrust
out. NKJV

Luke 13:23-28
23 Someone asked him, "Lord, are only a few people going
to be saved?" He said to them, 24 "Make every effort to
enter through the narrow door, because many, I tell you,
will try to enter and will not be able to. 25 Once the owner
of the house gets up and closes the door, you will stand
outside knocking and pleading, 'Sir, open the door for us.'
"But he will answer, 'I don't know you or where you come
from.' 26 "Then you will say, 'We ate and drank with
you, and you taught in our streets.' 27 "But he will reply,
'I don't know you or where you come from. Away from
me, all you evildoers!' 28 "There will be weeping there,
and gnashing of teeth, when you see Abraham, Isaac and
Jacob and all the prophets in the kingdom of God, but you
yourselves thrown out. NIV

Make every effort to enter the Kingdom of God. How important is holding to the teachings and to putting to death the misdeeds of the body through the Spirit? When we know the truth, it becomes our number one ambition.

Take a stand
What are you going to do with what I have shown you so far? Are you going to shrink back and hide the verses allowing hundreds of people around you to go their way, or are you going to take a stand for what is right and help people who do not know what is written?

Why would any man be willing to take a stand against what God has said in the very Bible he has been carrying for years? Let the verses below answer that question.

John 12:42-43
42 Nevertheless even among the rulers many believed in
Him, but because of the Pharisees they did not confess

Him, lest they should be put out of the synagogue; 43 for they loved the praise of men more than the praise of God. NKJV

John 12:42-43
42 Yet at the same time many even among the leaders believed in him. But because of the Pharisees they would not confess their faith for fear they would be put out of the synagogue; 43 for they loved praise from men more than praise from God. NIV

We don't know what our Bible says, and yet we readily take a stand alongside someone that only seems to know. What do we do when our eyes are opened, and we can see the truth again? Do we stand up for the truth or stand up for our desire to fit in with the crowd?

I wish that everyone on earth knew the truth. I'm asking you to side with the living Word, even if you don't understand everything right now. I'm asking you to take a stand for the truth regardless of where you gather. I'm asking you to make disciples of Jesus wherever you may be on this planet. If I can help you, please contact me.

KINGDOM

Do you see the condition in the verses below?

John 3:15-16
15 that whoever believes in Him should not perish but have eternal life. 16 For God so loved the world that He gave His only begotten Son, that whoever believes in Him should not perish but have everlasting life. NKJV

John 3:15-16
15 that everyone who believes in him may have eternal life. 16 For God so loved the world that he gave his one and only Son, that whoever believes in him shall not perish but have eternal life. NIV

Everywhere I teach I ask the people if there is a condition in John 3:16 and almost everyone in the room will answer "no." Can you see the condition?

I teach people according to what the Bible says and not according to what seems right. When I mention John 3:16, I tell people that they have to believe, or they will not have eternal life. When I speak about being saved, I tell them that they are saved exactly how and where the Word of God says they are saved, and that is seated with Christ in His Kingdom (Ephesians 2:6-8).

We have to be born again to even see the Kingdom of God (John 3:3). In other words, now that we are in Christ, we have to be born again through the Word of truth (1 Peter 1:22-25) in order to be able to see and then enter the Kingdom of God (John 3:6). The Words "eternal life" are not in Romans chapter ten or in Ephesians chapter two, verses one through ten. If that doesn't match what you have heard then go back and ask for the verses that say exactly what you are hearing.

The Thessalonians were thought worthy to enter the Kingdom of God only after their faith was growing exceedingly, and their love toward one another was abounding (2 Thessalonians 1:3-5). Check it! They were born again, and the evidence proved it. Do we have a different promise than they did?

Now that we are saved and seated with Christ, we are working out our salvation with fear and trembling (Philippians 2:12), because Jesus is the Author of eternal salvation for those who obey Him (Hebrews 5:9). Therefore, we are obeying the doctrine that delivers us from sins that lead to death in order that we will inherit the Kingdom of God. Here is a list of sins that will keep the people who continue to commit them out of the Kingdom of God.

Galatians 5:19-21
19 Now the works of the flesh are evident, which are: adultery, fornication, uncleanness, lewdness, 20 idolatry, sorcery, hatred, contentions, jealousies, outbursts of wrath, selfish ambitions, dissensions, heresies, 21 envy, murders, drunkenness, revelries, and the like; of which I tell you beforehand, just as I also told you in time past,

*that those who practice such things will not inherit the
kingdom of God. NKJV*

Galatians 5:19-21
*19 The acts of the sinful nature are obvious: sexual
immorality, impurity and debauchery; 20 idolatry and
witchcraft; hatred, discord, jealousy, fits of rage, selfish
ambition, dissensions, factions 21 and envy; drunkenness,
orgies, and the like. I warn you, as I did before, that those
who live like this will not inherit the kingdom of God. NIV*

Those who practice such sins will not inherit the Kingdom of God,
but we come as we are. Who can stop sinning before they accept Jesus
as Lord? It's easy to enter the Kingdom of Christ, but not everyone in the
Kingdom of Christ will make it into the Kingdom of God or the Kingdom
of Heaven. In the end Jesus will send out His angels to weed out of His
Kingdom all who sin and do evil according to Matthew 13:41. Check it!

The Apostle Paul warned the Ephesians for three years that false
teachers were coming (Acts 20:29-31). There is definitely no shortage
of them today just as it is written in 2 Timothy 4:3-4 below. A time will
come when people will not want to hear what is written, but only what
pleases their ears.

2 Timothy 4:3-4
*3 For the time will come when they will not endure sound
doctrine, but according to their own desires, because
they have itching ears, they will heap up for themselves
teachers; 4 and they will turn their ears away from the
truth, and be turned aside to fables. NKJV*

2 Timothy 4:3-4
*3 For the time will come when men will not put up with
sound doctrine. Instead, to suit their own desires, they
will gather around them a great number of teachers to say
what their itching ears want to hear. 4 They will turn their
ears away from the truth and turn aside to myths. NIV*

False teachers always look the part and seem right until you test what they say (2 Corinthians 11:13-15, Matthew 7:15-20). Therefore, close your eyes and listen. Test everything (1 Thessalonians 5:21).

The person whom God sends to speak to you, will speak in accordance with God's Word, point, blank, period (John 3:34, Jeremiah 23:22). Are you hearing what is written, or are you hearing what you want to hear in accordance with 2 Timothy 4:1-4? If what you are hearing is directly against the verses we have covered so far in this book, then you will know that God did not send that person to speak.

There is a way that seems right to us, but in the end it leads to death (Proverbs 14:12, 16:25). Don't follow what seems right or the path that everybody is taking, but follow what the Bible actually says, because many, although saved into the Kingdom of Christ, will not enter the Kingdom of God (Luke 13:22-29). In the end, Jesus will send out His angels and they will gather out of His Kingdom all who practice sin and do evil (Matthew 13:41). Check the verses.

Read this passage of scripture and then I will ask you a question.

Revelation 21:6-8
6 And He said to me, "It is done! I am the Alpha and the Omega, the Beginning and the End. I will give of the fountain of the water of life freely to him who thirsts. 7 He who overcomes shall inherit all things, and I will be his God and he shall be My son. 8 But the cowardly, unbelieving, abominable, murderers, sexually immoral, sorcerers, idolaters, and all liars shall have their part in the lake which burns with fire and brimstone, which is the second death." NKJV

Revelation 21:6-8
6 He said to me: "It is done. I am the Alpha and the Omega, the Beginning and the End. To him who is thirsty I will give to drink without cost from the spring of the water of life. 7 He who overcomes will inherit all this, and I will be his God and he will be my son. 8 But the cowardly, the unbelieving, the vile, the murderers, the sexually immoral, those who

practice magic arts, the idolaters and all liars their place will be in the fiery lake of burning sulfur. This is the second death." NIV

In Revelation 21:6-8 above, Jesus said the person who overcomes would inherit what He promises, but there is a list of people who He will cast into the lake of fire. Surely we can accept Jesus as Lord while we are wicked, but if "all liars" are cast into the lake of fire, doesn't that tell you that at some point during the Christian life we need to change? Our faith overcomes the world (1 John 5:4). Got faith?

My name is Alan P. Ballou. I am a servant. If you have questions, or need help with what I have explained in this book, please contact me at www.howtostopsinning.com.

3. Through Love

Remaining in Christ
It's a command
Remain in death
Access by faith into grace
Nothing can make us stumble
To the point of suffering
Follow Me
Cannot be snatched
Know Jesus
Turn him back
Love is
Don't tell me you love me
We are not saved by good works
Good works benefit us
Slave to righteous acts
Whoever does God's will
Associations
Recognize ans warn
Righteous acts as filthy rags

3

THROUGH LOVE

ಬುⱰಜ

If we were seeking to wholeheartedly obey the form of teaching that would set us free from sin mentioned in Romans 6:17-18, we would have to love one another. Part of the doctrine that delivers Christians from sin is love. In this chapter we will cover the effect that love has on our ability to stop sinning.

Love is directly connected to our ability to come out of darkness, see clearly (1 John 2:8-11), bear fruit (John 15:4-6), overcome the world (1 John 5:2-5), know Jesus (1 John 2:3), abide in the vine (John 15:10, 1 John 3:24), and have Jesus make His home in us (John 14:21-23). Check the verses. Love is the most excellent way (1 Corinthians 12:31).

Not any of these things happen for the person who does not love in the way described in the Bible. Therefore, whoever is lacking in love, is without a doubt caught up in all sorts of sins. They may not be obvious, but without a doubt they are there.

REMAINING "IN CHRIST"

Ask the average church attendant if we have to remain in Jesus and he will not answer you with anything that sounds like John 15:1-6. We assume that Jesus can't possibly be referring to the same people He was soon to die for, but that's who He was talking to; disciples. Jesus declared that God the Father would cut off every branch "in Him" (in Christ) that bears no fruit (John 15:1-6 below). Unsaved people are not "in Christ;" made alive in Christ, nor seated with Him in His Kingdom (Ephesians 2:1-8).

Now that we are in Christ, we have to bear fruit in order to remain in Him (John 15:5). The branches that do not remain in Jesus are cut off and burned in the end (John 15:6, Romans 11:22, Hebrews 6:7-8). We didn't work to enter the Kingdom of Christ, but we were created in Him to serve Him (John 15:16, Ephesians 2:10, 2 Corinthians 5:15). Check the verses.

John 15:1-6
1 "I am the true vine, and My Father is the vinedresser.
2 Every branch in Me that does not bear fruit He takes away; and every branch that bears fruit He prunes, that it may bear more fruit. 3 You are already clean because of the word which I have spoken to you. 4 Abide in Me, and I in you. As the branch cannot bear fruit of itself, unless it abides in the vine, neither can you, unless you abide in Me. 5 "I am the vine, you are the branches. He who abides in Me, and I in him, bears much fruit; for without Me you can do nothing. 6 If anyone does not abide in Me, he is cast out as a branch and is withered; and they gather them and throw them into the fire, and they are burned. NKJV

John 15:1-6
1 "I am the true vine, and my Father is the gardener. 2 He cuts off every branch in me that bears no fruit, while every branch that does bear fruit he prunes so that it will be even more fruitful. 3 You are already clean because of the word I have spoken to you. 4 Remain in me, and I will

remain in you. No branch can bear fruit by itself; it must remain in the vine. Neither can you bear fruit unless you remain in me. 5 "I am the vine; you are the branches. If a man remains in me and I in him, he will bear much fruit; apart from me you can do nothing. 6 If anyone does not remain in me, he is like a branch that is thrown away and withers; such branches are picked up, thrown into the fire and burned. NIV

It is impossible to bear the right kind of fruit unless we remain in the vine. The vine is Jesus, and if we do not remain in Jesus, we will be cut off (Romans 11:22, John 15:1-6 above).

This is one of the reasons many fall back into sins that lead to death a few years after being set free from sin. By not remaining (abiding) in Jesus (the vine) we can't do anything (John 15:5 above). The only way Christians can remain in Jesus, in Christ, is to obey His commands (John 15:10, 1 John 3:24 below).

John 15:10
10 If you keep My commandments, you will abide in My love, just as I have kept My Father's commandments and abide in His love. NKJV

John 15:10
10 If you obey my commands, you will remain in my love, just as I have obeyed my Father's commands and remain in his love. NIV

1 John 3:24
24 Now he who keeps His commandments abides in Him, and He in him. And by this we know that He abides in us, by the Spirit whom He has given us. NKJV

1 John 3:24
24 Those who obey his commands live in him, and he in them. And this is how we know that he lives in us: We know

it by the Spirit he gave us. NIV

The only way to remain in the vine is to obey His commands (John 15:10, 1 John 3:24 above). That's how we remain. Every branch (disciple) that does not bear good fruit will be cut off (John 15:1-6). Every tree (person) that does not bear good fruit will be cut down, thrown into the fire and burned (Matthew 7:19, Acts 26:20, Luke 3:8-9).

IT'S A COMMAND

It's not a suggestion, or part of the Ten Commandments, but it's a new command to love one another. It's not the sum of the Laws of Moses, which is to love your neighbor as you love yourself, but it's a new command for one disciple to love another disciple; love one another (John 13:34-35, 15:12-17 below).

John 13:34-35
34 "A new commandment I give to you, that you love one another; as I have loved you, that you also love one another. 35 By this all will know that you are My disciples, if you have love for one another." NKJV

John 13:34-35
34 "A new command I give you: Love one another. As I have loved you, so you must love one another. 35 By this all men will know that you are my disciples, if you love one another." NIV

John 15:12-17
12 This is My commandment, that you love one another as I have loved you. 13 Greater love has no one than this, than to lay down one's life for his friends. 14 You are My friends if you do whatever I command you. 15 No longer do I call you servants, for a servant does not know what his master is doing; but I have called you friends, for all things that I heard from My Father I have made known to you. 16 You did not choose Me, but I chose you and appointed

you that you should go and bear fruit, and that your fruit should remain, that whatever you ask the Father in My name He may give you. 17 These things I command you, that you love one another. NKJV

John 15:12-17
12 My command is this: Love each other as I have loved you. 13 Greater love has no one than this, that he lay down his life for his friends. 14 You are my friends if you do what I command. 15 I no longer call you servants, because a servant does not know his master's business. Instead, I have called you friends, for everything that I learned from my Father I have made known to you. 16 You did not choose me, but I chose you and appointed you to go and bear fruit — fruit that will last. Then the Father will give you whatever you ask in my name. 17 This is my command: Love each other. NIV

We will know the disciples of Jesus by their love for one another. That's one disciple loving another disciple. We recognize disciples of Jesus by this type of fruit, and not by how they look, how long they have been in church, their title, or their position (Matthew 7:15-20, 2 Corinthians 5:16, 11:3-4).

If Jesus is the Lord of our life, then He is in control. Therefore, we may have to deny ourselves in order to do what He commanded us (Matthew 16:24-25). If Jesus is the Lord of our life, then love is the fruit we are bearing, which proves that we are His disciples.

REMAIN IN DEATH

The person who does not obey Jesus' commands does not abide, or remain in Him (in Christ). It's not that they were not saved, but they chose not to remain in Jesus. Those who remain in Jesus pass from death to life, but those who do not abide in Jesus remain in death, and do not have eternal life in them (1 John 3:14-15 below).

1 John 3:14-15
14 We know that we have passed from death to life, because we love the brethren. He who does not love his brother abides in death. 15 Whoever hates his brother is a murderer, and you know that no murderer has eternal life abiding in him. NKJV

1 John 3:14-15
14 We know that we have passed from death to life, because we love our brothers. Anyone who does not love remains in death. 15 Anyone who hates his brother is a murderer, and you know that no murderer has eternal life in him. NIV

Obeying Jesus is not optional. We have to love one another in order to remain, and those who do not love remain in death. They don't need to be saved again, since they are seated with Christ in His Kingdom until the end of the age when they will be weeded out, but they need to repent (Matthew 13:40-43). Those who do not repent, do not accept Jesus' Words or God's will for their life, which is to believe in the Son (John 6:28-29).

When saved people refuse to obey Jesus over a period of time, they will be cut off. Land that drinks the rain (grace) and produces a useful crop receives a blessing, but land that bears thorns and briers is in danger of being cursed, and in the end it will be burned (Hebrews 6:7-8).

ACCESS BY FAITH INTO GRACE

What about grace? God gives grace to the humble, but He opposes the proud (James 4:5, 1 Peter 5:5). Can we speak directly against Jesus, Who is the Word, and say that God approves of our message? Can we insult the Spirit of grace and receive grace (Hebrews 10:26-30)? Check and see.

Only through faith in Jesus do we gain access into grace (Romans 5:2), and faith in Jesus expresses itself through love (Galatians 5:6). Anyone who claims to be in the light, but hates his brother is in darkness (1 John 2:10-11). Anyone who claims to have fellowship with God, but walks in darkness lies (1 John 1:6).

Therefore, if we say that we are living by faith in Jesus Christ, but we do not love one another, we are lying. That would be the same as if Noah could have faith in God without building the Ark (Hebrews 11:7).

Building the Ark was proof that Noah had faith in God, just like taking Isaac to the mountain was proof of Abraham's faith (James 2:2-24, Hebrews 11:17-19). In the same way, loving one another proves that we have faith in Jesus, and it fulfills our faith (Galatians 5:6). Faith in Jesus will produce love, and without faith, we have no access to grace (Romans 5:2). Check the verses.

Don't be deceived by the multitudes that reject what Jesus said and have formed their own version of the Gospel message. It is a part of God's plan, that all who desire to continue in wickedness and reject the truth will be condemned (2 Thessalonians 2:9-15 below).

2 Thessalonians 2:9-15
9 The coming of the lawless one is according to the working of Satan, with all power, signs, and lying wonders, 10 and with all unrighteous deception among those who perish, because they did not receive the love of the truth, that they might be saved. 11 And for this reason God will send them strong delusion, that they should believe the lie, 12 that they all may be condemned who did not believe the truth but had pleasure in unrighteousness. 13 But we are bound to give thanks to God always for you, brethren beloved by the Lord, because God from the beginning chose you for salvation through sanctification by the Spirit and belief in the truth, 14 to which He called you by our gospel, for the obtaining of the glory of our Lord Jesus Christ. 15 Therefore, brethren, stand fast and hold the traditions which you were taught, whether by word or our epistle. NKJV

2 Thessalonians 2:9-15
9 The coming of the lawless one will be in accordance with the work of Satan displayed in all kinds of counterfeit miracles, signs and wonders, 10 and in every sort of evil

73

that deceives those who are perishing. They perish because they refused to love the truth and so be saved. 11 For this reason God sends them a powerful delusion so that they will believe the lie 12 and so that all will be condemned who have not believed the truth but have delighted in wickedness. 13 But we ought always to thank God for you, brothers loved by the Lord, because from the beginning God chose you to be saved through the sanctifying work of the Spirit and through belief in the truth. 14 He called you to this through our gospel, that you might share in the glory of our Lord Jesus Christ. 15 So then, brothers, stand firm and hold to the teachings we passed on to you, whether by word of mouth or by letter. NIV

According to the Bible, the sanctifying work of the Spirit and belief in the truth are parts of the Gospel (verse 13-14 above). If you have not heard about it, then you have not heard a complete Gospel. Get the Gospel straight out of the Bible and forget about what you can see with your eyes. Do not allow signs and wonders to deceive you, since the devil is capable of producing them for that purpose (Matthew 24:24 below).

Matthew 24:24
24 For false christs and false prophets will rise and show great signs and wonders to deceive, if possible, even the elect. NKJV

Matthew 24:24
24 For false Christs and false prophets will appear and perform great signs and miracles to deceive even the elect if that were possible. NIV

Jesus gave the fig tree in Luke 13:6-9, four years to bear fruit. Once that period of time had passed, it was to be cut down. There is no reason to allow a barren tree to continue to use up the nutrients in the soil (grace) and the same is true for us. Check the verses.

If you have not remained in Christ in accordance with what is written, ask the Father in the name of Jesus to forgive you. Repent of anything that comes to mind and start over, but this time do it according to what is written. Always test what anyone tells you (1 Thessalonians 5:21). Make it a habit to always carry a Bible, and use whatever free time you have to read it.

You are responsible for what you believe. The Spirit will confirm it. Ask the Father in Jesus' name to forgive you of your sins and wash your conscience clean with the blood of Jesus (Hebrews 9:14, 10:22). Once you complete that, when you hear the truth, do not reject it (Hebrews 3:7-15).

NOTHING CAN MAKE US STUMBLE

How is love connected to sin? If you asked someone filled with human wisdom if we could rid ourselves of anything within us that could make us sin simply by loving other disciples of Jesus, what do you think they would say? They would probably laugh, since the world's ways do not rely on spiritual principles, and a man without the Holy Spirit, cannot possibly rely on the thoughts, wisdom, or understanding that comes from Him (1 Corinthians 2:6-15).

However, the wisdom of this world is foolishness to God (1 Corinthians 3:18-19), and what is highly valued to men is detestable in God's sight (Luke 16:15). Check the verses. We have written evidence in the Word of God that love can clear away the darkness that is within those who abide in Jesus Christ.

1 John 2:8-11
8 Again, a new commandment I write to you, which thing is true in Him and in you, because the darkness is passing away, and the true light is already shining. 9 He who says he is in the light, and hates his brother, is in darkness until now. 10 He who loves his brother abides in the light, and there is no cause for stumbling in him. 11 But he who hates his brother is in darkness and walks in darkness, and does not know where he is going, because the darkness has blinded his eyes. NKJV

1 John 2:8-11
8 Yet I am writing you a new command; its truth is seen in him and you, because the darkness is passing and the true light is already shining. 9 Anyone who claims to be in the light but hates his brother is still in the darkness. 10 Whoever loves his brother lives in the light, and there is nothing in him to make him stumble. 11 But whoever hates his brother is in the darkness and walks around in the darkness; he does not know where he is going, because the darkness has blinded him. NIV

Love makes us abide (remain) in the light to the point that there will never be anything in us that can make us stumble (verse 10 above). Love gives us the power to stand against sin since it takes the desire to sin out of us. From that point on, we would have to fall out of love, or allow someone or something to talk us into creating a desire to sin just like the serpent tempted Eve (Genesis 3:1-7).

Most sin starts with a desire from within us (James 1:13-15). If we were placed in a position where we had absolutely no desire within us to commit sins, then we would have a clear mind. We could go from thinking about crack cocaine every waking moment, to singing Christian songs in our mind all day long (Ephesians 5:19). Imagine that.

That's the power that love has over darkness. The person who obeys Jesus and remains in love will come out of darkness. That's a spiritual principle that works whether we know it or not.

TO THE POINT OF SUFFERING

If we were willing to deny ourselves and remain in love in all situations, even to the point of suffering, then we would be done with sin for good (1 Peter 4:1-4 below). In other words, sin can no longer rule over a Christian who is willing to obey Jesus to the point of suffering in his body, just as Jesus resisted sin to the point of shedding His blood (Hebrews 12:4).

1 Peter 4:1-4
1 Therefore, since Christ suffered for us in the flesh,

76

arm yourselves also with the same mind, for he who has suffered in the flesh has ceased from sin, 2 that he no longer should live the rest of his time in the flesh for the lusts of men, but for the will of God. 3 For we have spent enough of our past lifetime in doing the will of the Gentiles when we walked in lewdness, lusts, drunkenness, revelries, drinking parties, and abominable idolatries. 4 In regard to these, they think it strange that you do not run with them in the same flood of dissipation, speaking evil of you. NKJV

1 Peter 4:1-4
1 Therefore, since Christ suffered in his body, arm yourselves also with the same attitude, because he who has suffered in his body is done with sin. 2 As a result, he does not live the rest of his earthly life for evil human desires, but rather for the will of God. 3 For you have spent enough time in the past doing what pagans choose to do living in debauchery, lust, drunkenness, orgies, carousing and detestable idolatry. 4 They think it strange that you do not plunge with them into the same flood of dissipation, and they heap abuse on you. NIV

Does that really say that we can be done with sin (verse 1 above)? Notice that the Christian, who is done with sin, does not live the rest of his life for evil human desires, but for God's will (verse 2 above). Sinful desires can no longer control him.

Your willingness to suffer at the hands of another person is a direct indicator to whether or not you are done with sin. If someone strikes you on one cheek, and you turn the other, then you are done with sin because you were willing to remain in love to the point of suffering. However, if you return evil for evil or insult for insult, then you are unwilling to suffer and consequently your desire for revenge will rule over you (Romans 12:17-21).

At whatever point we do not remain in love through our actions, we are unwilling to suffer, and consequently, we are not done with sin. Therefore, Christians who remain in love do not bite and devour one another, since they know that it can destroy them (Galatians 5:13-15).

Galatians 5:13-15
13 For you, brethren, have been called to liberty; only do not use liberty as an opportunity for the flesh, but through love serve one another. 14 For all the law is fulfilled in one word, even in this: "You shall love your neighbor as yourself." 15 But if you bite and devour one another, beware lest you be consumed by one another! NKJV

Galatians 5:13-15
13 You, my brothers, were called to be free. But do not use your freedom to indulge the sinful nature; rather, serve one another in love. 14 The entire law is summed up in a single command: "Love your neighbor as yourself." 15 If you keep on biting and devouring each other, watch out or you will be destroyed by each other. NIV

Notice that we can be destroyed by each other (verse 15 above). Once we begin to love one another, we have to remain in love.

The Bible says that when you bring your gift before the Lord, and there remember that your brother has something against you, first go and be reconciled with your brother, and then give (Matthew 5:23-24). Love is more important than giving, although you would have never guessed it this day and age.

Once a Christian who remains in Christ is willing to suffer in his body in order to be done with sin, the only effective attack the enemy has is to make him fall out of love. Recognize that, because the unwillingness to suffer has made many well-meaning Christians fall.

Even among church people, the ones who are not free "in Christ" will persecute the ones who are (Galatians 4:29). All who choose to live a godly life will be persecuted (treated unfairly) by the people who are not going to make it (2 Timothy 3:12, Philippians 1:27-29).

We are called to suffer in order that we would inherit a blessing (1 Peter 3:9). In fact, the amount of suffering we face is a direct indicator of our reward in Heaven (Matthew 5:11-12, Romans 8:17, Acts 5:41).

Perfect love drives out fear of punishment for sins, since those who remain in love are done with sin (1 John 4:12-21, 1 Peter 4:1-2).

Suffering is a part of the Christian process, or the doctrine that delivers us from sin which all of us must go through. It's not only a calling, but it's an opportunity that has been given to us in order that we might share in Christ's glory (Romans 8:17, John 17:22). Check the verses before you speak. It is also a sign to those who cause us to suffer (Philippians 1:27-29 below).

Philippians 1:27-29
27 Only let your conduct be worthy of the gospel of Christ, so that whether I come and see you or am absent, I may hear of your affairs, that you stand fast in one spirit, with one mind striving together for the faith of the gospel, 28 and not in any way terrified by your adversaries, which is to them a proof of perdition, but to you of salvation, and that from God. 29 For to you it has been granted on behalf of Christ, not only to believe in Him, but also to suffer for His sake. NKJV

Philippians 1:27-29
27 Whatever happens, conduct yourselves in a manner worthy of the gospel of Christ. Then, whether I come and see you or only hear about you in my absence, I will know that you stand firm in one spirit, contending as one man for the faith of the gospel 28 without being frightened in any way by those who oppose you. This is a sign to them that they will be destroyed, but that you will be saved and that by God. 29 For it has been granted to you on behalf of Christ not only to believe on him, but also to suffer for him. NIV

Those who cause us to suffer will be destroyed, if they do not repent of their ways. This is why the Bible says in 1 John 3:13, "Do not be surprised my Brothers if the world hates you." Jesus told His disciples that the people of this world would hate them, because they were His disciples

(John 15:18-21). In 1 Peter 4:12 the Bible tells us not to be shocked at suffering, but rejoice that we participate in the sufferings of Christ.

If your faith is growing, and the love you have for other disciples is increasing, even through the persecutions and trials, then that is the evidence that you will be counted worthy of the Kingdom of God (2 Thessalonians 1:3-9 below).

2 Thessalonians 1:3-9
3 We are bound to thank God always for you, brethren, as it is fitting, because your faith grows exceedingly, and the love of every one of you all abounds toward each other, 4 so that we ourselves boast of you among the churches of God for your patience and faith in all your persecutions and tribulations that you endure, 5 which is manifest evidence of the righteous judgment of God, that you may be counted worthy of the kingdom of God, for which you also suffer; 6 since it is a righteous thing with God to repay with tribulation those who trouble you, 7 and to give you who are troubled rest with us when the Lord Jesus is revealed from heaven with His mighty angels, 8 in flaming fire taking vengeance on those who do not know God, and on those who do not obey the gospel of our Lord Jesus Christ. 9 These shall be punished with everlasting destruction from the presence of the Lord and from the glory of His power. NKJV

2 Thessalonians 1:3-9
3 We ought always to thank God for you, brothers, and rightly so, because your faith is growing more and more, and the love every one of you has for each other is increasing. 4 Therefore, among God's churches we boast about your perseverance and faith in all the persecutions and trials you are enduring. 5 All this is evidence that God's judgment is right, and as a result you will be counted worthy of the kingdom of God, for which you are suffering. 6 God is just: He will pay back trouble to those who trouble

you 7 and give relief to you who are troubled, and to us as well. This will happen when the Lord Jesus is revealed from heaven in blazing fire with his powerful angels. 8 He will punish those who do not know God and do not obey the gospel of our Lord Jesus. 9 They will be punished with everlasting destruction and shut out from the presence of the Lord and from the majesty of his power. NIV

Those who do not know God, and do not obey the Gospel will be punished with everlasting destruction and shut out from the presence of the Lord (verse 8-9 above). God will pay back trouble for those who trouble us, point, blank, period (verse 6 above).

Decide today which side of the fence you are on because you may never be able to see what I am explaining to you again. Darkness makes us blind to the point that we cannot see (1 John 2:8-11 above). As it is written, "Whoever hates his brother is in darkness and walks around in darkness." "He does not know where he is going because the darkness has blinded him." Repent, pick up your cross and follow Jesus who left us an example" (1 Peter 2:21-24).

1 Peter 2:21-24
21 For to this you were called, because Christ also suffered for us, leaving us an example, that you should follow His steps: 22 "Who committed no sin, Nor was deceit found in His mouth;" 23 who, when He was reviled, did not revile in return; when He suffered, He did not threaten, but committed Himself to Him who judges righteously; 24 who Himself bore our sins in His own body on the tree, that we, having died to sins, might live for righteousness by whose stripes you were healed. NKJV

1 Peter 2:21-24
21 To this you were called, because Christ suffered for you, leaving you an example, that you should follow in his steps. 22 "He committed no sin, and no deceit was found in his mouth." 23 When they hurled their insults at him, he

did not retaliate; when he suffered, he made no threats. Instead, he entrusted himself to him who judges justly. 24 He himself bore our sins in his body on the tree, so that we might die to sins and live for righteousness; by his wounds you have been healed. NIV

Remain in love with everyone, and as much as it depends of you, be at peace with everyone (Romans 12:18, Colossians 3:15). Walking away is always an option.

Being a Christian doesn't necessarily mean that you are a pushover. You are called to suffer in order that you may inherit a blessing (1 Peter). However, if someone breaks the law, which causes you to suffer, dial 911 (Romans 13:1-7). Always leave room for God's wrath, which is relying on Him for your revenge (Romans 12:17-21).

After you suffer a while, God will restore you and make you stronger (1 Peter 5:8-10 below).

1 Peter 5:8-10
8 Be sober, be vigilant; because your adversary the devil walks about like a roaring lion, seeking whom he may devour. 9 Resist him, steadfast in the faith, knowing that the same sufferings are experienced by your brotherhood in the world. 10 But may the God of all grace, who called us to His eternal glory by Christ Jesus, after you have suffered a while, perfect, establish, strengthen, and settle you. NKJV

1 Peter 5:8-10
8 Be self-controlled and alert. Your enemy the devil prowls around like a roaring lion looking for someone to devour. 9 Resist him, standing firm in the faith, because you know that your brothers throughout the world are undergoing the same kind of sufferings. 10 And the God of all grace, who called you to his eternal glory in Christ, after you have suffered a little while, will himself restore you and make you strong, firm and steadfast. NIV

Those who attack you will be the very ones you will be exalted over, if you are willing to suffer through the persecutions (Isaiah 54:14-17). However, if you do not leave room for God's wrath, He will not be your avenger and you will not be restored (Romans 12:19). Take the blessing (1 Peter 3:9)!

FOLLOW ME

People in the dark don't necessarily know it (1 John 2:8-11 above). According to those verses, we could be in darkness and not know it since darkness blinds us. Therefore, it is conceivable that a person could attend church for years and still be living in darkness simply because they hate a believer. Imagine that.

I'm not saying they have not been saved. The church building is full of saved people. In fact, some go through the motions of being saved over and over again, but only those who follow Jesus come out of darkness to the point of stopping sin.

The church building is full of people who have accepted Jesus as their savior, which frees them from the power of darkness (Colossians 1:12-13), but that doesn't mean they choose to come out of darkness. As it is written, "Light has come into the world, but men loved darkness instead of light because their deeds were evil (John 3:19).

We hear things like, "Jesus forgives sins" over and over again, but we rarely hear a complete message. Therefore, many have come to interpret passages of scripture like the woman caught in adultery (John 8:1-13), as an excuse to say that if we continue in sin, Jesus will not condemn us. What they are missing is that Jesus is trying to show us the way, or the path we must take to be delivered from sin (John 14:6).

One morning while Jesus was teaching the people, the scribes and Pharisees brought in a woman caught in adultery (John 8:1-12). You know the story, but look at what Jesus told her afterwards, concerning sin.

John 8:10-12
10 When Jesus had raised Himself up and saw no one but the woman, He said to her, "Woman, where are those accusers of yours? Has no one condemned you?" 11 She said, "No one, Lord." And Jesus said to her, "Neither do I

condemn you; go and sin no more." 12 Then Jesus spoke to them again, saying, "I am the light of the world. He who follows Me shall not walk in darkness, but have the light of life." NKJV

John 8:10-12
10 Jesus straightened up and asked her, "Woman, where are they? Has no one condemned you?" 11 "No one, sir," she said. "Then neither do I condemn you," Jesus declared. "Go now and leave your life of sin." 12 When Jesus spoke again to the people, he said, "I am the light of the world. Whoever follows me will never walk in darkness, but will have the light of life." NIV

When Jesus had finished addressing the woman, He spoke again to the people that had witnessed what had transpired saying, "Whoever follows me will never walk in darkness." Jesus did not condemn the woman in accordance with the Laws of Moses, but He did not condone the sin either. In fact, He corrected her by telling her to stop sinning, and gave her the method in which to accomplish it; follow Me.

It is impossible to follow Jesus and walk in darkness. Who can say, "I followed Jesus and He led me into sin?" If we were following Jesus, our life would show it since we would come out of darkness.

As Christ followers, we are called to deny our own desires, pick up our cross daily, and follow Jesus (Matthew 16:24-25). Whoever loses his life in this way, will find life and keep it for eternal life. Whoever does not deny himself and follow Jesus to the point of coming out of darkness, rejects Jesus as Lord of his life.

We don't condemn those caught up in sins that lead to death, but we do try and correct them in order to save their soul from death (James 5:19-20). Those who are spiritual (Galatians 6:1-2), and have taken the plank out of their own eye (Matthew 7:5), are to instruct those who live in error in the hope that God will grant them repentance (2 Timothy 2:24-26). May the Lord have mercy on all who allow this teaching to reach them for the truth, in the name of Jesus. Amen.

CANNOT BE SNATCHED

Many have received the wrong message. Now that they are saved, they believe that nothing can snatch them out of Jesus' hand (John 10:28). He did promise that, but like so many promises that are misinterpreted as "all inclusive," so it is with that one. Read the verses below to see who the sheep are that Jesus made that promise to. Does it include all saved people or the ones who hear His voice, know Him, and follow Him?

John 10:27-28
27 My sheep hear My voice, and I know them, and they follow Me. 28 And I give them eternal life, and they shall never perish; neither shall anyone snatch them out of My hand. NKJV

John 10:27-28
27 My sheep listen to my voice; I know them, and they follow me. 28 I give them eternal life, and they shall never perish; no one can snatch them out of my hand. NIV

If you read verse 28 without reading verse 27 first, the interpretation can be twisted. The sheep that cannot be snatched out of Jesus' hand listen to Him, know Him, and follow Him (verse 27 above). Do you reject or accept what Jesus has said? Those who accept His Word hear His Word and do not avoid it.

Draw a large circle on a piece of paper, and a smaller circle inside of it. On the outside of the large circle write "unsaved people." Inside the large circle write "saved people." Inside the inner circle write "Jesus' sheep." They are among the sheep that cannot be snatched out of Jesus' hand (John 5:24, 6:53-63).

The prodigal son was welcomed home and His Father ran to meet him (Luke 15:11-32). Praise God! That's true, but while the son was away he was dead, and when he returned his father said, "He is alive again" (Luke 15:32). Now, which circle are we in? Being saved gives us the right to become children of God (John 1:12). As it is written for those who are in the Kingdom of Christ, "We have been qualified to share in the inheritance" (Colossians 1:12-13). Check the verses.

85

Yes, Jesus came to save sinners (1 Timothy 1:15). Praise God! However, His Word will condemn those who reject it in the end according to John 12:46-49. Who would call Jesus the truth and the life in one breath, but a liar in the next? Only those who do not hear His Word would do that (John 6:60-69).

KNOW JESUS

Do you know Jesus? One of the questions I ask during a seminar is how can we be sure that we know Jesus? At the end of the age some people will hear, "Away from Me, I never knew you" (Matthew 7:21-23, Luke 13:27). I don't want anyone that I have had the opportunity to teach, fail to come to know Jesus in accordance with what is written.

1 John 2:3-5
3 Now by this we know that we know Him, if we keep His commandments. 4 He who says, "I know Him," and does not keep His commandments, is a liar, and the truth is not in him. 5 But whoever keeps His word, truly the love of God is perfected in him. By this we know that we are in Him. NKJV

1 John 2:3-5
3 We know that we have come to know him if we obey his commands. 4 The man who says, "I know him," but does not do what he commands is a liar, and the truth is not in him. 5 But if anyone obeys his word, God's love is truly made complete in him. This is how we know we are in him: NIV

The people who do not obey Jesus' command to love one another, cannot possibly know Him (1 John 2:3-5), and they are in danger of hearing, "Away from Me, I never knew you" in the end (Matthew 7:15-21).

Those who obey Jesus' command to love remain in Him, and come out of darkness to the point of nothing being in them that can make them stumble. According to verse five above, those who obey His Word have the love of God perfected in them. Does that describe you? Further evidence of this is found in Ephesians 4:20-24 below.

86

Ephesians 4:20-24
20 But you have not so learned Christ, 21 if indeed you have heard Him and have been taught by Him, as the truth is in Jesus: 22 that you put off, concerning your former conduct, the old man which grows corrupt according to the deceitful lusts, 23 and be renewed in the spirit of your mind, 24 and that you put on the new man which was created according to God, in true righteousness and holiness. NKJV

Ephesians 4:20-24
20 You, however, did not come to know Christ that way. 21 Surely you heard of him and were taught in him in accordance with the truth that is in Jesus. 22 You were taught, with regard to your former way of life, to put off your old self, which is being corrupted by its deceitful desires; 23 to be made new in the attitude of your minds; 24 and to put on the new self, created to be like God in true righteousness and holiness. NIV

Those who put off their former conduct, renew their mind to the point of putting on the new person are the ones who come to know Jesus Christ according to Ephesians 4:20-24 above. The Apostle Paul is telling the people of Ephesus that this is how they were taught. Does that match what you have been taught?

Jesus is the source of eternal salvation for those who obey Him (Hebrews 5:9), but when we harden our hearts by refusing to change, we become separated from the life of God (Ephesians 4:17-19). We must deny ourselves, put off our old way of life, and allow Jesus, Who is the Word made flesh (John 1:14), to give us life (John 6:63).

TURN HIM BACK

Can you see that many people have placed their hope into being treated like the woman caught in adultery as if we can willfully live our entire life in sins that lead to death and be forgiven as we walk through the pearly gates of Heaven? They don't know the truth. Many Christians believe that they cannot be snatched out of Jesus' hand also, and they too don't know the truth.

These people are in line to hear "Away from Me, I never knew you" on the last day and they don't even realize it. No wonder there will be weeping and gnashing of teeth, but in the new Heaven and the new earth, the things of old will not be remembered or come to mind (Isaiah 65:17). We will not remember the people we see now who will not make it.

My heart goes out to them and my prayer is that through this book I might reach all of them. We should try to reach the people among us who have placed their hope in promises that do not even apply to them (James 5:19-20).

James 5:19-20
19 Brethren, if anyone among you wanders from the truth, and someone turns him back, 20 let him know that he who turns a sinner from the error of his way will save a soul from death and cover a multitude of sins. NKJV

James 5:19-20
19 My brothers, if one of you should wander from the truth and someone should bring him back, 20 remember this: Whoever turns a sinner from the error of his way will save him from death and cover over a multitude of sins. NIV

Those verses say that if someone is going the wrong way it will end in death. A sinner has to be turned from error in order to save his soul and cover his sins. Israel was on fire for God, but not according to knowledge (Romans 10:2). Shouldn't we try to reach people who have trusted their eternal future to misinterpreted promises?

The "You are okay, I'm okay" philosophy just isn't working. Somebody has to stand up and correct the error in accordance with what is written. Why did the Apostle Paul rebuke the Apostle Peter to his face?

Galatians 2:14
14 But when I saw that they were not straightforward

about the truth of the gospel, I said to Peter before them all,... NKJV

Galatians 2:14
14 When I saw that they were not acting in line with the truth of the gospel, I said to Peter in front of them all...
NIV

Those in authority who are caught in sin, from the position of elder upward, should be corrected (rebuked) in front of all that the rest may fear (1 Timothy 5:20). Check the verses.

LOVE IS

What is love according to the Bible? If you do not know the scriptures, then you might think that love is hugging people you don't necessarily want to hug, and shaking hands with people that you do not want to associate with, but that's not necessarily the case. A person who is good at socializing may be considered faithful, when all the while he doesn't really love anyone, and may even be on the list of people that we are instructed not to associate with.

Hugging each other and shaking hands can be considered a sign of love since love includes brotherly kindness (Ephesians 4:32, 1 Corinthians 13:4-7 below). So, go ahead and hug anyone you want, but know that it can be a show of worldly affection without Christian love according to what is written in the Bible.

1 Corinthians 13:4-7
4 Love suffers long and is kind; love does not envy; love does not parade itself, is not puffed up; 5 does not behave rudely, does not seek its own, is not provoked, thinks no evil; 6 does not rejoice in iniquity, but rejoices in the truth; 7 bears all things, believes all things, hopes all things, endures all things. NKJV

1 Corinthians 13:4-7
4 Love is patient, love is kind. It does not envy, it does not

boast, it is not proud. 5 It is not rude, it is not self-seeking, it is not easily angered, it keeps no record of wrongs. 6 Love does not delight in evil but rejoices with the truth. 7 It always protects, always trusts, always hopes, always perseveres. NIV

The last time we were impatient, we fell out of love, because love is patient. Patience in trials reveals maturity, and a genuine faith (James 1:2-4, 1 Peter 1:6-7).

The last time we were rude, we fell out of love because love is kind. Being rude is a sign that we are unwilling to suffer. Repent of that and turn back the other way (Ephesians 4:32).

Love forgives everybody because it keeps no record of wrong, and so on. The person who does not forgive others is in rebellion. He refuses to suffer at the cost of his own life (Matthew 6:14-15). You can be sure that he is nowhere close to being done with sin or living for the will of God (1 Peter 4:1-3).

The person, who does not forgive everyone, does not have the kind of love that God requires. He may hug everyone in the church, but he has failed the test of love. Do you see how affection can be mistaken for love or a cover-up for love?

The most impatient person in the world can flip that "smile switch" on, right before he gets out of his car in the church parking lot. These days a "smile switch" is standard equipment in the majority of cars driven in the United States.

A person who is good at socializing might smile and say all the right words in church, but curse the waitress out at the restaurant soon after. That's clearly not the love of God. A spring does not produce both fresh water and salt water (James 3:9-12).

This could very well happen to a spiritual person that doesn't know to remain in love. He may not realize that his faith will be tested until proven genuine (1 Peter 1:6-7, James 1:2-4). The trial has come to test his faith in order that he will realize where he is in the faith. God knows where he is, but the test should make him realize that something is not right in his life.

Just as Abraham's faith was tested by offering his son (Hebrews

11:17), so too our faith in Jesus will be tested to see if we are going to remain in the faith. God doesn't tempt us into sin, but He tests us (1 Thessalonians 2:4, Proverbs 17:3, 1 Chronicles 29:17).

We who are spiritual should know that we have to pass the testing of our faith. We can seem as spiritual as angels, but without love we are absolutely nothing (1 Corinthians 13:1-3). We can have prophecy, faith, knowledge, giving, speaking in tongues, and laying hands on people, down pat, but if we don't have love, we operate in the flesh (1 John 15:4-6), and are absolutely nothing.

God's gifts and callings are irrevocable (Romans 11:29) and work in proportion to a person's faith (Romans 12:6). Therefore, even though a person's gift works, it doesn't mean that they are in the will of God or have come to know the Lord (Matthew 7:21-23, Ephesians 4:20-24). Apart from the vine, a branch operates for his own glory (John 7:18, Acts 20:29-31).

In fact, if anyone comes to us, or we listen to them, and they do not mention the doctrine of Jesus we should not welcome them regardless of how spiritual they may seem (2 John 9-11 below). This should be a sign that they are working for their own glory (John 7:18).

2 John 9-11
9 Whoever transgresses and does not abide in the doctrine of Christ does not have God. He who abides in the doctrine of Christ has both the Father and the Son. 10 If anyone comes to you and does not bring this doctrine, do not receive him into your house nor greet him; 11 for he who greets him shares in his evil deeds. NKJV

2 John 9-11
9 Anyone who runs ahead and does not continue in the teaching of Christ does not have God; whoever continues in the teaching has both the Father and the Son. 10 If anyone comes to you and does not bring this teaching, do not take him into your house or welcome him. 11 Anyone who welcomes him shares in his wicked work. NIV

Just because there are signs and wonders for everyone to rant and rave over, it doesn't mean that God is in it or that He approves of the message. If the doctrine of Jesus is not mentioned you can be sure the intentions are not to free people from sin, but to make followers of the speaker (Acts 20:29-31).

Many seem very spiritual with prophecy and signs this day and time, but they do not teach people to remain in Jesus by obeying Him, which is crucial for making disciples of Jesus (Matthew 28:19-20). If we were taught to obey Jesus we would love one another, and if we loved one another we would remain in Christ and come out of darkness. I believe that it would be fair to say that only disciples of Jesus, make disciples of Jesus.

If you find patience, forgiveness, and meekness in a Christian who is not proud, or easily angered, and does not tell dirty jokes, or speak against the Word of God, then hug that person for me would you? However, we can't look at someone and say with certainty that they are in Christ.

By their fruits we recognize them, and fruit includes what they do (Colossians 1:10, Matthew 7:15-20), and what they say (Matthew 12:33-37, James 3:9-12, Hebrews 13:15).

DON'T TELL ME YOU LOVE ME

There is one fruit that is unmistakable evidence. If the love of God has been poured into a person's heart, he will most certainly love in the way described in 1 John 3:16-19 below.

1 John 3:16-19
16 By this we know love, because He laid down His life for us. And we also ought to lay down our lives for the brethren. 17 But whoever has this world's goods, and sees his brother in need, and shuts up his heart from him, how does the love of God abide in him? 18 My little children, let us not love in word or in tongue, but in deed and in truth. 19 And by this we know that we are of the truth, and shall assure our hearts before Him. NKJV

1 John 3:16-19
16 This is how we know what love is: Jesus Christ laid down his life for us. And we ought to lay down our lives for our brothers. 17 If anyone has material possessions and sees his brother in need but has no pity on him, how can the love of God be in him? 18 Dear children, let us not love with words or tongue but with actions and in truth. 19 This then is how we know that we belong to the truth, and how we set our hearts at rest in his presence. NIV

According to verse 19 above, this is how we know for sure that we belong to the truth. If the love of God is in us, we will love our brothers by sharing our provisions with them.

Loving with words is not the type of love Jesus commanded us to have according to verse 18 above. The type of love Jesus commanded us requires that we help other disciples (Christ followers, brothers) with their needs according to verse 17 above, and James 2:14-17 below.

James 2:14-17
14 What is the use (profit), my brethren, for anyone to profess to have faith if he has no [good] works [to show for it]? Can [such] faith save [his soul]? 15 If a brother or sister is poorly clad and lacks food for each day, 16 And one of you says to him, Good-bye! Keep [yourself] warm and well fed, without giving him the necessities for the body, what good does that do? 17 So also faith, if it does not have works (deeds and actions of obedience to back it up), by itself is destitute of power (inoperative, dead). AMP

James 2:14-17
14 What good is it, my brothers, if a man claims to have faith but has no deeds? Can such faith save him? 15 Suppose a brother or sister is without clothes and daily food. 16 If one of you says to him, "Go, I wish you well; keep warm and well fed," but does nothing about his

93

physical needs, what good is it? 17 In the same way, faith by itself, if it is not accompanied by action, is dead. NIV

This is how those who have faith in Jesus love one another. The verses say to give a brother what is needed for the body (James 2:16); food, clothing, and shelter. People who will inherit salvation have one thing in common; they help the Saints, who are the faithful in Christ Jesus (Hebrews 6:9-10). As it is written, "These things accompany salvation."

Hebrews 6:9-12
9 But, beloved, we are confident of better things concerning you, yes, things that accompany salvation, though we speak in this manner. 10 For God is not unjust to forget your work and labor of love which you have shown toward His name, in that you have ministered to the saints, and do minister. 11 And we desire that each one of you show the same diligence to the full assurance of hope until the end, 12 that you do not become sluggish, but imitate those who through faith and patience inherit the promises. NKJV

Hebrews 6:9-12
9 Even though we speak like this, dear friends, we are confident of better things in your case things that accompany salvation. 10 God is not unjust; he will not forget your work and the love you have shown him as you have helped his people and continue to help them. 11 We want each of you to show this same diligence to the very end, in order to make your hope sure. 12 We do not want you to become lazy, but to imitate those who through faith and patience inherit what has been promised. NIV

What accompanies salvation? Those who will inherit salvation work for and love God by continuing to help His people to the very end (verse 10 above). Who do you work for, and can God forget your work? Tough question, but you need to know the truth.

According to what we have learned so far regarding love, a person can attend church, hug everybody, smile, kiss all the babies, and still not help anyone, or love anyone. Therefore, he may have faith, but it is a dead faith that cannot save. Sometimes what we see in the natural is exactly the opposite of the truth (Galatians 5:17).

I'm not saying that there is anything wrong with giving hugs, shaking hands, and smiling, but it seems like we have replaced the Bible's explanation of what love is with it. We should clothe ourselves with compassion, kindness, humility, and patience, and to greet the saints (faithful in Christ) with a holy kiss. However, that same passage of scripture also says, "above all these things" we should love one another (Colossians 3:12-15).

Therefore, start by giving to the least of God's people out of what you have to give. Find people who are reading their Bible and helping others. Search for those who are putting to death their sinful nature without making excuses to continue in sin (Romans 8:12-14). Help children who believe in Jesus at children shelters, or the homeless who believe in Jesus at local shelters, and help them with food, clothing, and shelter.

Don't tell them you love them, but show them (James 2:14-17). Whatever you do for the least of Jesus' "brothers," or God's people, you do for Him (Matthew 25:41, Hebrews 6:9-12). He will not forget it (Colossians 3:24). Check the verses.

WE ARE NOT SAVED BY GOOD WORKS

We are not saved by good works, since we were saved before we were appointed to do good works. However, the reward for sowing to please the Spirit is eternal life (Galatians 6:8, Colossians 3:24, Romans 6:20-22). Check what is written and then speak accordingly. If Jesus is our Lord, He tells us what to do (John 15:16, Luke 6:46).

We are saved by grace through faith (Ephesians 2:8-10), but dead faith cannot save (James 2:14-17) since it does not have the right deeds (love) to back up that person's statement of faith (James 2:20-24). Therefore, Christians who do not love one another as described above, have a dead faith in Jesus, which means that they accepted Jesus as Lord, but they do not allow Him to be their Lord. Faith in Jesus will produce love (Galatians 5:6).

God prepared good works in advance for each one of us to accomplish once we were saved (Ephesians 2:10, John 15:16-17, Titus 3:16). Basically, we are saved "to do" good works, or we have been appointed to do good works according to John 15:16.

Ephesians 2:8-10
8 For by grace you have been saved through faith, and that not of yourselves; it is the gift of God, 9 not of works, lest anyone should boast. 10 For we are His workmanship, created in Christ Jesus for good works, which God prepared beforehand that we should walk in them. NKJV

Ephesians 2:8-10
8 For it is by grace you have been saved, through faith — and this not from yourselves, it is the gift of God— 9 not by works, so that no one can boast. 10 For we are God's workmanship, created in Christ Jesus to do good works, which God prepared in advance for us to do. NIV

We are created in Christ Jesus "to do" good works, which God prepared in advance for us to do. That means the will of God for our life includes accomplishing good works that He specifically created for us to do.

That means that we are not a mistake or here by chance, but there is something that God wants each one of us to do. According to Acts 17:26, the time and place we were born was determined by God. Therefore, to refuse our obligation would be as if Noah had told God that he wasn't going to build the ark.

Imagine Noah telling God that he didn't see the need to build the ark since God could simply hold him out of the water until the flood waters dried, or build a higher mountain for him to live on. Human wisdom and deceptive philosophy makes us think like that (1 Corinthians 2:14, 2 Peter 2:1-3).

In the same way, some people believe we can ignore everything Jesus said and be like the thief on the cross, but we were never instructed to be like the thief. Jesus' covenant didn't start until His death on the cross (Hebrews 9:15-17). Now, under the New Covenant, God requires all people to repent (Acts 17:30). Check it!

GOOD WORKS BENEFIT US

There are countless people who are against good works, but they obviously do not know the truth. Good works and love benefit us. For example, love covers a multitude of sins according to 1 Peter 4:8.

1 Peter 4:8
8 And above all things have fervent love for one another, for "love will cover a multitude of sins." NKJV

1 Peter 4:8
8 Above all, love each other deeply, because love covers over a multitude of sins. NIV

If you have had a sin problem in the past, as all of us have, then love will deliver you from the effects of your sins. We can be forgiven for almost anything, but the problem is that we reap exactly what we sow (Galatians 6:7-10).

My grandmother used to say, "Alan, your sins will find you out!" I used to think that was just what she thought, but I found it in my Bible (Numbers 32:23), and let me assure you that it will happen. Your sin will catch up with you no matter where you go. However, there is something that we can do.

Jesus forgives us if we confess our sins (1 John 1:9), and forgive others (Matthew 6:14-15), but we still reap what we sow (Galatians 6:7-8). If we plant tomatoes, then tomatoes are going to grow. We can pray, shout halleluiah twenty times, do a holy dance, claim the blood of Jesus over our sin, and whatever else, but if we planted tomatoes, then tomatoes are going to grow. If we sow it, we will also reap it.

The only way to rectify what you've sown, once you've sown something that you don't want to reap, is to seed over it with something else. Loving one another, showing mercy toward others who wrong you (James 2:12-13), and sowing acts of righteousness to those who cannot repay you, produce mercy (Hosea 10:12, Matthew 25:34-39). All three of these will produce mercy for your mistakes, and they can be summed up as love.

We love in proportion to our sins. The person who has been forgiven of much, simply loves much.

Luke 7:47
47 Therefore I say to you, her sins, which are many, are forgiven, for she loved much. But to whom little is forgiven, the same loves little." NKJV

Luke 7:47
47 Therefore, I tell you, her many sins have been forgiven for she loved much. But he who has been forgiven little loves little." NIV

God doesn't punish us according to what our sins deserve (Lamentations 3:22, Psalm 103:30, 130:3), and He gives us plenty of time to repent (Romans 2:4). This is the reason why bank robbers don't get struck by lightning on the way out the door of the bank. God's kindness and patience is meant to lead us to repentance (Romans 2:4).

If God struck bank robbers with lightning as soon as they left the bank, He would have to treat us the same way. God does not show favoritism, or as it is written, "He is no respecter of persons" (Acts 10:34, Romans 2:11).

If we judged ourselves in accordance with God's righteous judgment, we would know that all of us deserve death (Romans 1:28-32). Check the verses! Therefore, since God gives us time to repent, He has to give everyone time to repent.

How much time do you need? Think about that before you judge those outside of the church (Matthew 7:1-2, Luke 6:37, 1 Corinthians 5:12-13). God will take care of them (Romans 13:1-7, 12:17-21). The land that lives in safety, will be the land that does God's will (Proverbs 1:33, 2 Chronicles 7:14, Psalm 91:14-16, Isaiah 58:6-11). Check it!

Learn these promises so that you can utilize them if you fall short in the future; love covers, mercy triumphs, and righteous acts produce mercy. Good works are an important part of being set free from sin, since they can control us in the same way sin can control us (Romans 6:20 below).

SLAVE TO RIGHTEOUS ACTS

Have you ever noticed that when people help others in need without any return from them, they are eager to do it again? The act of love or the act of doing good created the desire in them to do more good just as sin controls the person who sins. In this way, obeying Jesus makes us a slave to righteousness and sets us free from the control of sin (Romans 6:15-22 below).

Romans 6:15-22
15 What then? Shall we sin because we are not under law but under grace? Certainly not! 16 Do you not know that to whom you present yourselves slaves to obey, you are that one's slaves whom you obey, whether of sin leading to death, or of obedience leading to righteousness? 17 But God be thanked that though you were slaves of sin, yet you obeyed from the heart that form of doctrine to which you were delivered. 18 And having been set free from sin, you became slaves of righteousness. 19 I speak in human terms because of the weakness of your flesh. For just as you presented your members as slaves of uncleanness, and of lawlessness leading to more lawlessness, so now present your members as slaves of righteousness for holiness. 20 For when you were slaves of sin, you were free in regard to righteousness. 21 What fruit did you have then in the things of which you are now ashamed? For the end of those things is death. 22 But now having been set free from sin, and having become slaves of God, you have your fruit to holiness, and the end, everlasting life. NKJV

Romans 6:15-22
15 What then? Shall we sin because we are not under law but under grace? By no means! 16 Don't you know that when you offer yourselves to someone to obey him as slaves, you are slaves to the one whom you obey whether you

are slaves to sin, which leads to death, or to obedience, which leads to righteousness? 17 But thanks be to God that, though you used to be slaves to sin, you wholeheartedly obeyed the form of teaching to which you were entrusted. 18 You have been set free from sin and have become slaves to righteousness. 19 I put this in human terms because you are weak in your natural selves. Just as you used to offer the parts of your body in slavery to impurity and to ever-increasing wickedness, so now offer them in slavery to righteousness leading to holiness. 20 When you were slaves to sin, you were free from the control of righteousness. 21 What benefit did you reap at that time from the things you are now ashamed of? Those things result in death! 22 But now that you have been set free from sin and have become slaves to God, the benefit you reap leads to holiness, and the result is eternal life. NIV

Good works is a part of the doctrine that delivers us from sin. We will cover more on sin later, but notice the advantage of becoming a slave to righteous acts in order that we will be set free from sin's control. Only a slave to righteousness is set free from sin (verse 18 above). As I mentioned before, if we love one another we will come out of darkness and there will be nothing in us that could make us stumble (James 2:8-11).

All of the verses fit together. The book of Romans, Luke, John, Matthew, Ephesians, Galatians, and First Peter are saying the same thing that the book of James and First John taught us earlier. Take a look at the book of Titus below.

Titus 3:8, 14
8 This is a faithful saying, and these things I want you to affirm constantly, that those who have believed in God should be careful to maintain good works. These things are good and profitable to men. 14 And let our people also learn to maintain good works, to meet urgent needs, that they may not be unfruitful. NKJV

Titus 3:8, 14
8 This is a trustworthy saying. And I want you to stress
these things, so that those who have trusted in God may be
careful to devote themselves to doing what is good. These
things are excellent and profitable for everyone. 14 Our
people must learn to devote themselves to doing what is
good, in order that they may provide for daily necessities
and not live unproductive lives. NIV

Not only does the Bible say that we should do good works, but that we should be devoted to doing good works and constantly verifying (confirming) that we all are (Titus 3:6, 14 above). If that one passage of scripture alone was observed among Christians, how many of us would come out of darkness?

Those who are against good works probably have not read the book of Titus yet, but Lord willing, when that day comes, millions of Christians who live in bondage to sin, will be liberated. Glory, halleluiah!

The Apostle Paul preached, "Do deeds that prove your repentance" according to Acts 26:20, and Jesus said, "I have appointed you to go and bear fruit" (John 15:16), and "Every tree that does not bear good fruit will be cut down and thrown into the fire" (Matthew 7:19, John 15:6).

John the Baptist preached the same things to the crowds coming to be baptized by him. He preached, "Produce fruit in keeping with repentance" (Luke 3:8-9 below).

Luke 3:8-9
8 Therefore bear fruits worthy of repentance, and do
not begin to say to yourselves, 'We have Abraham as
our father.' For I say to you that God is able to raise up
children to Abraham from these stones. 9 And even now the
ax is laid to the root of the trees. Therefore every tree
which does not bear good fruit is cut down and thrown into
the fire." NKJV

Luke 3:8-9
8 Produce fruit in keeping with repentance. And do not

begin to say to yourselves, 'We have Abraham as our father.' For I tell you that out of these stones God can raise up children for Abraham. 9 The ax is already at the root of the trees, and every tree that does not produce good fruit will be cut down and thrown into the fire." NIV

Face it. Good works are a part of the Christian process, and it's mentioned everywhere in the New Testament. We would have to be blind or purposely ignore the verses not to see it.

Before you were baptized, you should have heard the message; "Produce fruit in keeping with repentance" (Luke 3:8 above). That means to purposely go out and do something that would show you have repented.

When the crowds asked John what to do, he told them to share their food and clothing with those who had none (Luke 3:10-11). He told the tax collectors to only collect what they were supposed to collect (Luke 3:13). He told the soldiers to be content with their pay, and not to intimidate anyone, or accuse them falsely (Luke 3:14). Essentially, they were to do what was right, just and fair.

WHOEVER DOES GOD'S WILL

When you are looking for a brother to help, look for someone who follows Jesus because disciple means follower of something, and disciples of Jesus follow Jesus. This day and time we consider everyone who walks in the door of a place called church to be a Christian, but ask them about following Jesus and you will get that "don't judge me" look.

Jesus identifies who our brothers are in Matthew 12:46-50 below.

Matthew 12:46-50
46 While He was still talking to the multitudes, behold, His mother and brothers stood outside, seeking to speak with Him. 47 Then one said to Him, "Look, Your mother and Your brothers are standing outside, seeking to speak with You." 48 But He answered and said to the one who told Him, "Who is My mother and who are My brothers?" 49 And He stretched out His hand toward His disciples and said, "Here are My mother and My brothers! 50 For whoever does the

will of My Father in heaven is My brother and sister and mother." NKJV

Matthew 12:46-50
46 While Jesus was still talking to the crowd, his mother and brothers stood outside, wanting to speak to him. 47 Someone told him, "Your mother and brothers are standing outside, wanting to speak to you." 48 He replied to him, "Who is my mother, and who are my brothers?" 49 Pointing to his disciples, he said, "Here are my mother and my brothers. 50 For whoever does the will of my Father in heaven is my brother and sister and mother." NIV

Jesus' earthly family was standing outside including His mother Mary, but He clearly identified who His real family was; His followers. He pointed to His followers (disciples) and identified them as His family and so should we.

That may be a hard pill to swallow, but that is the truth, and feelings do not change the truth. Jesus said that His followers should not call anyone on earth father (Matthew 23:9). When Jesus' earthly parents were searching for Him, He said, "Didn't you know I must be about My Father's business" (Luke 2:49)? We willingly follow Jesus to the point that we become uncomfortable, and then we shrink back. Is John 6:60-69 written for us?

Whoever does the will of the Father is our brother. The will of the Father is to believe in and know the Son (John 6:28-29, Matthew 7:21-23), to do good even in the face of suffering (1 Peter 2:15, 3:17), to avoid sexual immorality, and to be holy (1 Thessalonians 4:3). Those who obey Jesus love Him, and Jesus will make His home in them, but those who do not keep His Word do not love Him, point, blank, period (John 14:21-23).

Even among Christians, there are many who do not do the will of the Father. They are not completely off the list of people that we should help, since we are to do good to all people. However, disciples are especially looking for those who belong to the family of believers; those who live by faith (Galatians 6:9-10).

Galatians 6:9-10
9 And let us not grow weary while doing good, for in due season we shall reap if we do not lose heart. 10 Therefore, as we have opportunity, let us do good to all, especially to those who are of the household of faith. NKJV

Galatians 6:9-10
9 Let us not become weary in doing good, for at the proper time we will reap a harvest if we do not give up. 10 Therefore, as we have opportunity, let us do good to all people, especially to those who belong to the family of believers. NIV

According to those verses, it should be obvious that we love other believers, and believers do not remain in darkness according to John 12:46. We should love all people, but our clear favorites should be Christians who "do the will of the Father." Jesus identifies these as His family. This is the evidence that we are disciples of Jesus, and that the love of God has been poured into our heart by the Holy Spirit (John 13:34-35, Romans 5:5, 1 John 3:10).

ASSOCIATIONS

We don't love people into the Kingdom of God. We plead with them to be reconciled to God through our Lord and Savior Jesus Christ, and then they make a decision based on the truth (2 Corinthians 5:20).

The church building is full of people, but not all of them believe and live by faith. We should love even our enemies, but that doesn't mean we are going to associate with everyone who walks through the church doors. Don't get me wrong, but please take a good look at the following instructions (1 Corinthians 5:9-13).

1 Corinthians 5:9-13
9 I wrote to you in my epistle not to keep company with sexually immoral people. 10 Yet I certainly did not mean with the sexually immoral people of this world, or with the covetous, or extortioners, or idolaters, since then

104

you would need to go out of the world. 11 But now I have written to you not to keep company with anyone named a brother, who is sexually immoral, or covetous, or an idolater, or a reviler, or a drunkard, or an extortioner not even to eat with such a person. 12 For what have I to do with judging those also who are outside? Do you not judge those who are inside? 13 But those who are outside God judges. Therefore "put away from yourselves the evil person." NKJV

1 Corinthians 5:9-13
9 I have written you in my letter not to associate with sexually immoral people— 10 not at all meaning the people of this world who are immoral, or the greedy and swindlers, or idolaters. In that case you would have to leave this world. 11 But now I am writing you that you must not associate with anyone who calls himself a brother but is sexually immoral or greedy, an idolater or a slanderer, a drunkard or a swindler. With such a man do not even eat. 12 What business is it of mine to judge those outside the church? Are you not to judge those inside? 13 God will judge those outside. "Expel the wicked man from among you." NIV

Who should we not associate with according to those verses? We should not associate with a brother who calls himself a Christian (Christ follower, Acts 11:26), who is caught up in sins that lead to death (verse 11 above). Do not even eat with such a person. Is that what your Bible says?

Does the church have the right to say something to you if you are caught up in sins that lead to death (verse 12 above)? Yes, they do according to 1 Corinthians 5:9-13 above, if you call yourself a Christian. Some churches hold their members accountable for much more than that, even their giving, but 1 Corinthians 5:9-13 above only deals with certain sins. However, if you have made a promise to allow someone to watch over your every move, such as an accountability partner, then it is a sin for you not to continue (Proverbs 6:1-5).

Yes, Jesus ate with sinners, but did He eat with people who claimed to be His followers and yet continued in sin? We put up with everything for the sake of the lost (1 Corinthians 9:19), but those rules do not apply to the rebellious. We're still going to love them, which means we will be patient, kind, not easily angered, but we're just not going to associate with them.

We are looking for people who are "willing" to die to sins and live for righteousness (1 Corinthians 15:33-34, 1 Peter 2:24). We're looking for people who don't throw the truth out the window when things aren't working, but they consult someone who knows the truth in order to figure out why it's not working for them, instead of making excuses (Colossians 3:16, 2 Thessalonians 3:13-15, Romans 15:14, James 5:16, Galatians 6:1-2, James 4:4-10). Check the verses.

Godly sorrow leads to repentance, but worldly sorrow leads to death (2 Corinthians 7:10-11). If they repent, then they should show evidence of their repentance, and then they can return. The person who was kicked out of the church in 1 Corinthians 5:9-13, was welcomed back in 2 Corinthians 2:6-7.

Christians who offer their body as a living sacrifice to God for what He has done for them begins with renewing their mind with the truth of God's Word (Romans 12:1-2, John 17:17). This proves repentance, and if they continue renewing their mind to the point of retaining the Word, many sins will automatically be eliminated (Romans 1:28-32).

If they repent, they will begin to obey Jesus, and consequently they will come out of darkness (1 John 2:8-10). You will be able to tell if someone truly repents, since they will receive grace and the grace that comes from God will teach them to say no to ungodliness (Titus 2:11-14). Grace will give them a godly attitude regarding sin.

Titus 2:11-14
11 For the grace of God that brings salvation has appeared to all men, 12 teaching us that, denying ungodliness and worldly lusts, we should live soberly, righteously, and godly in the present age, 13 looking for the blessed hope and glorious appearing of our great God and Savior Jesus Christ, 14 who gave Himself for us, that He might redeem

us from every lawless deed and purify for Himself His own special people, zealous for good works. NKJV

Titus 2:11-14
11 For the grace of God that brings salvation has appeared to all men. 12 It teaches us to say "No" to ungodliness and worldly passions, and to live self-controlled, upright and godly lives in this present age, 13 while we wait for the blessed hope the glorious appearing of our great God and Savior, Jesus Christ, 14 who gave himself for us to redeem us from all wickedness and to purify for himself a people that are his very own, eager to do what is good. NIV

The grace of God itself teaches us to reject worldly passions and makes us eager to do good works. Anyone who has experienced grace described in the Bible, can look back over their life and find a time when they rejected the world's ways, and eagerly did good works. Jesus says, "Repent and do the things you did at first" (Revelation 2:5).

RECOGNIZE AND WARN

You might be thinking that it is not right to judge, but according to 1 Corinthians 5:9-13 above, Christ followers should make judgments concerning those in the church, but not those outside the church (1 Corinthians 5:12-13 above). Mature Christians, who have the mind of Christ, should make judgments about all things in the church (1 Corinthians 2:15-16).

We do exactly the opposite. We picket gay marches, and refuse to instruct those inside the church who continue in sins that lead to death. Isn't that backwards? Do not judge people outside the church (1 Corinthians 5:12-13), but preach the Word (1 Timothy 4:1-4). If God enables them to come, they will be ready for His Word (John 6:44, Acts 2:37, 1 Corinthians 1:17-18).

Clearly according to the verses above, we cannot claim to be a brother and yet continue in sins that lead to death. That should be recognized as a process failure, and those people need to be instructed to repent in order that they be restored if they are willing (Galatians 6:1-2, Colossians 3:16).

Every brother who does not live according to the instructions should be identified and warned. We should note that person and withdraw from him (2 Thessalonians 3:6, 13-15 below).

2 Thessalonians 3:6, 13-15
6 But we command you, brethren, in the name of our Lord Jesus Christ, that you withdraw from every brother who walks disorderly and not according to the tradition which he received from us. 13 But as for you, brethren, do not grow weary in doing good. 14 And if anyone does not obey our word in this epistle, note that person and do not keep company with him, that he may be ashamed. 15 Yet do not count him as an enemy, but admonish him as a brother. NKJV

2 Thessalonians 3:6, 13-15
6 In the name of the Lord Jesus Christ, we command you, brothers, to keep away from every brother who is idle and does not live according to the teaching you received from us. 13 And as for you, brothers, never tire of doing what is right. 14 If anyone does not obey our instruction in this letter, take special note of him. Do not associate with him, in order that he may feel ashamed. 15 Yet do not regard him as an enemy, but warn him as a brother. NIV

Note that person who does not obey the instructions and warn him. Do not associate with him if he does not change. Some use this verse to hold people in bondage to the Law. We will cover the Law in the next chapter.

We should recognize and warn those who cause divisions in the body and offenses "contrary to the written doctrine" and avoid them if they do not change (Romans 16:17). Some use this verse in the wrong way, since they leave out "contrary to the written doctrine." Differences in the church must come so that those who are approved may be recognized (1 Corinthians 11:19).

We should recognize and warn those who are obscene, tell dirty jokes, are sexually immoral, or who worship idols (love and adore anything more than God). Do not be partners with them if they do not change. As it is written, "They have no inheritance in the Kingdom of God" (Ephesians 5:3-7). Check the verses.

We should recognize and warn those who boast about themselves, love money, and disobey their parents, as well as those who are unforgiving, slanderers, unholy, unthankful, have no self-control, and those that deny the power of God (2 Timothy 3:1-7). My goodness, who is going to be left? Lord have mercy on us!

We should reject anyone who is disruptive, conflict-ridden, or wants to continually argue against the Word of God. If they cannot see the verses, and will not hear them, you can be sure that they are blind. Let the wicked, continue to be wicked still, and let the righteous continue to be righteous (Revelation 22:11). Those who belong to God hear His Word (John 8:47), and the Lord's servant does not argue (2 Timothy 2:24-26).

RIGHTEOUS ACTS AS FILTHY RAGS

Repentance is a change of mind that leads to a change in behavior. A change in behavior, in line with righteous acts, proves repentance. John the Baptist and the Apostle Paul were basically saying that if the people truly repented, then they would willingly do deeds in line with their repentance (Acts 26:20, Luke 3:8-9).

Some are in the habit of calling righteous acts, filthy rags, and therefore they frown on performing them. Consequently, they do not come out of darkness, and do not sow mercy for their mistakes.

Obviously, they do not understand righteousness (Hebrews 5:11-14), and how it can control Christians to stop sinning (Romans 6:15-24, 1 Corinthians 15:33-34), since they have hardened their heart against it (Ephesians 4:17-19). When they interpret Isaiah, they speak directly against Ezekiel.

Anyone with Ezekiel chapter 18 and chapter 33 living in them can hear the violations immediately. A righteous man's sins are not remembered as long as he continues in righteous acts.

Read those chapters to see if I speak in line with scripture. I do not have room to place every verse I would like to in this book, but you will see it if you read those chapters. Righteous acts are required.

Does the Bible really say that all of "our" righteous acts are as filthy rags, meaning everyone's righteous acts, or those who continue in sin (Isaiah 64:5-6 below)?

Isaiah 64:5-6
5 You meet him who rejoices and does righteousness, Who remembers You in Your ways. You are indeed angry, for we have sinned In these ways we continue; And we need to be saved. 6 But we are all like an unclean thing, And all our righteousnesses are like filthy rags; We all fade as a leaf, And our iniquities, like the wind, Have taken us away. NKJV

Isaiah 64:5-6
5 You come to the help of those who gladly do right, who remember your ways. But when we continued to sin against them, you were angry. How then can we be saved? 6 All of us have become like one who is unclean, and all our righteous acts are like filthy rags; we all shrivel up like a leaf, and like the wind our sins sweep us away. NIV

Who is included in the group of people whose righteous acts are as filthy rags? God meets with (gathers with) those who do what is right (righteous acts), but He is angry with those who continue in sin (verse 5 above). The Amplified Bible makes this clearer.

Isaiah 64:5-6
5 You meet and spare him who joyfully works righteousness (uprightness and justice), [earnestly] remembering You in Your ways. Behold, You were angry, for we sinned; we have long continued in our sins [prolonging Your anger]. And shall we be saved? 6 For we have all become like one who is unclean [ceremonially, like a leper], and all our righteousness (our best deeds of rightness and justice) is like filthy rags or a polluted garment; we all fade like a leaf, and our iniquities, like the wind, take us away [far from God's favor, hurrying us toward destruction]. AMP

Those who continue in sin have "become" like one who is unclean. They may perform righteous acts, but they refuse to allow those acts to control them in doing good for one reason or other (Romans 6:20).

Isaiah says, "Although grace is shown to the wicked, they do not learn righteousness" (Isaiah 26:10). They never learn about righteous acts, and never become slaves to righteousness (Romans 6:15-22, Proverbs 11:18). Therefore, they are never completely free from the control of sin. Perhaps that is why they testify that nobody can stop sinning.

People who never learn righteousness may simply speak against righteous acts and consequently, they cannot understand them. As we learned in the last chapter, speaking against the faith, can lead us away from the faith (1 Timothy, James 3:2-12, Romans 10:6-8).

People who only perform righteous acts in order to receive their due on earth, do not receive anything from God (Matthew 6:1:-4 below).

Matthew 6:1-4
1 "Take heed that you do not do your charitable deeds before men, to be seen by them. Otherwise you have no reward from your Father in heaven. 2 Therefore, when you do a charitable deed, do not sound a trumpet before you as the hypocrites do in the synagogues and in the streets, that they may have glory from men. Assuredly, I say to you, they have their reward. 3 But when you do a charitable deed, do not let your left hand know what your right hand is doing, 4 that your charitable deed may be in secret; and your Father who sees in secret will Himself reward you openly. NKJV

Matthew 6:1-4
1 "Be careful not to do your 'acts of righteousness' before men, to be seen by them. If you do, you will have no reward from your Father in heaven. 2 "So when you give to the needy, do not announce it with trumpets, as the hypocrites do in the synagogues and on the streets, to be honored by men. I tell you the truth, they have received their reward in full. 3 But when you give to the needy, do

111

not let your left hand know what your right hand is doing,
4 so that your giving may be in secret. Then your Father,
who sees what is done in secret, will reward you. NIV

Good works or righteous acts cannot be hidden (1 Timothy 5:25), but as much as it depends on us they can be. We should give in secret (verse 4 above) without announcing it (verse 3 above). How God has changed our life, is what we allow to shine before men, and when they see our good deeds, it glorifies God (Matthew 5:14-16).

Hypocrites give, and their gift can be used for good, but they do it for the reward. There isn't a problem with sowing in order to reap (Matthew 7:12), but they sound the trumpet before men for the purpose of personal gain (verse 3 above, 1 Corinthians 13:3, 1 Timothy 6:5). Most of them are neither hot or cold, but still in danger of not remaining, since they do not allow their deeds to reap a reward from Heaven (verse 1 above, Revelation 3:15-20).

The sacrifice of people without God (pagans) is not used for good, but to promote the wrong message (1 Corinthians 10:20); the message of demons (1 Timothy 4:1-2). They promote messages that they want to hear (2 Timothy 4:3-4), and since the devil controls the world system through the spirit of disobedience (1 John 5:19, Ephesians 2:1-3), organizations who receive their support are enormous (Matthew 4:8). Check it!

The bottom line is that those who continue "in Christ" do not continue in sin (1 John 3:5). By their fruits you will recognize them.

1 John 3:6
6 Whoever abides in Him does not sin. Whoever sins has
neither seen Him nor known Him. NKJV

1 John 3:6
6 No one who lives in him keeps on sinning. No one who
continues to sin has either seen him or known him. NIV

"A good tree cannot bear bad fruit" (Matthew 7:18-19). You would have to be blind to miss that type of teaching, or avoid about half of the New Testament. Wherever you find the doctrine of Jesus missing, you can be sure that the doctrine of demons is present (1 Timothy 4:1-2, 2 John 1:8-11, 2 Thessalonians 2:9-11).

A Christian who has the hope of remaining a son of God, purifies himself (1 John 3:1-3), from everything that contaminates his body and spirit (1 Corinthians 7:1, James 4:8-9), by the grace of God that is in him (Titus 2:11-14).

Now tell me what would happen if your church followed what is clearly written in the Bible? These instructions could seriously change bowling night, and we wouldn't want that (John 12:42-43).

My name is Alan P. Ballou. I am a servant. If you have questions about anything covered in this chapter please contact me at www.how-tostopsinning.com. I serve Christians free of charge.

4. The Law

Many different laws
Christ's law
Moses leads us to Christ
Stumble over the stumbling stone
Righteousness is still required
Law gives sin power
Fall away from grace
The hope of glory
Die to the Law and be released
Tablets of stone or the new law
Teachers of the law
Faith credited righteousness
Back and forth
The good I want to do
Lawlessness or Christ's law
Obey the Gospel
Understanding

4

THE LAW

෨෨෬

Law is one of those touchy subjects that people like to avoid. Sometimes it separates close friends, somewhat like politics, since one may be under part of the Law, and the other is not.

I want everyone who reads this chapter to walk away with a basic knowledge of the Law, and how it is connected to our ability to stop sinning. All Christians should at least know that.

MANY DIFFERENT LAWS

The law of the Spirit sets us free from the law of sin and death (Romans 8:2). The perfect law gives freedom (James 1:25), and if we keep the royal law, we do well (James 2:8). There are many laws mentioned in the Bible; eight in the book of Romans alone. Therefore, I will not cover every law, but only the ones we need to know in order to stop sinning.

A law is simply a list of rules, commandments, regulations, or judgments. When the Bible speaks about "the Law," it is talking about the laws that God gave Moses for the Israelites to follow. Some people call it, "Old Testament Law."

At different times, God gave commandments, regulations, judgments, and instructions to Moses and he in turn spoke to the people. All of these are recorded in Exodus, Leviticus, Numbers, and Deuteronomy, the sum of which is called, "The Laws of Moses," or simply "The Law."

The Ten Commandments are a part of the Laws that came through Moses. Grace and the truth, that sets us free, came through Jesus Christ (John 1:17).

John 1:17
17 For the law was given through Moses, but grace and truth came through Jesus Christ. NKJV

John 1:17
17 For the law was given through Moses; grace and truth came through Jesus Christ. NIV

There are many different laws in the New Testament as well. However, they are not necessarily a list of commandments. They are more like rules, verdicts, or decrees. In other words, if we do that, this will happen.

For example, if we follow the law of the Spirit it will set us free from the law of sin and death (Romans 8:2, Ezekiel chapter 18). The soul of the person who sins shall die (Ezekiel 18:4, 20), but the law of the Spirit sets those who are in Christ, free from that verdict (decree).

This doesn't mean that the law of the Spirit gives us approval to continue in sin. If we live by the Spirit we will not sin by following the desires of our sinful nature (Galatians 5:16). We will cover that later in this book.

Other laws include the law of sin, the law of God, the law of righteousness, the law of the mind, and so on. A number of these laws are an alternate way of describing other laws.

For example the "law of righteousness" mentioned in Romans 9:31 simply describes pursuing righteousness by attempting to obey all the Laws of Moses. If anyone could obey the whole Law, they would be declared righteous (Romans 2:13). However, nobody can, and therefore to pursue righteousness through Law, rather than by faith, is considered stumbling over the stumbling stone (Romans 9:30-33).

CHRIST'S LAW

Another example would be Christ's law. Jesus Christ taught us many things, including, love one another, love our enemies, pray for those who treat us unfairly, turn the other cheek to those who strike us, give to those who ask, and don't stand in the way of an evil person (Matthew 5:39-48). That's totally different from the Laws of Moses which demands an eye for an eye, a tooth for a tooth, and a hand for a hand (Deuteronomy 16-19:21, Leviticus 24:17-20).

God has made us ministers of a New Covenant (Matthew 26:28, 2 Corinthians 3:6), which is better than the Old Covenant, and built on better promises (Hebrews 8:6-7). God found fault with the Old Covenant (Hebrews 8:7), and having replaced it with the new, He makes the old obsolete (Hebrews 8:13). Check the verses before you speak, and allow them to judge your attitudes and thoughts (Hebrews 4:12).

We don't throw the Old Testament away, since there is much more in the Old Testament than the Laws of Moses. The Lord is the same yesterday, today, and forever (Hebrews 13:8). Therefore, there is much to learn in the Old Testament (Romans 15:4), and the things that happened to Israel in the desert were written down as warnings for us (1 Corinthians 10:6-12). However, we can certainly know all there is to know about the Old Testament and still miss Kingdom teaching.

Now we preach the Kingdom of God, which is the Kingdom we should seek first in order to have all of our needs met (Matthew 6:33). Kingdom teaching is found in the New Testament (Luke 16:16).

Luke 16:16
16 "The law and the prophets were until John. Since that time the kingdom of God has been preached, and everyone is pressing into it. NKJV

Luke 16:16
16 "The Law and the Prophets were proclaimed until John. Since that time, the good news of the kingdom of God is

being preached, and everyone is forcing his way into it. NIV

The Law and the prophets were preached until John the Baptist, but since that time the Kingdom of God is being preached. The Laws of Moses are still in effect (Matthew 5:17-20), but they are only for those who are still under the Law (Romans 3:19), and not for those who have fulfilled the Law through Christ's law (Romans 13:8-10, Galatians 5:13-15, 1 Timothy 1:9-11).

The Apostle Paul was under Christ's law (1 Corinthians 9:21). He only became like one under the Law, when he was trying to win people who were under the Law (1 Corinthians 9:20). Christ's law fulfills the Laws of Moses and any other command, no matter what it may be (Romans 13:8-10).

Romans 13:8-10
8 Owe no one anything except to love one another, for he who loves another has fulfilled the law. 9 For the commandments, "You shall not commit adultery," "You shall not murder," "You shall not steal," "You shall not bear false witness," "You shall not covet," and if there is any other commandment, are all summed up in this saying, namely, "You shall love your neighbor as yourself." 10 Love does no harm to a neighbor; therefore love is the fulfillment of the law. NKJV

Romans 13:8-10
8 Keep out of debt and owe no man anything, except to love one another; for he who loves his neighbor [who practices loving others] has fulfilled the Law [relating to one's fellowmen, meeting all its requirements]. 9 The commandments, You shall not commit adultery, You shall not kill, You shall not steal, You shall not covet (have an evil desire), and any other commandment, are summed up in the single command, You shall love your neighbor as [you do] yourself. [Ex 20:13-17; Lev 19:18.] 10 Love does no wrong to one's neighbor [it never hurts anybody].

Therefore love meets all the requirements and is the fulfilling of the Law. AMP

Notice that love fulfills the Ten Commandments, as well as any other command there may be; "and if there is any other commandment" (verse 9 above). No matter what you do spiritually, love is more important (1 Corinthians 13:1-3).

"Love your neighbor as you love yourself" means that if you like to eat, then you should help feed people who do not have a means to eat, and so on. Love "as" you love yourself. This can be done through local charities that actually help people who are in need. Under the Old Covenant, food was given out by the church; "Bring all of the tithes into the storehouse, that there might be food in My house" (Malachi 3:10).

Some will ask, "What if you don't love yourself?" However, the Bible says that no man hates himself (Ephesians 5:29). If you hate yourself, stop eating, but if you feed yourself, help feed your neighbor.

Christ's law goes a step further in saying, love your enemies and do not repay anyone evil for evil, or insult for insult (1 Peter 3:8, 1 John 17:20). However, that doesn't mean that we have to associate with anyone who insults us or treats us with evil.

Love itself fulfills the Law because love does no harm to a neighbor (Romans 13:8-10 above). If we buy a house and pay it off, the lender will send us a letter stating that we have "fulfilled" our obligation. In the same way, if we would simply obey Jesus Christ, Who taught us to love our enemies, pray for those who treat us unfairly, turn the other cheek to those who strike us, give to those who ask, and especially love other disciples, we would fulfill the Law.

Obeying Jesus fulfills or fully meets the requirements of the Law, as if we had kept all of the commandments, regulations, judgments, and instructions ourselves, including the Ten Commandments (Romans 13:8-10). Christ's law doesn't nullify (cancel out) the Laws of Moses, but in this way, faith in Jesus upholds (maintains) the Law (Romans 3:31).

Even though Christians uphold the Laws of Moses by obeying Christ's law, some feel the need to obey parts of the Law and require it of those they teach (1 Timothy 1:3-11). The Bible says that we shouldn't argue with them (Titus 3:9-10, Philippians 2:14). In these cases we are

119

called to do whatever leads to peace (Colossians 3:15, Romans 14:19).

MOSES LEADS US TO CHRIST

Once we know what the Laws of Moses are, it becomes evident that everyone needs a Savior. In fact, the purpose of the law is to lead us to Christ so that we may be justified (declared righteous) through faith in Jesus (Galatians 3:24).

We look at people as being good or evil, depending on what they have done, but nobody is good when we compare ourselves to the Laws that came through Moses (Romans 3:10-19). As you will see, all of us, no matter how good we may think we are, have sinned and fallen short of God's righteous decree.

The Laws of Moses state that whoever uses the Lord's name in vain is to be stoned to death (Leviticus 24:11-16). There is no, "Oops, I'm sorry," but that one and only instance is it; you sin, you die. The same holds true for anyone who curses his father or mother (Leviticus 20:9), a son who does not obey his parents (Deuteronomy 21:18-21), and a woman who loses her virginity before marriage (Deuteronomy 22:17-21).

How many people would be alive today in this country if these were the only laws? There would be so few of us, that we would probably still be living near Massachusetts where the pilgrims landed.

I'm sure that a considerable number of people did not stone their family members in accordance with the Law, but concealed their sins. Jesus bent down to write on the ground and the Pharisees, who had brought in a woman caught in adultery, left one by one, conscience-stricken (John 8:9). Jesus knew their sins, and obviously it was a specific act deserving the same punishment considering the Law. Who are we holding to the fire, and what would Jesus write on the ground about us that would make us walk away? Think about that.

The eye opener is not that Jesus didn't condemn the woman, but that she and the Pharisees were in the same boat (position). "He who is without sin among you, let him be the first to throw a stone at her" (John 8:7)! Their effort in obeying the Law, did not free them from sin, or the penalty of sin which is death, and the same is true for us today (Romans 8:1-4).

If you have ever eaten chicken you have broken the Law. According to the Laws of Moses you cannot eat chicken, pork, or any meat from an animal that doesn't chew grass and have split hooves. You cannot eat fish that doesn't have fins and scales, (Deuteronomy 14:3-21). Catfish is against the Law (Laws of Moses)!

Those who trim the edge of their beard, or cut the hair on the sides of their head, such as those in the military are guilty of breaking the Laws of Moses (Leviticus 19:26). Tattoos and cutting parts of the body for the purpose of conforming to this world is against the Law (Leviticus 19:28). How popular is that these days?

Think about how some militaries are set up to break the Laws of Moses simply by the appearance of there soldiers. The terrorist knows more about violating the Law than we do, and I am sure he uses that knowledge to his advantage.

If two groups of people are fighting and neither are in Christ, which one is more righteous in God's sight? Pray for whoever is in office (1 Timothy 2:1-2). Not for the sake of a particular party, but for the benefit of soldiers who may not know spiritual laws.

How did David know that he would be victorious over Goliath? He knew that the battle was a spiritual matter and not the result of what was taking place on the battlefield (1 Samuel 17:47).

If the Lord has decreed that a certain nation will win a war, but there are only wounded men left in that nation, then those wounded men will rise up to be victorious (Jeremiah 37:6-10, Psalm 127:1). Therefore, it is far better to know spiritual laws rather than to assume that God is on your side. Righteous blood will never go unpunished (Matthew 23:35-36).

Those who practice divination, or sorcery are worthy of death. This includes fortunetelling, witchcraft, omens, horoscopes, ouija boards, and the like (Exodus 22:18, Leviticus 19:26). This is the reason that the Lord drove the wicked nations out of the land of Canaan to begin with (Deuteronomy 18:9-14).

How many people innocently get caught up in sins like these? It starts off as fun and games, and curiosity draws us in, but sin is deceptive. It makes us think one thing and delivers another. Witchcraft and sorcery are still on the list of sins that lead to death, which we will cover later (Galatians 5:19-21).

The Law condemns the person who is simply wearing a shirt made from two different types of material. That's right, according to the Laws of Moses, we cannot wear a garment made of different types of cloth, such as cotton and wool (Deuteronomy 22:11). Imagine that.

Most of us do not own apparel that is made of only one type of fabric, and yet we think that we are pleasing to God when we look our best. God looks at the heart (Jeremiah 17:10, 2 Corinthians 5:12, Acts 15:8). If our clothes make our heart proud, we should swap them with someone who needs clothing before we go before the Lord, so that we will not be defiled; made useless (Matthew 15:17-20). God tests our heart (1 Thessalonians 2:4).

Every seventh year, we would not be allowed to plant a garden, or to pick the fruit from the trees. Whatever grows on its own that year is to be gathered and used by the workers, the poor, and the strangers of the land (Leviticus 25:1-7). Imagine farmers taking a year off and allowing the poor, the workers, and the strangers in their town to gather from their land. Would that wipe out hunger in the world?

If that didn't wipe out hunger then tithing would. Every third year, the tithe, which is a requirement under the Laws of Moses (Hebrews 7:5), is to be stored in that person's town, and given to the priest, the strangers, the fatherless, and the widows of that town (Deuteronomy 14:28-29).

Under the Law, the tithe was always food, and the only time it could be changed into money, was when the journey was too far to take the food. At that time the tithe could be exchanged for money and then turned back into food when the person arrived at the place that the Lord would show them (Deuteronomy 14:24-26, 12:17-18). The tithe was not used to construct a building. Offerings were used for such things.

Abraham gave a tithe (tenth) of the goods that he gained through the defeat of the Kings to the priest Melchizedek (Genesis 14:16-20), but not in accordance with the Laws of Moses, since they were 430 years later (Galatians 3:17). The difference is that the Law commands a tenth of the things that can be used as food (Leviticus 27:30, Deuteronomy 14:22-23) , but Abraham gave a tenth of the plunder willingly and not grudgingly or out of necessity (2 Corinthians 9:7).

There is nothing wrong with giving a tenth, but the "command" to give a tenth is certainly through the Laws of Moses, which is not based on faith (Hebrews 7:5, Galatians 3:10). However, if you have pledged a tenth or made any other promise by oath and do not fulfill your vow, it is a violation of the Law and against God (Numbers chapter 30, Proverbs 6:1-5).

STUMBLE OVER THE STUMBLING STONE

Many who are under the Law today only observe parts of it, which is another violation of the Laws of Moses. The Law can not be changed, or observed in parts. No one can add to it, or take away from it (Deuteronomy 12:32). We can't obey a third of it, or half of it and be right in God's eyes because at whatever point we break one part of the Law, we are guilty of breaking "the" Law (James 2:10 below).

James 2:10
10 For whoever shall keep the whole law, and yet stumble in one point, he is guilty of all. NKJV

James 2:10
10 For whosoever keeps the Law [as a] whole but stumbles and offends in one [single instance] has become guilty of [breaking] all of it. AMP

Therefore, it doesn't matter how many commands, regulations, and judgments anyone can obey. Even if someone could obey 99% of them, they are still guilty of breaking the Law and consequently remain under the curse for disobedience, which includes sickness and disease (Deuteronomy 28:53-63).

Certainly the person who obeys part of the Law is more righteous than the one who is not under any law at all (Matthew 7:21, Genesis 38:26, 1 Samuel 24:17). However, it is far better to fulfill all the Law's commands through Christ's law, since now that Christ has come, our righteousness has to exceed that of the Pharisees and the teachers of the Law (Matthew 5:20). Nobody will be declared righteous by observing the Law (Romans 3:20).

If anyone could keep the whole Law without stumbling, they would be declared righteous (Romans 2:13), but no one could. This is what is meant by the term, "all have sinned and fallen short of the glory of God"

(Romans 3:23 below). Christ is the only way (John 14:6).

Therefore, those who try to be justified by the Law are under obligation to obey all of it, since that is the path they have chosen instead of allowing the Law to lead them to Christ (Galatians 5:4-5). If righteousness could have been gained through the Law, then Christ died for nothing (Galatians 2:21). In other words, there was no reason for Christ to die for our sins if we could be righteous through observing the Law.

Galatians 2:19-21
19 For I through the law died to the law that I might live to God. 20 I have been crucified with Christ; it is no longer I who live, but Christ lives in me; and the life which I now live in the flesh I live by faith in the Son of God, who loved me and gave Himself for me. 21 I do not set aside the grace of God; for if righteousness comes through the law, then Christ died in vain." NKJV

Galatians 2:19-21
19 For through the law I died to the law so that I might live for God. 20 I have been crucified with Christ and I no longer live, but Christ lives in me. The life I live in the body, I live by faith in the Son of God, who loved me and gave himself for me. 21 I do not set aside the grace of God, for if righteousness could be gained through the law, Christ died for nothing!" NIV

We die to the Law in order to live for God (verse 19 above). We will cover more on this later in this chapter, but notice the contrast between trying to obey the Law and living by faith in the Son of God (verse 20 above). We either do one or the other, but not both.

Those who are under the Law are obligated to obey the whole Law (Galatians 3:10), and they will not be declared righteous (Romans 3:20). Those who die to the Law, believe, and put faith in Jesus Christ instead, will be declared righteous (Romans 3:21-26).

The Law simply makes us realize that we are all heathens; conscious of sin (Romans 7:7, 3:20). Some of us don't realize it yet, since we don't know the Law. We're all wicked and need a Savior. We may not rob banks, but what if we planted our garden with two types of seeds (Deuteronomy 22:9)? We can't do that according to the Laws of Moses, and by breaking the Law at just one point, we are guilty of disobeying all of it.

I don't have time to cover even a tenth of the Laws of Moses. Nevertheless, one thing is clear. Beginning with the little old lady who would never hurt a flea, to the worst sinner in the world, we all need a Savior and that is what the Law is designed to do; make us run to Jesus (Galatians 3:24).

If someone remains under the Law and refuses to fully submit to God's new way of righteousness, it is a sign that they do not know the Law. They are the ones who stumble over the stumbling stone (Romans 9:30-33). Check the verses.

We cannot be righteous by observing the Law, since we would have to keep the whole Law (Romans 2:13). However, the Gospel reveals a new way of obtaining righteousness, which is through faith (Romans 1:16).

Romans 1:16-17
16 For I am not ashamed of the gospel of Christ, for it is the power of God to salvation for everyone who believes, for the Jew first and also for the Greek. 17 For in it the righteousness of God is revealed from faith to faith; as it is written, "The just shall live by faith." NKJV

Romans 1:16-17
16 I am not ashamed of the gospel, because it is the power of God for the salvation of everyone who believes: first for the Jew, then for the Gentile. 17 For in the gospel a righteousness from God is revealed, a righteousness that is by faith from first to last, just as it is written: "The righteous will live by faith." NIV

Notice that "in the Gospel" the righteousness of God is revealed or made known (verse 17 above). If you have not heard about this new way of righteousness, then you have not heard a complete Gospel (Romans 15:19, Acts 20:26-27). The new Heaven, new earth, and the eternal Kingdom of Christ are all about righteousness (2 Peter 3:13, 1:11, Hebrews 1:8).

RIGHTEOUSNESS IS STILL REQUIRED

Even though no flesh (person) will be justified (declared righteous, made right) in God's sight by observing the Law (Romans 3:20), righteousness is still a requirement in order to enter the Kingdom of Heaven (Matthew 5:20).

Matthew 5:20
20 For I say to you, that unless your righteousness exceeds the righteousness of the scribes and Pharisees, you will by no means enter the kingdom of heaven. NKJV

Matthew 5:20
20 For I tell you that unless your righteousness surpasses that of the Pharisees and the teachers of the law, you will certainly not enter the kingdom of heaven. NIV

God's righteousness, which is the same righteousness that we are supposed to seek first (Matthew 6:33), comes by faith in Jesus Christ to all who believe (Romans 3:21-26 below). Again, the Gospel reveals this new way of obtaining righteousness, which is through faith (Romans 1:16), and separate (totally apart) from the Law.

Romans 3:21-26
21 But now the righteousness of God apart from the law is revealed, being witnessed by the Law and the Prophets, 22 even the righteousness of God, through faith in Jesus Christ, to all and on all who believe. For there is no difference; 23 for all have sinned and fall short of the glory of God, 24 being justified freely by His grace through the redemption that is in Christ Jesus, 25 whom God set forth as a propitiation by His blood, through faith, to demonstrate His righteousness, because in His forbearance God had passed over the sins that were previously committed, 26 to demonstrate at the present time His

righteousness, that He might be just and the justifier of the one who has faith in Jesus. NKJV

Romans 3:21-26
21 But now a righteousness from God, apart from law, has been made known, to which the Law and the Prophets testify. 22 This righteousness from God comes through faith in Jesus Christ to all who believe. There is no difference, 23 for all have sinned and fall short of the glory of God, 24 and are justified freely by his grace through the redemption that came by Christ Jesus. 25 God presented him as a sacrifice of atonement, through faith in his blood. He did this to demonstrate his justice, because in his forbearance he had left the sins committed beforehand unpunished 26 he did it to demonstrate his justice at the present time, so as to be just and the one who justifies those who have faith in Jesus. NIV

Notice that it starts with the words, "but now." That's what I mean by new, but actually it is not new, since it was announced in advance to Abraham (Galatians 3:8), and all of the saints of old, including Noah, Isaac, Jacob, Moses, Gideon, Barak, Samson, Jephthah, David, Samuel, all the prophets, and even Rahab the prostitute were righteous by faith (Hebrews chapter 11). It is "new to us" (made known to us) through the Gospel.

According to Romans 3:21 above, the Law and God's righteousness are separate. The righteousness that comes by the Law comes by keeping the whole Law, which no human can do (Romans 3:20). The righteousness of God comes through faith in Jesus (Romans 3:21-26, Philippians 3:9).

Philippians 3:9
9 and be found in Him, not having my own righteousness, which is from the law, but that which is through faith in Christ, the righteousness which is from God by faith. NKJV

Philippians 3:9
9 and be found in him, not having a righteousness of my own that comes from the law, but that which is through faith in Christ the righteousness that comes from God and is by faith. NIV

That's two totally different paths. It's like saying, "The bridge is out up ahead, and therefore, we will have to go the other way." We have to go the other way since the Law is not made for the righteous (1 Timothy 1:9). Therefore, we must seek to be righteous through faith in Jesus Christ.

LAW GIVES SIN POWER

What can the Law do for a sinner? Law makes sin increase (Romans 5:20). Sinful passions are aroused by the Law so that those under the Law cannot stop sinning (Romans 7:5). With every violation of the Law, sin increases in strength (1 Corinthians 15:56 below). Therefore, those who serve under the Law have no hope of stopping sin, since no one can keep the whole Law.

1 Corinthians 15:56
56 The sting of death is sin, and the strength of sin is the law. NKJV

1 Corinthians 15:56
56 The sting of death is sin, and the power of sin is the law. NIV

1 Corinthians 15:56
56 Now sin is the sting of death, and sin exercises its power [upon the soul] through [the abuse of] the Law. AMP

Law gives sin power over us to control us through the trespassing of its commands. Every time a person who is under the Laws of Moses breaks the Law at one point, he consequently gives sin more power over himself (1 Corinthians 15:56). This is how sin grows and becomes exceedingly wicked (Romans 7:13).

128

Imagine what would happen if every time you ate chicken, cut your hair on the sides, checked your horoscope, called a psychic, got a tattoo, planted a garden, bought a new dress, or ate catfish you increased sins ability to make you commit one of the following sins that lead to death; sexual immorality, idolatry, witchcraft, hatred, discord, jealousy, fits of rage, drunkenness, orgies, prostitution, homosexuality, stealing, slandering, swindling, obscenity, foolish talk, coarse joking, rebellion, debauchery, which is sinful behavior, and the like. That is exactly what you will end up with once sin controls you (Romans 6:20-22, Galatians 6:7-9).

Go ahead and blame these sins on whatever you want to blame them on, but the bottom line is that we were given over to sin, and by trespassing of the Law, sin increased in power to control us. The more we sin, the more power it has. Don't you want another tattoo?

Those who die with Christ through their baptism, are able to live a new life (Romans 6:1-4, 7:4-6). They offer the parts of their body to Him as instruments of righteousness (Romans 6:11-14). They gain access into grace by faith (Romans 5:1-2).

Those who offer themselves in obedience to the Laws of Moses will have sin as their master (Romans 6:14).

Romans 6:14
14 For sin shall not have dominion over you, for you are not under law but under grace. NKJV

Romans 6:14
14 For sin shall not be your master, because you are not under law, but under grace. NIV

The bottom line is that those who are under the Law will never be able to control sin in their life no matter what they attempt (Romans 6:14). Sin itself will have dominion (authority and power) over them to make them sin; causing their own destruction. It's just a matter of time.

However, apart from the Law sin is dead, and has no power over us to control us (Romans 7:8). Under the Law, sin comes alive. Sinful passions are aroused by the Law (Romans 7:5). In other words, sin within us, which is awakened by what the Law makes sin (i.e. eating chicken, pork, etc., explained above), will produce all sorts of wicked desires that would not even come to mind if we were not under the Law (Romans 7:8).

A passion is an uncontrollable desire, which can be mistaken as an addiction. Many people, who are still under the Law, live with these so-called addictions and have no idea that it is sin that is controlling them. They don't know how to come out of it, and they are destined for wrath (Romans 4:14-15).

They simply cannot stop sinning, and every time they trespass one of the Laws of Moses, they give sin more power. God's people are destroyed for lack of knowledge (Hosea 4:6).

The world system is set up to feed these violations. The devil controls the people of the world (1 John 5:19) through the spirit of disobedience (Ephesians 2:1-3). It would be easy to see why certain things are popular in our culture today, if we knew the Law. The spirit of disobedience is simply leading the people of this world to go against the law of God, which has been placed in our heart (Hebrews 10:16). We will cover this in more detail later.

FALL AWAY FROM GRACE

The Christian life is lived by faith from start to finish (Romans 1:16-17), and only those of faith are blessed (Galatians 3:9). Those who rely on observing the Law are under a curse (Galatians 3:10). Those who continue in the Laws of Moses after coming to the Lord, fall away from grace (Galatians 5:4), and reject faith (Romans 4:14-15, Galatians 3:12)..

In Galatians 4:9, the Apostle Paul asked the Galatians, "How is it that you are turning back to those weak and miserable principles?" "Do you wish to be enslaved by them all over again?" In Galatians 3:1-2 he asked, "Who has tricked (bewitched) you?" "Did you receive the Spirit by the Law or by the hearing of faith?" Do you live by faith, or by the Law?

If the Law leads us to Christ, who yelled "Wait, come back" after we started the Christian life by faith? According to Galatians 3:12, the Law is not based on faith.

We were given the faith to come to the Lord; saved by grace through faith (Ephesians, 2:6-8, John 6:44). We gain access by faith into grace (Romans 5:2). God's righteousness comes through faith (Romans 3:22), and those who are righteous live by faith (Romans 1:17). What part of faith comes from the Law?

Those who are led by the Holy Spirit are not under the Law (Galatians 5:18). Check the verse. Once someone is filled with the Holy Spirit by faith, He doesn't lead them back to observe the Law's regulations (Galatians 5:16). The Apostle Paul calls that foolishness (Galatians 3:2-3 below).

Galatians 3:2-3
2 This only I want to learn from you: Did you receive the Spirit by the works of the law, or by the hearing of faith? 3 Are you so foolish? Having begun in the Spirit, are you now being made perfect by the flesh? NKJV

Galatians 3:2-3
2 I would like to learn just one thing from you: Did you receive the Spirit by observing the law, or by believing what you heard? 3 Are you so foolish? After beginning with the Spirit, are you now trying to attain your goal by human effort? NIV

Where the Spirit of the Lord is, there is freedom from the Law (2 Corinthians chapter 3). Therefore, if the spirit you received is not leading you to die to the Law, and to serve in the new way of the Holy Spirit (Romans 7:4-6), then you may be following a deceiving spirit (1 Timothy 4:1-2). Check the verses.

THE HOPE OF GLORY

In fact, now that Christ has come, we will not make it by observing the Law, but only through faith in Jesus Christ will we be made right in God's sight. Those who live by the Law are not heirs. In other words, they do not inherit eternal life, since the Law cannot free us from sin, death, or condemnation (Romans 4:14-15 below).

Romans 4:14-15
14 For if those who are of the law are heirs, faith is made

void and the promise made of no effect, 15 because the law brings about wrath; for where there is no law there is no transgression. NKJV

Romans 4:14-15
14 For if those who live by law are heirs, faith has no value and the promise is worthless, 15 because law brings wrath. And where there is no law there is no transgression. NIV

Those who live by the Law will not be heirs since Law cannot save us from God's wrath (Romans 4:14 above), or set us free from sin (Romans 8:1-4). In fact, Law makes our faith void or useless, and brings wrath upon those of us who are under it.

Where there is no Law, there is no account for sin. In other words, sin is not charged to man's account where there is no Law (Romans 5:13). In this way the sinner becomes the righteous through faith in Jesus, and grace reigns for the righteous (Romans 5:19-20). Jesus became sin for us that we might become the righteousness of God (2 Corinthians 5:21).

If there weren't any speed limit signs, the highway would become a freeway. Without a speed limit we would not be known as "speeders," since it would be impossible to travel faster than "no limit." Where there is "no Law" we cannot break "The Law" (Romans 5:13). However, we are not without law toward God, but we are under Christ's law (1 Corinthians 9:21).

In the same way, those who are free (from the Law) in Christ, cannot be known as transgressors (sinners), since they have fully met all of the requirements of the Law through faith in Jesus (Romans 13:8-10, Galatians 5:13-14).

Galatians 5:13-14
13 For you, brethren, have been called to liberty; only do not use liberty as an opportunity for the flesh, but through love serve one another. 14 For all the law is fulfilled in one word, even in this: "You shall love your neighbor as yourself." NKJV

Galatians 5:13-14
13 You, my brothers, were called to be free. But do not use your freedom to indulge the sinful nature; rather, serve one another in love. 14 The entire law is summed up in a single command: "Love your neighbor as yourself." NIV

We are called to be free from the Law, but that doesn't mean that we can willfully continue to sin and expect God to willfully supply grace, especially after we know the truth (Hebrews 10:26-30). God doesn't give grace to the proud, but only to the humble or contrite (James 4:4-10). To be humble and contrite concerning sin is to have a godly sorrow for sin with a determination not to sin again. The proud have an attitude that says, "I know God will forgive me," even before they sin.

If we fully meet the requirements of the Law through faith by serving one another (verse 13 above), we will fulfill the Law (verse 14 above), and obtain the glory of God that we fell away from by trespassing the Law. This is our hope as Christians (Romans 5:2, John 17:22, Colossians 1:27). It is what we are seeking (Romans 2:7-10, 8:17-18), and as we are being conformed into the likeness of Christ, it is what we are receiving (2 Corinthians 3:18). Check the verses.

DIE TO THE LAW AND BE RELEASED

We can't say that we are not under the Law, until we die to it and serve in this new way. We have to die to the Law in order to be "delivered" from sin's power (Romans 7:8) and serve in the "new way" of the Spirit (Romans 7:4-6 below).

Romans 7:4-6
4 Therefore, my brethren, you also have become dead to the law through the body of Christ, that you may be married to another to Him who was raised from the dead, that we should bear fruit to God. 5 For when we were in the flesh, the sinful passions which were aroused by the law were at work in our members to bear fruit to death. 6 But now we have been delivered from the law, having died to what we were held by, so that we should serve in the

133

newness of the Spirit and not in the oldness of the letter.
NKJV

Romans 7:4-6
4 So, my brothers, you also died to the law through the
body of Christ, that you might belong to another, to him
who was raised from the dead, in order that we might
bear fruit to God. 5 For when we were controlled by the
sinful nature, the sinful passions aroused by the law were
at work in our bodies, so that we bore fruit for death. 6
But now, by dying to what once bound us, we have been
released from the law so that we serve in the new way of
the Spirit, and not in the old way of the written code. NIV

We have to die to the Law in order to be "released" from it (verse 6 above). If we are still hanging on to parts of the Law we can end up being enslaved by it again (Galatians 4:9).

Now we serve in the new way of the Spirit (mind set), and not by the letter written on tablets of stone (Deuteronomy 27:1-6). This new way is discussed later in this book. Jesus Christ is the end of the Law for those who believe (Romans 10:4).

Romans 10:4
4 For Christ is the end of the law for righteousness to
everyone who believes. NKJV

Romans 10:4
4 Christ is the end of the law so that there may be
righteousness for everyone who believes. NIV

For those who believe, Christ is the end of the Law. If that isn't clear, then read Ephesians 2:15. Jesus abolished the Law with its commandments for those who are in Christ. According to Colossians 2:14, He wiped the requirements of the Law away, and nailed them to the cross.

If you are in Christ then you cannot be a transgressor, since you continually keep the Law's requirements through Christ's law discussed in chapter 3. Therefore, instead of the curses for disobeying the Law, now you will receive blessings for obedience.

These blessings include blessings that will overtake everything that belongs to you, victory against those who rise up against you, and so on. Your land will be blessed, and the work of your hands will be blessed (Deuteronomy 28:1-26).

TABLETS OF STONE OR THE NEW LAW

Some will say that Jesus told us to keep the Ten Commandments, and use verses such as Luke 10:25-28 as evidence.

Luke 10:25-28
25 And behold, a certain lawyer stood up and tested Him, saying, "Teacher, what shall I do to inherit eternal life?" 26 He said to him, "What is written in the law? What is your reading of it?" 27 So he answered and said, "'You shall love the Lord your God with all your heart, with all your soul, with all your strength, and with all your mind,' and 'your neighbor as yourself.'" 28 And He said to him, "You have answered rightly; do this and you will live." NKJV

Luke 10:25-28
25 On one occasion an expert in the law stood up to test Jesus. "Teacher," he asked, "what must I do to inherit eternal life?" 26 "What is written in the Law?" he replied. "How do you read it?" 27 He answered: "'Love the Lord your God with all your heart and with all your soul and with all your strength and with all your mind'; and, 'Love your neighbor as yourself.'" 28 "You have answered correctly," Jesus replied. "Do this and you will live." NIV

When Jesus was questioned about eternal life in the verses above, He in turn asked what was written in the Law? The lawyer answered quoting part of the Ten Commandments that came through Moses. The lawyer's answer was correct at the time because the New Covenant did not take effect until Jesus' death on the cross (Hebrews 9:15-17).

Jesus' commands are to love one another, and to believe in His name (John 13:34-35, 15:12, 17, 1 John 3:23). There is power in the name of Jesus Christ for those who accept His Words (John 17:8-12, Psalm 50:16-21, Proverbs 1:23-33).

1 John 3:23
23 And this is His commandment: that we should believe on the name of His Son Jesus Christ and love one another, as He gave us commandment. NKJV

1 John 3:23
23 And this is his command: to believe in the name of his Son, Jesus Christ, and to love one another as he commanded us. NIV

That doesn't look like the Ten Commandments, does it? The Ten Commandments came through Moses, but Jesus' covenant, which brings a change in law (Hebrews 7:12), started at His death (Hebrews 9:15-17). The new law is to love one another and believe in the name of Jesus.

Now that Christ has come, the will of the Father is to believe in the Son (John 6:28-29). There is no other way to the Father (John 14:6) now that Jesus' ministry has started. God requires repentance (Acts 17:30), and doing works that show repentance (Acts 26:20, Luke 3:8-9, John 15:16-17, Ephesians 2:10, Titus 3:14). That's not part of the Law, and we can't obtain that by obeying the Ten Commandments.

It's two totally separate ministries. The Law, engraved on tablets of stone kills, but the Spirit gives life (verse 6 below). The Law produced death in us, but putting to death the misdeeds of the body through the Spirit leads to righteousness (Romans 8:12-14, 6:17, 2 Corinthians 3:3-11 below).

2 Corinthians 3:3-11
3 clearly you are an epistle of Christ, ministered by us, written not with ink but by the Spirit of the living God, not on tablets of stone but on tablets of flesh, that is, of the heart. 4 And we have such trust through Christ toward

God. 5 Not that we are sufficient of ourselves to think of anything as being from ourselves, but our sufficiency is from God, 6 who also made us sufficient as ministers of the new covenant, not of the letter but of the Spirit; for the letter kills, but the Spirit gives life. 7 But if the ministry of death, written and engraved on stones, was glorious, so that the children of Israel could not look steadily at the face of Moses because of the glory of his countenance, which glory was passing away, 8 how will the ministry of the Spirit not be more glorious? 9 For if the ministry of condemnation had glory, the ministry of righteousness exceeds much more in glory. 10 For even what was made glorious had no glory in this respect, because of the glory that excels. 11 For if what is passing away was glorious, what remains is much more glorious. NKJV

2 Corinthians 3:3-11
3 You show and make obvious that you are a letter from Christ delivered by us, not written with ink but with [the] Spirit of [the] living God, not on tablets of stone but on tablets of human hearts. [Ex 24:12; 31:18; 32:15,16; Jer 31:33.] 4 Such is the reliance and confidence that we have through Christ toward and with reference to God. 5 Not that we are fit (qualified and sufficient in ability) of ourselves to form personal judgments or to claim or count anything as coming from us, but our power and ability and sufficiency are from God. 6 [It is He] Who has qualified us [making us to be fit and worthy and sufficient] as ministers and dispensers of a new covenant [of salvation through Christ], not [ministers] of the letter (of legally written code) but of the Spirit; for the code [of the Law] kills, but the [Holy] Spirit makes alive. [Jer 31:31.] 7 Now if the dispensation of death engraved in letters on stone [the ministration of the Law], was inaugurated with such glory and splendor that the Israelites were not able to look steadily at the face of Moses because of its brilliance,

[a glory] that was to fade and pass away, [Ex 34:29-35.] 8 Why should not the dispensation of the Spirit [this spiritual ministry whose task it is to cause men to obtain and be governed by the Holy Spirit] be attended with much greater and more splendid glory? 9 For if the service that condemns [the ministration of doom] had glory, how infinitely more abounding in splendor and glory must be the service that makes righteous [the ministry that produces and fosters righteous living and right standing with God]! 10 Indeed, in view of this fact, what once had splendor [the glory of the Law in the face of Moses] has come to have no splendor at all, because of the overwhelming glory that exceeds and excels it [the glory of the Gospel in the face of Jesus Christ]. 11 For if that which was but passing and fading away came with splendor, how much more must that which remains and is permanent abide in glory and splendor! AMP

Now, which ministry has God given us? Are we Christ's ambassadors? Did He send us to force people to remain under the Law? Why did the Apostle Paul rebuke Peter in front of everyone? Read Galatians 2:14-21 a few times and see if you can figure out what Peter was doing wrong.

When the Apostle Paul saw that Peter was teaching the non-Jews to follow Jewish customs he corrected him (verse 14). He reminded Peter that we have to be justified (made acceptable) by faith in Jesus Christ and not by observing the Law (verses 15-16).

If we return and rebuild, or start over under the Law through our practice of it, we prove (show, confirm) our desire to remain under it (verses 17-18). The Law led us to Christ, since it put us to death (verse 19). Now we live by faith, because righteousness, which is still required to enter the Kingdom of Heaven (Matthew 5:20), could not be gained through the Law (verses 20-21).

We cannot attempt to be righteous by observing the Law, and by having faith in Jesus. The two do not blend together (Romans 4:14-15). Now that faith has come, or rather has been revealed, we are no longer subject to the Law (Galatians 3:22-25).

Galatians 3:22-25
22 But the Scripture has confined all under sin, that the promise by faith in Jesus Christ might be given to those who believe. 23 But before faith came, we were kept under guard by the law, kept for the faith which would afterward be revealed. 24 Therefore the law was our tutor to bring us to Christ, that we might be justified by faith. 25 But after faith has come, we are no longer under a tutor. NKJV

Galatians 3:22-25
22 But the Scripture declares that the whole world is a prisoner of sin, so that what was promised, being given through faith in Jesus Christ, might be given to those who believe. 23 Before this faith came, we were held prisoners by the law, locked up until faith should be revealed. 24 So the law was put in charge to lead us to Christ that we might be justified by faith. 25 Now that faith has come, we are no longer under the supervision of the law. NIV

Those who have accepted Jesus as Lord are no longer under the Law. They live by faith and not by the written code. Sons of God follow the Holy Spirit into putting to death the misdeeds of the body (Romans 8:12-14), instead of trying to keep the Laws of Moses. If the Holy Spirit is not leading them to remain under the Law, then who is (Galatians 5:18)?

TEACHERS OF THE LAW

I don't have a problem with people teaching the Law. We should teach the Law in order to lead people to Christ, so that Christians will understand the "Christian life."

People who only quote a sinner's prayer may be confused by the implied message; just say Jesus is Lord and believe in your heart that God raised Him from the dead (Romans 10:10-13). They may believe that by simply quoting a sinner's prayer, they have eternal life.

However, when only Romans 10:10-13 is used to explain life in Christ, the listener knows nothing about the righteousness that comes by faith, which Romans 9:30 through Romans 10:8 describes. Consequently, they naturally reject righteousness through faith which includes speaking in line with the faith (Romans 10:6-8), and lean toward a law of righteousness (Romans 10:6), or a man-made doctrine.

If the Law is taught, then this shouldn't be a problem, since a law of righteousness cannot be humanly attained (Romans 9:30-33). However, teachers of the Law do not use the Law to lead people to Christ, but to make them obey parts of it.

1 Timothy 1:7-11
7 desiring to be teachers of the law, understanding neither what they say nor the things which they affirm. 8 But we know that the law is good if one uses it lawfully, 9 knowing this: that the law is not made for a righteous person, but for the lawless and insubordinate, for the ungodly and for sinners, for the unholy and profane, for murderers of fathers and murderers of mothers, for manslayers, 10 for fornicators, for sodomites, for kidnappers, for liars, for perjurers, and if there is any other thing that is contrary to sound doctrine, 11 according to the glorious gospel of the blessed God which was committed to my trust. NKJV

1 Timothy 1:7-11
7 They want to be teachers of the law, but they do not know what they are talking about or what they so confidently affirm. 8 We know that the law is good if one uses it properly. 9 We also know that law is made not for the righteous but for lawbreakers and rebels, the ungodly and sinful, the unholy and irreligious; for those who kill their fathers or mothers, for murderers, 10 for adulterers and perverts, for slave traders and liars and perjurers and for whatever else is contrary to the sound doctrine 11 that conforms to the glorious gospel of the blessed God, which he entrusted to me. NIV

The Law is not made for the righteous (verse 9 above). In other words, the Law is not made for the people who are going to Heaven, but

140

for the ones who will not make it (Matthew 5:20).

Who doesn't know what they are talking about according to verse 7 above? The Law is contrary to sound doctrine found in the Gospel (verses 10-11 above). Therefore, when a teacher tries to keep his listeners under the Law, it becomes obvious that it is for personal gain rather than leading them to Christ (1 Timothy 6:3-5, Acts 20:29-31, Galatians 3:24).

The Law is still in effect, and God will judge the people of this world by it. Through the Law the whole world will be held accountable to God (Romans 3:19), but the righteous go free (Proverbs 10:2, 11:21). Their sins are never counted against them (Romans 4:6-8). They go free as if there was never a law that opposed them.

FAITH CREDITED RIGHTEOUSNESS

Do you want to be righteous, or remain a sinner saved by grace? Sinners remain under the Law which identifies them as sinners as they trespass its commands, but where there is no Law, there cannot be any trespassing of the Law. Being a sinner saved by grace is simply the beginning of the process of being conformed into the likeness of Christ (Romans 8:12-14, 29, 2 Corinthians 3:18).

Jesus became our sin in order that we "might" become God's righteousness through faith in Jesus (2 Corinthians 5:21, Romans 5:19).

2 Corinthians 5:21
21 For He made Him who knew no sin to be sin for us, that we might become the righteousness of God in Him. NKJV

2 Corinthians 5:21
21 God made him who had no sin to be sin for us, so that in him we might become the righteousness of God. NIV

Some people take the word "might" out of that verse and declare that we are the righteousness of God. I don't have a problem with that, but I don't think the listeners know that the promise is not fulfilled until we pass the test (James 2:20-24). Therefore, it should be preached like it is written.

Abraham believed God concerning his descendants, and it was

credited to him as righteousness (Genesis chapter 15). However, Abraham's faith was tested many years later when Isaac was old enough to walk (Hebrews 11:17). God asked Abraham to offer up his only son, Isaac (Genesis 22:1-19). Check the verses.

Once Abraham obeyed God, the scripture was fulfilled which says, "Abraham believed God, and it was credited to him as righteousness" (James 2:20-24). It is the same with our faith.

James 2:20-24
20 Are you willing to be shown [proof], you foolish (unproductive, spiritually deficient) fellow, that faith apart from [good] works is inactive and ineffective and worthless? 21 Was not our forefather Abraham [shown to be] justified (made acceptable to God) by [his] works when he brought to the altar as an offering his [own] son Isaac? [Gen 22:1-14.] 22 You see that [his] faith was cooperating with his works, and [his] faith was completed and reached its supreme expression [when he implemented it] by [good] works. 23 And [so] the Scripture was fulfilled that says, Abraham believed in (adhered to, trusted in, and relied on) God, and this was accounted to him as righteousness (as conformity to God's will in thought and deed), and he was called God's friend. [Gen 15:6; 2 Chron 20:7; Isa 41:8.] 24 You see that a man is justified (pronounced righteous before God) through what he does and not alone through faith [through works of obedience as well as by what he believes]. AMP

James 2:20-24
20 You foolish man, do you want evidence that faith without deeds is useless? 21 Was not our ancestor Abraham considered righteous for what he did when he offered his son Isaac on the altar? 22 You see that his faith and his actions were working together, and his faith was made complete by what he did. 23 And the scripture was fulfilled that says, "Abraham believed God, and it was credited to

him as righteousness," and he was called God's friend. 24 You see that a person is justified by what he does and not by faith alone. NIV

The scripture is not fulfilled until we pass the test by obeying Jesus. That is why it is written, "We eagerly wait through the Spirit, for the righteousness in which we hope" (Galatians 5:5). If we eagerly wait for it, how is it that we already have it?

We receive imputed righteousness as a gift because we believe in the way Abraham believed (Romans 4:24), and then our faith is tested until we remain in the faith (1 Peter 1:6-7, James 1:2-4). If we remain in the faith, our faith is going to produce the right actions; love (Galatians 5:6).

The right actions (obedience to the faith), combined with our faith produces a complete faith. It is written, "faith and his actions were working together, and his faith was made complete by what he did" (verse 22 above). Only after Abraham's faith was complete, was the scripture fulfilled concerning his righteousness, and so it is with us.

In this way, righteousness comes through faith in Jesus Christ to all who believe (Romans 3:22). The goal of our faith is the salvation of our souls (1 Peter 1:9), and the "righteousness of God" that we are supposed to seek is through faith (Matthew 6:33).

Think about this. If our faith was tested today, would the scripture be fulfilled concerning us? Obedience to the faith is very important. Most of us do not realize that our faith has anything to do with the Christian life once we are saved, but now we have to live by faith. If we don't, then we will shrink back to destruction (Hebrews 10:37-39)? This could very well answer the question, "Why do bad things happen to good people?"

It is written, "obedience leads to righteousness" (Romans 6:16). Those who love Jesus obey His teaching (John 14:21-23). Baby Christians and those who speak against the scriptures concerning righteousness, cannot understand the righteousness of God (Hebrews 5:11-14, 1 Timothy 6:20-21). By their fruits you will recognize them.

BACK AND FORTH

We have to fight in order to keep the faith (1 Timothy 1:18-19). It's an everyday challenge to remain in love since each day has enough trouble of its own (Matthew 6:34). We have to continually obey Jesus in order to remain under Christ's law.

When we disobey Jesus, or refuse to follow Him, we are once again convicted by the Law as a Law breaker (James 2:8-13, 4:11-12). At whatever point we do not remain in love, we are not fulfilling the Law, but back under it.

James 2:8-13
8 If you really fulfill the royal law according to the Scripture, "You shall love your neighbor as yourself," you do well; 9 but if you show partiality, you commit sin, and are convicted by the law as transgressors. 10 For whoever shall keep the whole law, and yet stumble in one point, he is guilty of all. 11 For He who said, "Do not commit adultery," also said, "Do not murder." Now if you do not commit adultery, but you do murder, you have become a transgressor of the law. 12 So speak and so do as those who will be judged by the law of liberty. 13 For judgment is without mercy to the one who has shown no mercy. Mercy triumphs over judgment. NKJV

James 2:8-13
8 If you really keep the royal law found in Scripture, "Love your neighbor as yourself," you are doing right. 9 But if you show favoritism, you sin and are convicted by the law as lawbreakers. 10 For whoever keeps the whole law and yet stumbles at just one point is guilty of breaking all of it. 11 For he who said, "Do not commit adultery," also said, "Do not murder." If you do not commit adultery but do commit murder, you have become a lawbreaker. 12 Speak and act as those who are going to be judged by the law that gives freedom, 13 because judgment without mercy will be shown to anyone who has not been merciful. Mercy triumphs over judgment! NIV

By showing favoritism, we no longer act in love as Jesus commanded

144

us (verse 9 above). Consequently, we go back under the Laws of Moses without even realizing it, until we receive more grace (James 4:4-10). If the truth were known, we probably all go back and forth a few times, switching between Christ's law and the Laws of Moses until we put to death the misdeeds of the body through the Spirit (Romans 8:12-14).

If someone attends a denomination that says they are not under the Law, it doesn't mean that they are not. We can say that we are not under the Laws of Moses, but the proof is if we fulfill the Law through faith in Jesus (Romans 13:8-10).

If we do not fulfill the Law through faith in Jesus, then we are by default still under it and subject to its curses, which includes prolonged sickness, diseases, plagues, and the like (Deuteronomy 28:58-63). Check the verses. This teaching can change health care in this country.

In order to remain "in Christ" we have to obey and remain in love (John 15:10, 1 John 3:24). When we listen to the Word and put it into practice, we are under the "perfect law" that gives freedom (James 1:22-25), or the "law of freedom" that frees us from being lawbreakers (sinners) mentioned above (James 2:8-13). We have to purposely speak and act in such a way as to remain in love; be patient, kind, not rude, not easily angered, etc. (1 Corinthians 13:4-8, Ephesians 4:29).

This is how the person who is willing to suffer in his body is done with sin according to 1 Peter 4:1-4. He follows Jesus no matter what comes his way. If someone strikes him on one cheek, he turns the other, and so on. This is what is meant by picking up our cross, and following Jesus (Matthew 16:24, 10:38, 1 Peter 2:21-24). Suffering is covered in detail in chapter 3.

Children of the devil do not rest until they make someone fall (Proverbs 4:16), and our faith will be tested until it is proven genuine (1 Peter 1:6-7). Therefore, as a part of the Christian process (God's will), we will have plenty of opportunities to suffer at the hands of someone who is controlled by the spirit of disobedience (1 Peter 4:12-19, 3 :13-17, Ephesians 2:1-3). Pass the test, and stop complaining like those who do not know this process (Philippians 2:14).

Imagine being called to the hospital to pray for a life-long Christian, whose illness is caused by violating the Laws of Moses. Are you going to instruct them to repent, remain in love, and perform deeds that prove repentance? You might, but if looks could kill, you might not make it. Keep in mind that by becoming sin for us, Jesus also took our infirmities (Isaiah 53:4-6, Matthew 8:17).

THE GOOD I WANT TO DO

Have you ever heard anyone say "The good I want to do, I cannot carry it out?" Some people use Romans chapter seven as an excuse, but when we find ourselves in a position where we cannot do the good we want to do, we should recognize that it is "sin" controlling us (Romans 7:20).

Romans 7:20
20 Now if I do what I will not to do, it is no longer I who do it, but sin that dwells in me. NKJV

Romans 7:20
20 Now if I do what I do not want to do, it is no longer I who do it, but it is sin living in me that does it. NIV

Romans 7:20
20 Now if I do what I do not desire to do, it is no longer I doing it [it is not myself that acts], but the sin [principle] which dwells within me [fixed and operating in my soul]. AMP

At this point we should recognize that it is sin within us that is controlling us, because we are under the Law, whether by choice, or by not remaining in love (James 2:8-13). Either way, "when we want to do good," but cannot carry it out, that is the sign that it is a Law problem.

This doesn't apply to those who do not desire to do good. If they do not have a desire to help the family of believers (Galatians 6:10), then the love of God is not in them, point, blank, period (1 John 3:16-18).

Many religious people, who are still under the Law, fall into sin at a time when they are trying their hardest in the flesh not to. They don't realize that by trying to obey the whole Law they are not submitting to God's way of righteousness, which requires that we die to the Law (Romans 10:1-4).

146

Romans 10:1-4
1 Brethren, my heart's desire and prayer to God for Israel is that they may be saved. 2 For I bear them witness that they have a zeal for God, but not according to knowledge. 3 For they being ignorant of God's righteousness, and seeking to establish their own righteousness, have not submitted to the righteousness of God. 4 For Christ is the end of the law for righteousness to everyone who believes.
NKJV

Romans 10:1-4
1 Brothers, my heart's desire and prayer to God for the Israelites is that they may be saved. 2 For I can testify about them that they are zealous for God, but their zeal is not based on knowledge. 3 Since they did not know the righteousness that comes from God and sought to establish their own, they did not submit to God's righteousness. 4 Christ is the end of the law so that there may be righteousness for everyone who believes. NIV

Israel was on fire for God, but they didn't do things according to what was written. Some seemingly religious individuals, who are under the Law, do the same things today and end up committing exceedingly wicked sins that are out of character for them. Everyone looks on in disbelief. However, none of us are immune to what our sinful nature is capable of.

These people need to know the truth and be set free, Lord willing, before sin controls them again. If you can get them to actually read the verses out loud a few times, that could break the stronghold in their thinking (2 Corinthians 10:3-5).

Keep in mind that the Word itself judges the thoughts and attitudes of the heart (Hebrews 4:12). Therefore, always mention the verses, which is the sword of the Spirit (Ephesians 6:17). It will cut like a knife, long after you have finished your conversation. One verse can make all the difference in the world, especially when speaking about the Law.

LAWLESSNESS OR CHRIST'S LAW

Some people declare that they are not under any law. When people say that they are not under any law, they are considered to be lawless or without law. However, they are probably just saying that they are not under the Laws of Moses, and don't really mean to say that they are without law.

A lawless person is not concerned with any law; he willingly, or unknowingly breaks any of them. Those who are not under any law will not enter the Kingdom of Heaven (Matthew 7:21-23 below).

Matthew 7:21-23
21 "Not everyone who says to Me, 'Lord, Lord,' shall enter the kingdom of heaven, but he who does the will of My Father in heaven. 22 Many will say to Me in that day, 'Lord, Lord, have we not prophesied in Your name, cast out demons in Your name, and done many wonders in Your name?' 23 And then I will declare to them, 'I never knew you; depart from Me, you who practice lawlessness!' NKJV

Matthew 7:21-23
21 "Not everyone who says to me, 'Lord, Lord,' will enter the kingdom of heaven, but only he who does the will of my Father who is in heaven. 22 Many will say to me on that day, 'Lord, Lord, did we not prophesy in your name, and in your name drive out demons and perform many miracles?' 23 Then I will tell them plainly, 'I never knew you. Away from me, you evildoers!' NIV

If we do not come to know Jesus Christ, He will say, "Away from Me I never knew you," on the day when the faithful are entering the Kingdom of Heaven (Matthew 7:21-23, Luke 13:22-30). The way we come to know Christ is by obeying what He commanded (1 John 2:3, John 14:21-23), and putting off our old self (Ephesians 4:20-24).

Obeying Jesus automatically puts us under His law or rule (Christ's law). The Apostle Paul was under Christ's law (1 Corinthians 9:21).

If you are under Christ's law then say that you are. Speak your faith! A lawless person will not enter the Kingdom of Heaven because Jesus is the only way, and the author of eternal salvation for those who obey Him (Hebrews 5:9). Check the verse.

OBEY THE GOSPEL

Read the verses below and ask yourself if there is a part of the Gospel that we must obey?

1 Peter 4:17-19
17 For the time has come for judgment to begin at the house of God; and if it begins with us first, what will be the end of those who do not obey the gospel of God? 18 Now "If the righteous one is scarcely saved, Where will the ungodly and the sinner appear?" 19 Therefore let those who suffer according to the will of God commit their souls to Him in doing good, as to a faithful Creator. NKJV

1 Peter 4:17-19
17 For it is time for judgment to begin with the family of God; and if it begins with us, what will the outcome be for those who do not obey the gospel of God? 18 And, "If it is hard for the righteous to be saved, what will become of the ungodly and the sinner?" 19 So then, those who suffer according to God's will should commit themselves to their faithful Creator and continue to do good. NIV

According to those verses, it appears that we don't need to settle with being a sinner saved by grace, but we need to be righteous. Being a slave to sin leads to death, but obedience leads to righteousness (Romans 6:16).

What will the end be for those who do not obey the Gospel of God? It's difficult for the righteous to be saved, so where will the ungodly and the sinner end up? That's an excellent question, don't you think? Is there a part of the Gospel that we must obey?

Let's look at another passage of scripture to determine if there is something specific in the Gospel that we need to obey. If there is a requirement that we must accomplish according to the Gospel, then we have not heard a complete Gospel until we know what is required of us.

Think about that.

2 Thessalonians 1:8-10
8 in flaming fire taking vengeance on those who do not know God, and on those who do not obey the gospel of our Lord Jesus Christ. 9 These shall be punished with everlasting destruction from the presence of the Lord and from the glory of His power, 10 when He comes, in that Day, to be glorified in His saints and to be admired among all those who believe, because our testimony among you was believed. NKJV

2 Thessalonians 1:8-10
8 He will punish those who do not know God and do not obey the gospel of our Lord Jesus. 9 They will be punished with everlasting destruction and shut out from the presence of the Lord and from the majesty of his power 10 on the day he comes to be glorified in his holy people and to be marveled at among all those who have believed. This includes you, because you believed our testimony to you. NIV

We already know that some people will hear, "Away from Me I never knew you on the last day" since they did not come to know Jesus by obeying His commands, but verse 8 above also includes those who do not obey the Gospel. Notice how they will be punished; with everlasting destruction (verse 9). Let me ask you again. Is there a part of the Gospel that we must obey?

If you have not put into practice what we have already covered, then start as soon as possible. Don't wait until you finish reading this book since what I have taught you, may not remain in you (Mark 4:24-25, Matthew 13:18-23, 1 John 2:24).

UNDERSTANDING

Any part of Kingdom teaching that you do not understand, the devil can snatch out of your heart (Matthew 13:19). If you have not retained

150

what we have already covered, it has probably been taken from you. Put this teaching into practice as you learn it so that you will see the results as you go, and so that you may receive the understanding that you need to continue.

This chapter may be difficult to understand if you have not invested time in the previous chapters. Attending church services for thirty years is irrelevant, if you are not practicing the basics. By their fruits we recognize Christians, and not according to their length of service, title, position, or degree (2 Corinthians 5:16).

If you are not practicing loving one another, being transformed through the Word, and seeking God's Kingdom and righteousness first, which is New Testament teachings, then your understanding will be darkened or cloudy at best (Ephesians 4:17-19).

Why couldn't the Apostle Paul speak to the Corinthians about certain spiritual things? It was because they were still worldly (1 Corinthians 3:1-3). Instead of remaining in love with one another, there was strife, envy, jealousy, and the like. Their way of life prevented them from understanding spiritual things, and so it is today.

The way we speak and act will determine how much we can receive and understand. We are not to conform (do the accepted thing) to this world any longer. We must put to death our old way of life, because a friend of the world becomes an enemy of God (James 4:4). When we bite and devour each other, we are not acting in love (Galatians 5:13-15, James 4:11-12, 5:9).

People who refuse to obey the Gospel, harden their hearts (rebellion), and will have a darkened understanding (Ephesians 4:17-19). On the other hand, people who believe and obey the precepts, will be given a good understanding; even more than their teachers (Psalm 111:10, 119:97-105). Their understanding is by faith and not by head knowledge.

When I hear someone who has been a Christian for more than four years say that they cannot understand the scriptures, what they are actually telling me is that they do not obey the Gospel. Somewhere along the way they did not live up to what they had attained (Philippians 3:16).

Jesus is our understanding (1 John 5:20). Anyone who is allowing Jesus to be the Lord of their life, will have an understanding.

151

Luke 24:45
45 And He opened their understanding, that they might comprehend the Scriptures. NKJV

Luke 24:45
45 Then he opened their minds so they could understand the Scriptures. NIV

How long do you think it would take Jesus to open our understanding according to those verses (Luke 24:45)? Why would Jesus open the disciple's understanding and not open the understanding of His disciples today if He is not a respecter of persons?

If we have the faith of the disciples, we would be treated like the disciples, and if we had the faith of David, the Lord would treat us like He treated David. If we had the faith of Daniel, God would treat us like He treated Daniel, and so on. He is no respecter of persons, meaning He does not play favorites (Romans 2:11, Acts 10:34, Galatians 2:6).

How do we come to know Jesus? We have to obey His commands (1 John 2:3), and put off our old self (Ephesians 4:20-24). We have to take ownership of the elementary things such as repentance from dead works (Hebrews 5:11- 6:3), and become mature before we are ready for spiritual things, such as our seal of righteousness (Colossians 2:11, Romans 2:29, 4:11). Lets get with it!

My name is Alan P. Ballou. I am a servant. If you have questions, or need help with what I have explained in this chapter, please contact me at www.howtostopsinning.com.

5. Sin's Control

What is sin

The start of sin

Slave to sin

Insignificant sins

The lust of the eyes

The pride of life

All sin is common

Sins that lead to death

Baptized into His death

The doctrine

Discipline

Reap what we sow

Pronounce your judgment

Time to repent

Sinning willfully

Once saved always saved

Falling away

5

SIN'S CONTROL

᪂ᑐᘓ

In certain circumstances sin is uncontrollable and cannot be avoided. If you are reading this chapter first, then you probably think that's a silly statement. A life filled with sin, is a life filled with destruction and there is nothing childish about destruction (Galatians 6:7-8).

When we sin, most of us have a logical sounding explanation. However, the Bible says that we stumble because we disobey the message (1 Peter 2:8). Does anyone ever say that they were only "hearers" of the Word of God and not "doers" and that is why they are experiencing destruction (James 1:22-24, Matthew 7:24-27, Luke 6:46-49)?

Anything can be blamed on something else such as an addiction, but it is our sin that brings about our destruction. I want you to think of alcohol, drugs, eating disorders, and whatever else, as the vehicle that drives us to destruction. In other words, they are just the method of destruction. Deal with the sin, and like a car that runs out of gas, the destruction will stop (Proverbs 19:3).

There is nothing wrong with receiving help. For example, if you are a drug addict and someone is helping you with your addiction, I say, "Praise God." However, until you change what is controlling you, then you will remain vulnerable to destruction until you decide to wholeheartedly obey the message (Romans 6:17).

I heard an old man say that when we teach someone to fish, we feed them for a lifetime. I'm not one for old wives tales, or to go beyond what is written, but there may be some truth to that one (1 Timothy 4:7).

I want the reader of this chapter to be able to identify what sin is, how it gains control over us, how to eliminate it, and what to do if we are caught up in it; damage control. The more we know, the more we can control sin in our life instead of it controlling us.

We need to be proactive in controlling sin instead of waiting to see what will happen, since the effects of sin are very predictable. Therefore, we do not have to wait.

WHAT IS SIN

What is sin? By definition, all sin is lawlessness, or violating what the Law makes sin. There are many things that are considered sin for those who are still under the Laws that came through Moses, as we have already discussed in chapter 4.

Whatever the Law says, it says to those who are under it (Romans 3:19) and those who are under the Law cannot stop sinning (Romans 6:14). However, apart from the Law sin within us is dead (Romans 7:8, 1 Corinthians 15:56).

For those in Christ, all wrong doing is sin (1 John 5:17) and anything that is not done by faith is sin (Romans 14:23). We may be free in Christ, but that doesn't mean that we can curse someone out. That would not be living by faith, since the Word in our new agreement says to not allow any unwholesome talk come out of our mouth (Ephesians 4:29). Living by faith causes us to live in accordance with the truth.

Ignoring the good that we know to do is sin (James 4:17) and whoever leads his Christian brother into doing something that he believes is wrong, sins (1 Corinthians 8:12, Romans 14:13-21). Check the verses. Anyone who knows the good he should be doing and doesn't do it sins.

156

This doesn't apply to the person who doesn't know.

Some Christians are not free in Christ. In fact, I would say that most are not. This means that we all have little areas that we are unsure about. Whatever a Christian believes he can do and can't do, without violating his faith is what he should do.

For example, if someone does not believe they can eat chicken, then for them it is a sin to eat it (1 Corinthians 8:7) and a sin for the one who approves the violation of that person's conscience (Romans 14:14-23). However, edifying him with the truth found in 1 Timothy 4:1-6 (below) so that he will grow up in his faith, is not a sin and is the mark of a good minister (verse 6 below).

1 Timothy 4:1-6
1 Now the Spirit expressly says that in latter times some will depart from the faith, giving heed to deceiving spirits and doctrines of demons, 2 speaking lies in hypocrisy, having their own conscience seared with a hot iron, 3 forbidding to marry, and commanding to abstain from foods which God created to be received with thanksgiving by those who believe and know the truth. 4 For every creature of God is good, and nothing is to be refused if it is received with thanksgiving; 5 for it is sanctified by the word of God and prayer. 6 If you instruct the brethren in these things, you will be a good minister of Jesus Christ, nourished in the words of faith and of the good doctrine which you have carefully followed. NKJV

1 Timothy 4:1-6
1 BUT THE [Holy] Spirit distinctly and expressly declares that in latter times some will turn away from the faith, giving attention to deluding and seducing spirits and doctrines that demons teach, 2 Through the hypocrisy and pretensions of liars whose consciences are seared (cauterized), 3 Who forbid people to marry and [teach them] to abstain from [certain kinds of] foods which God created to be received with thanksgiving by those who

believe and have [an increasingly clear] knowledge of the truth. 4 For everything God has created is good, and nothing is to be thrown away or refused if it is received with thanksgiving. 5 For it is hallowed and consecrated by the Word of God and by prayer. 6 If you lay all these instructions before the brethren, you will be a worthy steward and a good minister of Christ Jesus, ever nourishing your own self on the truths of the faith and of the good [Christian] instruction which you have closely followed. AMP

There are many Christians who are trapped by false teachings. When I first met my wife, Lucie, she could not eat certain types of bread or she would become ill. For fourteen years she was kept in bondage. She hasn't had that problem since she has learned the truth from this passage of scripture. Praise the Lord!

Besides these, as long as we do everything in love (1 Corinthians 16:14), all things are permissible, but not all things are helpful or edify and bring glory to God (1 Corinthians 6:12, 10:23, 31). Therefore, even though we are free in Christ, we are still concerned with the building up (edifying) of those who do not know the truth.

How many Christians live in bondage to something everyday? This book is an attempt to free all who read it.

God has given us a conscience, and when we violate our conscience it is sin for us. Not only have we made a pledge to keep a clear conscience before God through our baptism (1 Peter 3:21), but we are to serve God with a clear conscience (1 Timothy 1:5, 18-19, 2 Timothy 1:3). Therefore, when our conscience is convicted, we should seek to repent and resolve the issue.

We know when we do wrong, unless we have fallen away to the point of losing our conscience (Ephesians 4:17-19). One sure sign that a person still has a conscience is if they hide their sin (John 16:8). Once a person's conscience is gone, they sin openly.

THE START OF SIN

Every sin that is in our control starts with a desire in our thinking

158

(James 1:13-15). It starts with thoughts from within us about something that we want. When we focus on an evil craving and decide to act upon it, then it is sin. We sin by participating in, or by planning to attain something we desire that is against God.

James 1:13-17
13 Let no one say when he is tempted, "I am tempted by God"; for God cannot be tempted by evil, nor does He Himself tempt anyone. 14 But each one is tempted when he is drawn away by his own desires and enticed. 15 Then, when desire has conceived, it gives birth to sin; and sin, when it is full-grown, brings forth death. 16 Do not be deceived, my beloved brethren. 17 Every good gift and every perfect gift is from above, and comes down from the Father of lights, with whom there is no variation or shadow of turning. NKJV

James 1:13-17
13 Let no one say when he is tempted, I am tempted from God; for God is incapable of being tempted by [what is] evil and He Himself tempts no one. 14 But every person is tempted when he is drawn away, enticed and baited by his own evil desire (lust, passions). 15 Then the evil desire, when it has conceived, gives birth to sin, and sin, when it is fully matured, brings forth death. 16 Do not be misled, my beloved brethren. 17 Every good gift and every perfect (free, large, full) gift is from above; it comes down from the Father of all [that gives] light, in [the shining of] Whom there can be no variation [rising or setting] or shadow cast by His turning [as in an eclipse]. AMP

Everything that is good and perfect for us will come from God. If something is right for us, we can attain it through faith in the promises written in scripture (2 Peter 1:3-4). If it is not perfect for us, then we attain it through fleshly means.

If we delight ourselves in the Lord, He will give us the desires of our heart (Psalm 37:4). When we seek first the Kingdom of God and God's righteousness, God will see to it that we have the things we worry about (Matthew 6:25-34, Psalm 34:10). If the Word remains in us and we remain in Jesus, we can ask what we wish (John 15:7). This would include bearing the fruit we are called to bear (John 15:16-17, 1 John 3:22-23). With promises like these, what could we possibly need or want?

Note that once our sinful nature is fully grown, it will put us to death (verse 15 above). Everyone has a divine appointment with death (Hebrews 9:27), but we can add to or take away from those years (Proverbs 3:2, 4:10, 5:9, 9:11). The wicked do not live out half of their years (Psalm 55:23). Check the verses.

SLAVE TO SIN

We have been taught that we have a free will. We do up to a certain point. Most of us can choose what we want to eat and if we want to go outside, but our freedom amounts to the ability to choose who we will serve (verse 16 below).

When those who are in Christ sin, they choose to sin instead of choosing God's way out of the temptation (1 Corinthians 10:13). This in turn gives them over to sin's control which is called being a slave to sin (Romans 6:16-18 below).

Romans 6:16-18
16 Do you not know that to whom you present yourselves slaves to obey, you are that one's slaves whom you obey, whether of sin leading to death, or of obedience leading to righteousness? 17 But God be thanked that though you were slaves of sin, yet you obeyed from the heart that form of doctrine to which you were delivered. 18 And having been set free from sin, you became slaves of righteousness. NKJV

Romans 6:16-18
16 Don't you know that when you offer yourselves to someone to obey him as slaves, you are slaves to the one whom you obey whether you are slaves to sin, which leads

to death, or to obedience, which leads to righteousness?
17 But thanks be to God that, though you used to be slaves
to sin, you wholeheartedly obeyed the form of teaching to
which you were entrusted. 18 You have been set free from
sin and have become slaves to righteousness. NIV

Once we choose obedience, then righteousness will control us to do good works (Romans 6:19). Only a slave to righteousness is set free from sin (Romans 6:18). Once we become a slave to sin by choosing to sin, it will control us for a period of time in order to make us sin again (16 above). This sin principle works whether we know it or not.

One thing is for certain. A slave to sin, will sin again. At this point, sin will determine what we will do next that will bring about our destruction (Galatians 6:7-9). That's how we end up doing things that we normally would not do. Let that sink in.

The way out is repentance from the heart, confessing our sins, turning away from them, and becoming a slave to righteousness (1 John 1:9). We can purposely become slaves to righteousness in order that we will not be a slave to sin.

What we choose determines what we will serve, and we choose by offering or presenting the parts of our body to sin or to righteous acts (Romans 6:11-13 below).

Romans 6:11-13
11 Likewise you also, reckon yourselves to be dead indeed
to sin, but alive to God in Christ Jesus our Lord. 12
Therefore do not let sin reign in your mortal body, that
you should obey it in its lusts. 13 And do not present your
members as instruments of unrighteousness to sin, but
present yourselves to God as being alive from the dead,
and your members as instruments of righteousness to God.
NKJV

Romans 6:11-13
11 In the same way, count yourselves dead to sin but alive
to God in Christ Jesus. 12 Therefore do not let sin reign in

your mortal body so that you obey its evil desires. 13 Do not offer the parts of your body to sin, as instruments of wickedness, but rather offer yourselves to God, as those who have been brought from death to life; and offer the parts of your body to him as instruments of righteousness. NIV

If you were determined to be a slave to righteousness in order to be set free from sin's control, then you would ask God what He wanted you to do with your hands, your mouth, your eyes, your feet, and so on.

We don't have to look very far to get an answer. Romans 12:1-2 declares that the first sacrifice that God wants each of us to do is offer the parts of our body to Him as a living sacrifice. He wants us to be holy in our body (1 Thessalonians 4:1-3), pleasing to Him (Ephesians 5:10), and He wants us to renew our mind with the truth, which is His Word (John 17:17).

Most of us do not give God what He wants, but like Cain, we give Him what we think He should be pleased with (Hebrews 11:4, Jude 1:11). When destruction hits we shout, "God loves me!" Praise God, halleluiah! However, do we love God, or have we laid what He requires aside, replacing it with the Law, or the traditions of men (Mark 7:8, 1 John 4:19-20)?

Christians who can see this process, run from sexual immorality, do the things that please God, and never set their Bible down, in accordance with Romans 12:1-2. It's time!

There is nothing wrong with playing dominoes, horseshoes, basketball, board games and the like, but fleshly things give birth to flesh (John 3:6). If we feed the flesh it will grow, just like the Spirit within us grows when we feed it (1 Peter 2:2). Only the Word grows us up spiritually (John 6:63) to the point of being born again, and born again Christians have one thing in common; they purify their soul by obeying the truth (1 Peter 1:22-25). Check it!

If you are a Christian with some sort of an addiction, the first thing you should do is repent of the past, and then offer to God the sacrifice He wants according to what is written, and you will no longer have an addiction, point, blank, period.

If you have followed the teachings in this book from the beginning, then you can kiss your addiction goodbye. Believe what is written even if you do not understand it yet. Do not speak against scripture (chapter 1). Force yourself to read the Word to the point of retaining it (chapter 2). Force yourself to love one another as described in chapter 3, and free yourself from the Laws of Moses described in chapter 4.

There are many things that you need to know, covered in those chapters, but the basics, combined with giving God the sacrifice He has asked, will deliver you in a matter of days; not months or years. However, you will have to be careful to continue in the doctrine (teachings).

It takes the full armor of God to stand against the devil's schemes (Ephesians 6:11-17). That is what I am teaching you in this book; truth, salvation, faith, love, remaining, peace, suffering, righteousness, testing, sin, baptism, denying ourselves, and spiritual forces. Therefore, if you have skipped the previous chapters, I believe that you will see results, but I am afraid that you will not stand firm. Please start at the beginning.

Any Christian can overcome an addiction and overcome sins that lead to death if they follow the doctrine. I want you to be totally set free from sins that lead to death without having to battle your whole lifetime.

INSIGNIFICANT SINS

Sin is deceitful. Our sinful nature makes us believe that we can sin and nobody will know. However, it's a trick, in order that our sinful nature may then control us to sin again, so that it can destroy us (Galatians 6:8, James 1:15).

The problem with the small sins is that they lead us to larger ones. Nobody knocks on the front door and says "Hey, let's go commit the biggest sin ever." No, it's the small acceptable things that place us under sin's control to do the bigger things.

Once we offer our body to sin, we can no longer see the outcome of our actions until sin has controlled us because wisdom is at the cross-roads where the paths meet (Proverbs 8:2). Therefore, we believe that we have everything under control until sin controls us for our destruction (Galatians 6:7-9).

This is why we can't reason with a person who is given over to sin. They really can't see that their next step will bring their destruction.

Once destruction hits and the process of control starts over again, then they can see. That's when they need the Word of God, which contains the power to change their life.

We don't have to tell a crack addict to stop smoking crack. Find out why he is given over, and show him how to prevent sin from controlling him according to what is written in the Bible. Then he will see lasting results that he can control.

Find the little sins that he never thought had anything to do with his situation (destruction) due to the deceitfulness of sin, and it will become an on/off switch in his hands. That's spiritual power!

Bank robbers don't start by robbing banks. They start with stealing insignificant things. They are enticed to steal something that they are sure they can get away with, and consequently they are given over to the next theft. A bank robber may have more money than he has ever had, but the sin principle makes him rob another bank until he is destroyed.

He may even live in comfort on stolen money, but his every waking thought will be on what he is given over to until it controls him again. The only thing he will truly enjoy is robbing another bank. The same is true for those who are given over to money unless they are rich in good deeds (1 Timothy 6:17-19).

Being a thief has nothing to do with whether or not the person has the money to purchase what they are stealing. The first sin has to do with whether or not he can get away with it in his mind, as the desire for it entices him (James 1:13-15). This is why so many employees steal, while the employer's focus is on those who look like criminals.

Sin has no social boundaries. Whoever is unfaithful in the little things, will be unfaithful with much (Luke 16:10). People who cheat while playing a simple board game, will cheat in other ways when you are not looking.

The employee who thinks it is harmless to occasionally take one roll of toilet paper from his employer, will eventually be controlled by sin to steal something that will bring about his destruction. That's when everyone who knows him will be in shock since what he will eventually do will be so out of character for him; so much so that he could possibly get away with it.

Swindlers start with little known information which allows them to gain advantage over the unsuspecting. Years ago, stores focused on selling a good product. Those days are nearly gone. Today, stores spend millions of dollars designing clever schemes based on human behavior in an attempt to make the unsuspecting customer spend more money and use credit cards for what they cannot afford. These are the ways of this world (1 John 2:15-17).

THE LUST OF THE EYES

People who will eventually commit physical adultery begin with allowing another individual to be pleasing to them, through the lust of the eyes (Luke 11:34), or through some other desire (1 John 2:15-17). Once their flesh has grown (John 3:6), their spouse will not satisfy them any longer.

Adultery has nothing to do with being unhappy at home, or the inabilities of the unsuspecting partner. How many wives and concubines did David have? Adultery is the effect (end result) of the desire created in the partner who cheats, but it is blamed on everything but that.

Sin starts with our own evil desires. Desires that lead us into sin, can be triggered by conversations with corrupt people (1 Corinthians 15:33), and through our senses, sight, hearing, taste, touch, and smell. The world system is set up to promote these desires through advertisements.

Sex sells, and advertisers use sex to grab our attention to promote a product, but the product is not the only thing the ad promotes. Sex, lifestyle, looks, and many other factors become a product of the advertisement through the lust of the eyes (1 John 2:15-17, Luke 11:34-35).

Luke 11:34-35
34 The lamp of the body is the eye. Therefore, when your eye is good, your whole body also is full of light. But when your eye is bad, your body also is full of darkness. 35 Therefore take heed that the light which is in you is not darkness. NKJV

Luke 11:34-35
34 Your eye is the lamp of your body. When your eyes are good, your whole body also is full of light. But when they

are bad, your body also is full of darkness. 35 See to it, then, that the light within you is not darkness. NIV

A person who is given over to the lust of the eyes will grow dark inside, which will make him blind. Blindness will take away his ability to see the outcome of his actions (1 John 2:11), and consequently, he will begin to live for the moment. His decision making will be ruled by what pleases him right here and right now.

He will grow tired of his relationship with his spouse, since it cannot meet the appealing standard in his mind, that was set by what his eyes have seen. At this point, an affair is simply a matter of time and opportunity. His eyes will be full of adultery, and his words promiscuous as he tests the waters with every worldly person he meets.

Sexual sins are always against the body (1 Corinthians 6:18). Every other sin a man may commit is outside his body, but sexual sins directly affect the body. A Christian who continues in sexual sins should expect some type of bodily ailment unless he repents (Revelation 2:20-23, Proverbs 6:26-32, Psalm 32:1-6).

Removing the television or computer from the home is certainly not the answer, either. Anything can be used for good or evil. We have to change rather than run from the world, since we are sent into the world (John 17:13-19) to reach God's people (Matthew 28:18-20, 1 Corinthians 5:9-10), but we are not to love this world (1 John 2:15-17 below).

1 John 2:15-17
15 Do not love the world or the things in the world. If anyone loves the world, the love of the Father is not in him. 16 For all that is in the world — the lust of the flesh, the lust of the eyes, and the pride of life — is not of the Father but is of the world. 17 And the world is passing away, and the lust of it; but he who does the will of God abides forever. NKJV

1 John 2:15-17
15 Do not love the world or anything in the world. If anyone loves the world, the love of the Father is not in

him. 16 For everything in the world — the cravings of sinful man, the lust of his eyes and the boasting of what he has and does — comes not from the Father but from the world. 17 The world and its desires pass away, but the man who does the will of God lives forever. NIV

Anyone who is given over to the things of this world does not have the love of the Father in Him (verse 15 above). There is no use in arguing with these people because they cannot see where they are going, but that verse is pretty clear. Therefore, do not be tricked.

The world's ways have slipped into the church, little by little. Now it is hard to tell the difference between the church and the local fitness, hunting, and country clubs. If the Word of God cannot be mentioned straight out of the Bible without it being offensive, then you can be sure that God is not the primary focus.

Church should be fun, or should it? I'm here to teach you a direction that your body is not going to want to go. You're going to have to deny yourself and lose your life in order to do what I am teaching you (Matthew 16:24, Mark 8:34, Luke 9:23, John 12:25-26). Read the verses below to see if it sounds like fun to you.

Matthew 16:24-25
24 Then Jesus said to His disciples, "If anyone desires to come after Me, let him deny himself, and take up his cross, and follow Me. 25 For whoever desires to save his life will lose it, but whoever loses his life for My sake will find it. NKJV

Matthew 16:24-25
24 Then Jesus said to His disciples, If anyone desires to be My disciple, let him deny himself [disregard, lose sight of, and forget himself and his own interests] and take up his cross and follow Me [cleave steadfastly to Me, conform wholly to My example in living and, if need be, in dying, also]. 25 For whoever is bent on saving his [temporal] life [his comfort and security here] shall lose it [eternal life];

and whoever loses his life [his comfort and security here] for My sake shall find it [life everlasting]. AMP

If you can make that fun without avoiding the message all together, then praise God. However, every time I teach it I see concerned looks, as people realize that they cannot continue living like the world.

Preach and teach the Word, which will turn God's people from the power of darkness to the power of God (Acts 26:18, 2 Timothy 4:1-4). If God enables a person to come to Him, he is ready for the Word of God (John 6:44-69).

Those who belong to God will hear God's Word (John 8:47, 18:37), but those who are of this world will not (1 John 4:5-6). This is how you can recognize the Spirit of truth, and the spirit of falsehood. Check the verses.

THE PRIDE OF LIFE

Idolatry begins with proclaiming the worth of earthly things, without acknowledging God, Who gives the ability to obtain. To worship is simply to acknowledge the worth of something.

Whatever you express adoration for, be sure that you mention that the Lord has allowed you to accomplish it, or receive it. Always give the glory to God. When the people declared that King Herod was a god, he did not in turn give glory to God, which brought about his ruin.

Acts 12:21-23
21 So on a set day Herod, arrayed in royal apparel, sat on his throne and gave an oration to them. 22 And the people kept shouting, "The voice of a god and not of a man!" 23 Then immediately an angel of the Lord struck him, because he did not give glory to God. And he was eaten by worms and died. NKJV

Acts 12:21-23
21 On an appointed day Herod arrayed himself in his royal robes, took his seat upon [his] throne, and addressed an oration to them. 22 And the assembled people shouted, It

is the voice of a god, and not of a man! 23 And at once an angel of the Lord smote him and cut him down, because he did not give God the glory (the preeminence and kingly majesty that belong to Him as the supreme Ruler); and he was eaten by worms and died. AMP

Do you think that the people saw the angel strike him down? I believe that they thought that he died from some kind of disease. Either way, he died because he received the praise of men, and did not give glory to God. That's very easy to do this day and age and those who live in idolatry have no idea that it is a sin that leads to death (Galatians 5:19-21).

For example, if you follow the ways of this world, then you are passionate about the Christmas season, but you do not give the glory to Jesus Christ. Imagine celebrating your birthday with lights, trees, and special decorations, but someone else is sitting in the seat of honor; santa, reindeer, snowmen, jack frost, etc. That's idolatry.

What birthday celebration honors the guests? Do not the guests honor the one celebrating the birthday? The name "Jesus Christ" is hidden during a season called Christmas even among Christian families.

If your friends visit you during the season called Christmas, or simply passerby, and they have to search for the name of Jesus Christ among your decorations, then Jesus is far removed from the seat of honor. These are the ways of this world.

It's very easy for the world's ways and what is acceptable to the world system to creep into a godly home. Jesus declared that whoever was ashamed of Him and His Word, He would be ashamed of them at His coming (Mark 8:38). Remember to always mention Jesus Christ and His Word. In all your ways acknowledge the Lord and He will make your paths straight (Proverbs 3:6).

ALL SIN IS COMMON

Actually all of us can look back over our life and find areas where we totally missed the mark of what was considered to be normal behavior. That's what I call a "What was I thinking" moment. The Bible calls it things that we are ashamed of and we all have them.

169

Romans 6:20-21
20 For when you were slaves of sin, you were free in regard to righteousness. 21 What fruit did you have then in the things of which you are now ashamed? For the end of those things is death. NKJV

Romans 6:20-21
20 When you were slaves to sin, you were free from the control of righteousness. 21 What benefit did you reap at that time from the things you are now ashamed of? Those things result in death! NIV

If all of our lives were laid out on the table for everyone to see, we would all have periods of time where sin controlled us to do something stupid. All sin is common to man (1 Corinthians 10:13). In other words, all of us have a sinful nature that is fully capable of controlling our body to the point of committing sins that we never imagined possible. We are all capable of being as evil as the worst sinner we know.

Look back over your life and you will find a "things that you are now ashamed of" moment. What allowed sin to control you in that way? Do you know which little sins gave you over to the big ones which made you liable to destruction (Joshua 7:11-12) ?

If you do not know what led you into being a slave to sin, then you are in line again, waiting for it to happen once again. We naturally think that it cannot happen to us, which places us back in the same line filled with those who are waiting for destruction (Joshua 7:11-12, 1 Corinthians 10:12 below).

1 Corinthians 10:12
12 Therefore let him who thinks he stands take heed lest he fall. NKJV

1 Corinthians 10:12
12 Therefore let anyone who thinks he stands [who feels sure that he has a steadfast mind and is standing firm], take heed lest he fall [into sin]. AMP

Don't think that since we have been in church for years that we are immune to the sins that have taken seasoned Christians down. Meeting in a church building once or twice a week for a lifetime does not guarantee that we will not be given over to sin. These things may not even be discussed in church (2 Timothy 4:3-4, John 12:42-43).

All of us need to pay close attention (take heed) to what is written and to be aware of how we are living, so that we don't fall. We need to become familiar enough with how sin works so that we can help those around us who want to stop sinning with godly wisdom rather than worldly philosophy. We cannot continue to ignore the consequences of sin, since it will collect its wages eventually (James 1:15, Romans 6:20-23). Get out of the line!

SINS THAT LEAD TO DEATH

All of us have committed sins that lead to death whether we know it or not. It doesn't have to be something like adultery, prostitution, or homosexuality, since sins such as slandering, idolatry and fits of rage are also among the sins that keep us out of the Kingdom of God if we do not change our lifestyle (1 Corinthians 6:9-10, Galatians 5:19-20, Ephesians 5:3-7).

If someone sees his brother commit sins that do not lead to death, he should pray for him, but we are not instructed to pray for the other (1 John 5:16-17). Therefore, sins that lead to death certainly carry more weight than others.

Some sins are obvious and some are not (1 Timothy 5:24). It's more dangerous to be guilty of the sins that are not obvious such as hatred, envy, and jealousy since most of us won't know that we are on the list of sins that lead to death. Those sins do not seem like they would keep someone out of the Kingdom of God, but we have to abide by what is written.

The methods we are covering in this book work on all sin, but clearly we want to stop sins that lead to death, which will keep us out of the Kingdom of God (Galatians 5:19-21 and 1 Corinthians 6:9-10 below). Here is a list of the verses that warn us about these sins.

Galatians 5:19-21
19 Now the works of the flesh are evident, which are:

171

adultery, fornication, uncleanness, lewdness, 20 idolatry, sorcery, hatred, contentions, jealousies, outbursts of wrath, selfish ambitions, dissensions, heresies, 21 envy, murders, drunkenness, revelries, and the like; of which I tell you beforehand, just as I also told you in time past, that those who practice such things will not inherit the kingdom of God. NKJV

Galatians 5:19-21
19 The acts of the sinful nature are obvious: sexual immorality, impurity and debauchery; 20 idolatry and witchcraft; hatred, discord, jealousy, fits of rage, selfish ambition, dissensions, factions 21 and envy; drunkenness, orgies, and the like. I warn you, as I did before, that those who live like this will not inherit the kingdom of God. NIV

1 Corinthians 6:9-10
9 Do you not know that the unrighteous will not inherit the kingdom of God? Do not be deceived. Neither fornicators, nor idolaters, nor adulterers, nor homosexuals, nor sodomites, 10 nor thieves, nor covetous, nor drunkards, nor revilers, nor extortioners will inherit the kingdom of God. NKJV

1 Corinthians 6:9-10
9 Do you not know that the wicked will not inherit the kingdom of God? Do not be deceived: Neither the sexually immoral nor idolaters nor adulterers nor male prostitutes nor homosexual offenders 10 nor thieves nor the greedy nor drunkards nor slanderers nor swindlers will inherit the kingdom of God. NIV

Ephesians 5:3-7
3 But fornication and all uncleanness or covetousness, let it not even be named among you, as is fitting for saints; 4 neither filthiness, nor foolish talking, nor coarse jesting,

which are not fitting, but rather giving of thanks. 5 For this
you know, that no fornicator, unclean person, nor covetous
man, who is an idolater, has any inheritance in the kingdom
of Christ and God. 6 Let no one deceive you with empty
words, for because of these things the wrath of God comes
upon the sons of disobedience. 7 Therefore do not be
partakers with them. NKJV

Ephesians 5:3-7
3 But among you there must not be even a hint of sexual
immorality, or of any kind of impurity, or of greed, because
these are improper for God's holy people. 4 Nor should
there be obscenity, foolish talk or coarse joking, which are
out of place, but rather thanksgiving. 5 For of this you can
be sure: No immoral, impure or greedy person such a man
is an idolater has any inheritance in the kingdom of Christ
and of God.   6 Let no one deceive you with empty words,
for because of such things God's wrath comes on those who
are disobedient. 7 Therefore do not be partners with them.
NIV

Most of these sins are self-explanatory and some of them are on all three lists. There are other lists in the New Testament, but they do not specifically say that those who live that way will not inherit the Kingdom of God. Therefore, I cannot state that. However, Galatians 5:21 does imply "sins like these" which means there are other sins that have the same effect. Some of the other lists include Colossians 3:5-9 and Romans 1:28-32.

BAPTIZED INTO HIS DEATH

Why would anyone want to continue in sin, if they didn't have to? Sin is connected to discipline, suffering, heartache, sickness, disabilities, and all types of destruction. Why would anyone need more of that in their life? Read the words of the Apostle Paul.

Romans 6:1-7
1 What shall we say then? Shall we continue in sin that

173

grace may abound? 2 Certainly not! How shall we who died to sin live any longer in it? 3 Or do you not know that as many of us as were baptized into Christ Jesus were baptized into His death? 4 Therefore we were buried with Him through baptism into death, that just as Christ was raised from the dead by the glory of the Father, even so we also should walk in newness of life. 5 For if we have been united together in the likeness of His death, certainly we also shall be in the likeness of His resurrection, 6 knowing this, that our old man was crucified with Him, that the body of sin might be done away with, that we should no longer be slaves of sin. 7 For he who has died has been freed from sin. NKJV

Romans 6:1-7
1 What shall we say, then? Shall we go on sinning so that grace may increase? 2 By no means! We died to sin; how can we live in it any longer? 3 Or don't you know that all of us who were baptized into Christ Jesus were baptized into his death? 4 We were therefore buried with him through baptism into death in order that, just as Christ was raised from the dead through the glory of the Father, we too may live a new life. 5 If we have been united with him like this in his death, we will certainly also be united with him in his resurrection. 6 For we know that our old self was crucified with him so that the body of sin might be done away with, that we should no longer be slaves to sin 7 because anyone who has died has been freed from sin. NIV

Being baptized into Christ Jesus means that we agree to die with Him in order that we may live a new life (Romans 6:1-4, 2 Corinthians 5:15). It means that we agree with the process He has chosen for us in order to put to death our sinful nature (Galatians 5:24).

Through our baptism we agreed (made a pledge) to keep a clear conscience toward God's ways (1 Peter 3:21). After making that pledge, can we now say that we disagree with God? I suppose we can, but we are warned not to in the parable of the two sons (Matthew 21:28-32). There were two sons, but only the son that obeyed did the will of the Father, and only those who do the will of the Father enter the Kingdom of Heaven (Matthew 7:21-23).

This is why Romans 6:5 begins with a condition; "if." If we are united with Him in His death, we will be united with Him in His resurrection (Romans 6:5). Through our baptism, Christ has freed us from sin's power, and therefore, we should choose not to be slaves to sin any longer (Romans 6:6-7, Colossians 2:12-13).

Obviously, the Apostle Paul knows something that we are not too familiar with this day and age. Paul is asking how can we, who have died to sin, live in it any longer? That's a question that needs to be asked of every baptized and faith professing Christian.

Some say that we do not have to be baptized, and use the thief on the cross as an example. Again I would ask, where is the verse that tells us to be like the thief? Think about this. If Jesus had said that all of His followers needed to wear a red hat, who do you think would approach us and say that we really didn't need to wear one, once Jesus left? If Jesus said be baptized, then do it, but don't call Him Lord if you have no intention of obeying Him (Luke 6:46-49).

Now that Christ has come, nobody can accept God's will for his life if he has not been baptized into Christ (Luke 7:29-30). This means that the people who are going to make it into the Kingdom of Heaven, which are those who do the will of the Father in Heaven, are baptized (Matthew 7:21-23).

Luke 7:29-30
29 And when all the people heard Him, even the tax collectors justified God, having been baptized with the baptism of John. 30 But the Pharisees and lawyers rejected the will of God for themselves, not having been baptized by him. NKJV

Luke 7:29-30
29 And all the people who heard Him, even the tax collectors, acknowledged the justice of God [in calling

*them to repentance and in pronouncing future wrath
on the impenitent], being baptized with the baptism of
John. 30 But the Pharisees and the lawyers [of the Mosaic
Law] annulled and rejected and brought to nothing God's
purpose concerning themselves, by [refusing and] not being
baptized by him [John]. AMP*

If you have not been baptized, I would suggest that you do so as soon as possible. Don't wait until the water temperature is just right for you, or for a particular day of the month, and don't allow anyone to talk you out of it once you have decided to be baptized.

The Christians that I have met over the past few years, who have not been baptized, do not accept what is written in their Bible, but they have come up with their own version of the Gospel. The same is true for those who do not continue in their baptismal vow, which is to keep a clear conscience before God (1 Peter 3:21).

THE DOCTRINE

Baptism is a part of the doctrine that we must obey. It's a part of making disciples for Jesus (Matthew 28:19-20). Continuing in our faith (chapter 2, By Faith), loving one another (chapter 3, Through Love), and dying to the Laws of Moses (chapter 4, The Law) are all a part of the doctrine that delivers us from sin.

The only reason that Christians would have to live in sin is if we were ignorant of the teachings (doctrine), we choose not to obey the teachings, or we are being controlled by the sins we have willfully committed. However, understand this. All those who belong to Christ continue in the doctrine to the point of crucifying (doing away with) their sinful nature (Galatians 5:24).

*Galatians 5:24
24 And those who are Christ's have crucified the flesh with its passions and desires. NKJV*

*Galatians 5:24
24 And those who belong to Christ Jesus (the Messiah) have*

crucified the flesh (the godless human nature) with its passions and appetites and desires. AMP

That's past tense; have crucified their sinful nature. We don't stop until we are free from sin. If we wholeheartedly obey the doctrine, then we will be set free from sin (Romans 6:17-18). We would have to stop following the teachings in order for it not to work.

DISCIPLINE

We would have to purposely leave the path of doing what is right in order for it not to be effective, which brings with it a new set of problems; discipline.

Proverbs 15:9-10
9 The way of the wicked is an abomination to the Lord, But He loves him who follows righteousness. 10 Harsh discipline is for him who forsakes the way, And he who hates correction will die. NKJV

Proverbs 15:9-10
9 The Lord detests the way of the wicked but he loves those who pursue righteousness. 10 Stern discipline awaits him who leaves the path; he who hates correction will die. NIV

Discipline (chastening) is correction that leads toward obedience. Therefore, the amount of discipline we receive is in direct proportion with how much pain and suffering it would take to make us obey. God disciplines everyone that belongs to Him in order that we will be righteous and holy (Hebrews 12:4-14 below).

Hebrews 12:4-14
4 You have not yet struggled and fought agonizingly against sin, nor have you yet resisted and withstood to the point of pouring out your [own] blood. 5 And have you [completely] forgotten the divine word of appeal

and encouragement in which you are reasoned with and addressed as sons? My son, do not think lightly or scorn to submit to the correction and discipline of the Lord, nor lose courage and give up and faint when you are reproved or corrected by Him; 6 For the Lord corrects and disciplines everyone whom He loves, and He punishes, even scourges, every son whom He accepts and welcomes to His heart and cherishes. 7 You must submit to and endure [correction] for discipline; God is dealing with you as with sons. For what son is there whom his father does not [thus] train and correct and discipline? 8 Now if you are exempt from correction and left without discipline in which all [of God's children] share, then you are illegitimate offspring and not true sons [at all]. [Prov 3:11,12.] 9 Moreover, we have had earthly fathers who disciplined us and we yielded [to them] and respected [them for training us]. Shall we not much more cheerfully submit to the Father of spirits and so [truly] live? 10 For [our earthly fathers] disciplined us for only a short period of time and chastised us as seemed proper and good to them; but He disciplines us for our certain good, that we may become sharers in His own holiness. 11 For the time being no discipline brings joy, but seems grievous and painful; but afterwards it yields a peaceable fruit of righteousness to those who have been trained by it [a harvest of fruit which consists in righteousness — in conformity to God's will in purpose, thought, and action, resulting in right living and right standing with God]. 12 So then, brace up and reinvigorate and set right your slackened and weakened and drooping hands and strengthen your feeble and palsied and tottering knees, [Isa 35:3.] 13 And cut through and make firm and plain and smooth, straight paths for your feet [yes, make them safe and upright and happy paths that go in the right direction], so that the lame and halting [limbs] may not be put out of joint, but rather may be cured. 14 Strive to live in peace with everybody and pursue that consecration and *holiness without which no one will [ever] see the Lord. AMP*

Hebrews 12:4-14
4 In your struggle against sin, you have not yet resisted to the point of shedding your blood. 5 And you have forgotten that word of encouragement that addresses you as sons: "My son, do not make light of the Lord's discipline, and do not lose heart when he rebukes you, 6 because the Lord disciplines those he loves, and he punishes everyone he accepts as a son." 7 Endure hardship as discipline; God is treating you as sons. For what son is not disciplined by his father? 8 If you are not disciplined (and everyone undergoes discipline), then you are illegitimate children and not true sons. 9 Moreover, we have all had human fathers who disciplined us and we respected them for it. How much more should we submit to the Father of our spirits and live! 10 Our fathers disciplined us for a little while as they thought best; but God disciplines us for our good, that we may share in his holiness. 11 No discipline seems pleasant at the time, but painful. Later on, however, it produces a harvest of righteousness and peace for those who have been trained by it. 12 Therefore, strengthen your feeble arms and weak knees. 13 "Make level paths for your feet," so that the lame may not be disabled, but rather healed. 14 Make every effort to live in peace with all men and to be holy; without holiness no one will see the Lord. NIV

Everyone who will enter the Kingdom of Heaven receives punishment for their sins here on earth, point, blank, period. Those who continue in sin without receiving discipline, do not belong to God (verse 8 above). According to 1 Peter 4:17-19, the family of God receives their due on earth. That's not the case for those who do not belong to God. For the most part, they store up wrath for the day of God's wrath (Romans 2:5-6).

Discipline may come in the form of punishment (verse 6), hardship (verse 7), or disabilities for those who do not heed the instructions (verses

179

12-13 above). The type of discipline it takes to conform us to the likeness of Jesus is the amount that we will receive, since that is what God is trying to mold us into (Romans 8:29). Imagine that.

It is written, "Why would any living man complain for the punishment of his sins" (Lamentations 3:39). That's God's point of view concerning discipline. What do we have to say (Philippians 2:14)? Father in Jesus' name, forgive us for not being all you have called us to be. Help us, through the power of your Spirit, to return to you. Amen.

All things work for the good of those who love God, and are called to do His will (Romans 8:28, Philippians 2:12-13, 1 Thessalonians 5:24). God will use whatever happens to us, including discipline, to turn us in the direction He wants us to go.

Once we have committed ourselves to Christ, there is no turning back. We have been bought at a price; the death of God's son Jesus Christ on a cross (1 Corinthians 6:20). He will pursue us with discipline until we are destroyed, if that is what it takes. Those who hate correction will die (Proverbs 15:9-10 above).

REAP WHAT WE SOW

Don't believe that ignorance is an excuse because it isn't. Our first sacrifice is to renew our minds with the truth (Romans 12:1-2). Rejecting those instructions is our own fault. God has already said that His people experience destruction in their life because of their lack of knowledge (Hosea 4:6). Therefore, in saying this, God has allowed those who do not know the truth to remain in destruction.

The bottom line is that we reap what we sow. Even though we can be forgiven for a sin, we still reap what we have sown in proportion with what we have heard and known (Luke 12:47-48, Hosea 7:12).

Luke 12:47-48
47 And that servant who knew his master's will, and did not prepare himself or do according to his will, shall be beaten with many stripes. 48 But he who did not know, yet committed things deserving of stripes, shall be beaten with few. For everyone to whom much is given, from him much will be required; and to whom much has been committed,

180

of him they will ask the more. NKJV

Luke 12:47-48
47 And that servant who knew his master's will but did not get ready or act as he would wish him to act shall be beaten with many [lashes]. 48 But he who did not know and did things worthy of a beating shall be beaten with few [lashes]. For everyone to whom much is given, of him shall much be required; and of him to whom men entrust much, they will require and demand all the more. [Num 15:29,30; Deut 25:2,3.] AMP

God usually doesn't discipline us in accordance with what our sins deserve (Psalm 103:10) unless we do not listen (Leviticus 26:21, Proverbs 15:10). However, one thing is for sure. If we sin, some type of change is on its way, since we reap what we sow.

If we sow to please our sinful nature, then "from that nature" we will reap destruction. In other words, sin will control us for our own ruin, and that is a spiritual principle that works whether we know it or not. Therefore, ignorance of how sin works, will keep us in bondage to it, and fill the rest of our life with one disaster after another.

Galatians 6:7-8
7 Do not be deceived, God is not mocked; for whatever a man sows, that he will also reap. 8 For he who sows to his flesh will of the flesh reap corruption, but he who sows to the Spirit will of the Spirit reap everlasting life. NKJV

Galatians 6:7-8
7 Do not be deceived: God cannot be mocked. A man reaps what he sows. 8 The one who sows to please his sinful nature, from that nature will reap destruction; the one who sows to please the Spirit, from the Spirit will reap eternal life. NIV

Galatians 6:7-8
7 Do not be deceived and deluded and misled; God will
not allow Himself to be sneered at (scorned, disdained,
or mocked by mere pretensions or professions, or by His
precepts being set aside.) [He inevitably deludes himself
who attempts to delude God.] For whatever a man sows,
that and that only is what he will reap. 8 For he who sows
to his own flesh (lower nature, sensuality) will from the
flesh reap decay and ruin and destruction, but he who sows
to the Spirit will from the Spirit reap eternal life. AMP

God cannot be mocked. In other words, nobody can say that they got away with a sin. Therefore, whoever thinks that it is acceptable to sin must be content with destruction. Think about that.

PRONOUNCE YOUR JUDGMENT

Sometimes God will allow us to pronounce our own judgment in the same way that we have judged others for the same type of sin. (Matthew 7:2).

Matthew 7:1-2
1 "Judge not, that you be not judged. 2 For with what
judgment you judge, you will be judged; and with the
measure you use, it will be measured back to you. NKJV

Matthew 7:1-2
1 "Do not judge, or you too will be judged. 2 For in the
same way you judge others, you will be judged, and with
the measure you use, it will be measured to you. NIV

When we judge other people with our tongue, we will be judged with the same measure we use. Imagine that. Before saying anything against anyone we should ask ourselves if we have done the same thing.

Such is the case with King David and Bathsheba, Uriah's wife. The Lord sent the prophet Nathan to David for the purpose of allowing David to judge himself (2 Samuel 12:1-14). David was forgiven, but his son died, his house was cursed with the sword, and his kingdom was taken for a period of time. That's serious stuff.

We should refuse to judge anyone and in doing so, set the bar (the standard) on the ground so that we can step over it. It is by our words we will be acquitted and by our words that we will be condemned (Matthew 12:37).

Therefore, we could have two identical people who have committed the same sin, but receive completely different punishments. Those who are very critical of others should pay close attention to this.

If we would judge ourselves before we are disciplined, we would not come under judgment (1 Corinthians 11:31-32).

1 Corinthians 11:31-32
31 For if we would judge ourselves, we would not be judged. 32 But when we are judged, we are chastened by the Lord, that we may not be condemned with the world.
NKJV

1 Corinthians 11:31-32
31 But if we judged ourselves, we would not come under judgment. 32 When we are judged by the Lord, we are being disciplined so that we will not be condemned with the world. NIV

We need to make a habit of judging ourselves using the Word of God as a guide (Hebrews 4:12). Once we sin and we are convicted in our conscience, we should judge ourselves so that we will not be judged by the Lord.

Look back over last week, last month, and your entire lifetime to see if you can figure out how sin controlled you. Learn from your mistakes and move on forgetting about the past. Ask the Lord to wash your conscience clean with the blood of Jesus Christ (Hebrews 9:14, 10:19-23). If you have been forgiven for your sins, then those sins will stop coming up in your conscience (Hebrews 10:2).

TIME TO REPENT

The Lord gives us plenty of time to repent (Romans 2:1-4, Revelation 2:21). If the convictions of the Spirit do not bring us to repentance (John 16:8), and we do not judge ourselves, using the Word of God as a ruler (Hebrews 4:12, 2 Corinthians 10:3-5), then we should expect a life changing event.

Revelation 2:20-23
20 Nevertheless I have a few things against you, because you allow that woman Jezebel, who calls herself a prophetess, to teach and seduce My servants to commit sexual immorality and eat things sacrificed to idols. 21 And I gave her time to repent of her sexual immorality, and she did not repent. 22 Indeed I will cast her into a sickbed, and those who commit adultery with her into great tribulation, unless they repent of their deeds. 23 I will kill her children with death, and all the churches shall know that I am He who searches the minds and hearts. And I will give to each one of you according to your works. NKJV

Revelation 2:20-23
20 But I have this against you: that you tolerate the woman Jezebel, who calls herself a prophetess [claiming to be inspired], and who is teaching and leading astray my servants and beguiling them into practicing sexual vice and eating food sacrificed to idols. [1 Kings 16:31; 2 Kings 9:22,30.] 21 I gave her time to repent, but she has no desire to repent of her immorality [symbolic of idolatry] and refuses to do so. 22 Take note: I will throw her on a bed [of anguish], and those who commit adultery with her [her paramours] I will bring down to pressing distress and severe affliction, unless they turn away their minds from conduct [such as] hers and repent of their doings. 23 And I will strike her children (her proper followers) dead [thoroughly exterminating them]. And all the assemblies (churches) shall recognize and understand that I am He

*Who searches minds (the thoughts, feelings, and purposes)
and the [inmost] hearts, and I will give to each of you [the
reward for what you have done] as your work deserves. [Ps
62:12; Jer 17:10.] AMP*

Even with all the wrong doing this self-proclaimed prophetess has
done, The Lord still gave her time to repent (verse 21). This is why we
should always check ourselves to make sure that we are within the faith
(2 Corinthians 13:5), especially if we instruct others. We who teach will
be judged more strictly (James 3:1).

Therefore, before you stand up to instruct others, make sure that
what you are saying is in line with what is written. Do not deny the truth
as you hear it (James 3:13-16), since you may not be able to hear it again
(Hebrews 3:7-18, Revelation 22:11). Repent as you go.

Notice all of the hardship, and punishment that was going to come
upon the people who tolerated the prophetess (Revelation 2:20-23).
Through her teachings, she led them into sin (verse 20 above). When we
hear something that is wrong, we need to do something about it rather
than support the wrong message as if we approve of it, or we may get
caught up in it (2 Corinthians 11:3-4 below).

2 Corinthians 11:3-4
*3 But I fear, lest somehow, as the serpent deceived Eve by
his craftiness, so your minds may be corrupted from the
simplicity that is in Christ. 4 For if he who comes preaches
another Jesus whom we have not preached, or if you
receive a different spirit which you have not received, or
a different gospel which you have not accepted — you may
well put up with it! NKJV*

2 Corinthians 11:3-4
*3 But I am afraid that just as Eve was deceived by the
serpent's cunning, your minds may somehow be led astray
from your sincere and pure devotion to Christ. 4 For if
someone comes to you and preaches a Jesus other than the
Jesus we preached, or if you receive a different spirit from*

185

***the one you received, or a different gospel from the one
you accepted, you put up with it easily enough. NIV***

Do not approve of the wrong message. I'm not saying that we should leave our church, since we are to remain in the place we were called, when we were called (1 Corinthians 7:20). However, do not approve of a message that is against what is written.

God sends the person who speaks His Word (John 3:34, Jeremiah 23:22). Differences may arise in order that the one whom God has approved may be recognized (1 Corinthians 11:19). Close your eyes and listen for the Word of God.

People who sow to please their sinful nature, will eventually live in destruction (Galatians 6:7-9). When they do not put God's Word into practice, their house is destroyed as soon as the flood hits (Matthew 7:24-27). Usually that's when most of them wake up, but many of them blame the devil and seek prayer to cast it out.

Let's assume that this prophetess brought her kids to you for prayer, since they were about to die for her sins. Would you ask her if she is caught up in sins that lead to death, or would you try to cast something out of the kids, and declare "by His stripes you are healed?"

As I have mentioned before, God has no problem protecting us from the devil (2 Thessalonians 3:3). If we do not sin, the devil cannot touch us (1 John 5:18). If we sin, we need to repent of that sin, and confess our sins that we may be healed (James 5:16).

Many ignore this teaching, never check to see if the person is in the will of God, and cast the spirit of infirmity out of them, only to watch it come back with friends (Luke 11:24-26). Check the verses. In these cases, many who have been healed, die of the same infirmities months later.

We are not instructed to pray for someone who is caught up in sins that lead to death (1 John 5:16-17). I believe that this is why the Bible says not to be in a hurry in laying hands on anyone (1 Timothy 5:22).

Fasting and prayer works, but fasting does not overcome sins that lead to death. Repent of those and then fast. Fasting is a method of forcing our body to submit to our will instead of the desires of the flesh. Our will should be in line with God's will. If it isn't, then that is more than likely the reason for the trouble.

True fasting is covered in Isaiah 58:6-11, and it will position you where God will answer your cry, assuming you are in the will of God. Read it and you will see many of the same things that I have shown you in this book already.

Keep in mind that the wicked have no right to proclaim the promises of God (Psalm 50:15-16), and nobody can speak and make it happen if the Lord has not decreed it (Lamentations 3:37). In other words, if the Lord has determined that someone will receive discipline, then no amount of praising, praying, fasting, anointing with oil, laying on hands, or casting out will rid that person of discipline until they repent (James 5:16).

It will work for those who are oppressed (under attack) by the devil, but not the former. Those who live against the will of God, must die to sins and live for righteousness (1 Peter 2:24). If they hate correction, they will die (Proverbs 15:9-10).

Perfect love drives out fear of punishment (1 John 4:16-21). If you want to be free of punishment, obey Jesus and love one another (discussed in chapter 3).

SINNING WILLFULLY

Jesus is the atoning sacrifice for everyone's sins and not just for Christians (1 John 2:1-2). The blood of Jesus washes our sins away (Colossians 1:14). The Spirit helps us in our weaknesses, and intercedes for those who are faithful in Christ in accordance with God's will (Romans 8:26-27). If we learned all of the appealing verses on sin and avoided the remaining, it could leave us thinking that we don't need to worry about it.

However, there may come a point where we could lose our right to the blood of Jesus, insult the Spirit of grace, and trample the Son of God under our feet by willfully continuing in sin after knowing the truth (Hebrews 10:26-31 below).

That's why we need to know all of the verses on any particular subject if that is how we study the Word of God. By reading the whole New Testament over and over again, we cannot be mislead by those who only mention the "goody-goody" verses in order to build their crowds (2 Timothy 4:3-4, Acts 20:29-31).

Hebrews 10:26-31
26 For if we sin willfully after we have received the knowledge of the truth, there no longer remains a sacrifice for sins, 27 but a certain fearful expectation of judgment, and fiery indignation which will devour the adversaries. 28 Anyone who has rejected Moses' law dies without mercy on the testimony of two or three witnesses. 29 Of how much worse punishment, do you suppose, will he be thought worthy who has trampled the Son of God underfoot, counted the blood of the covenant by which he was sanctified a common thing, and insulted the Spirit of grace? 30 For we know Him who said, "Vengeance is Mine, I will repay," says the Lord. And again, "The Lord will judge His people." 31 It is a fearful thing to fall into the hands of the living God. NKJV

Hebrews 10:26-31
26 If we deliberately keep on sinning after we have received the knowledge of the truth, no sacrifice for sins is left, 27 but only a fearful expectation of judgment and of raging fire that will consume the enemies of God. 28 Anyone who rejected the law of Moses died without mercy on the testimony of two or three witnesses. 29 How much more severely do you think a man deserves to be punished who has trampled the Son of God under foot, who has treated as an unholy thing the blood of the covenant that sanctified him, and who has insulted the Spirit of grace? 30 For we know him who said, "It is mine to avenge; I will repay," and again, "The Lord will judge his people." 31 It is a dreadful thing to fall into the hands of the living God. NIV

We should be working out our own salvation with fear and trembling (Philippians 1:12). This way we will be safe, but if we willfully continue in sin, no sacrifice for sins is left (Hebrews 10:26).

If we walk in the light, the blood of Jesus purifies us of all sin (1

John 1:7). However, if we deliberately continue in sin, we are in danger of losing our right as Christians to the blood of Jesus, according to the Word of the Lord written in Hebrews 10:26 above.

To intentionally continue in sin after knowing the truth is the same as rejecting the process altogether, since the purpose of the doctrine is to set us free from sin (Romans 6:1-22). Knowing it and then rejecting it is like telling God that He made a mistake in sending His Son to die for us.

We are the ones who needed a savior to deliver us from sin's power in order that we could choose Him over our sinful nature (Romans 6:1-22). Once we know the truth and then deliberately choose sin, which is rejecting God's way out, we have made our choice (2 Peter 2:20-21). The wages sin pays is death, but the gift of God is eternal life in Christ (Romans 6:23).

According to the verses above, the promises concerning the forgiveness of sins are different for people who try to use the grace of God as fire insurance, but have no intention of stopping sin in their life. Jesus, living inside us, wants to destroy the devil's work in us (1 John 3:8). He will not be used as an excuse to continue in sin.

Therefore, the person who has accepted Jesus as Lord, and has experienced the blood of Jesus delivering him from darkness, and is once again entangled up in sin is worse than if he had not known the way of righteousness (2 Peter 2:20-22).

2 Peter 2:20-22
20 For if, after they have escaped the pollutions of the world through the knowledge of the Lord and Savior Jesus Christ, they are again entangled in them and overcome, the latter end is worse for them than the beginning. 21 For it would have been better for them not to have known the way of righteousness, than having known it, to turn from the holy commandment delivered to them. 22 But it has happened to them according to the true proverb: "A dog returns to his own vomit," and, "a sow, having washed, to her wallowing in the mire." NKJV

2 Peter 2:20-22
20 If they have escaped the corruption of the world by knowing our Lord and Savior Jesus Christ and are again entangled in it and overcome, they are worse off at the end than they were at the beginning. 21 It would have been better for them not to have known the way of righteousness, than to have known it and then to turn their backs on the sacred command that was passed on to them. 22 Of them the proverbs are true: "A dog returns to its vomit," and, "A sow that is washed goes back to her wallowing in the mud." NIV

He doesn't need to be saved all over again, but he needs to repent of his ways. He needs to get back on course since he is worse off now than when he started. Christians who are caught up in sins that lead to death don't need to get saved again. They need to obey the teachings.

ONCE SAVED ALWAYS SAVED

"Once saved always saved" is not written in the Bible. Certainly the Christian life is designed to be "once saved," since all we need is to be saved once, but "once saved always saved" is not written and there are many scriptures that I have shown you so far in this book that are directly against it. We should never go beyond what is written unless we are stating what we believe and not explaining what is written (1 Corinthians 4:6-7, Acts 20:29-31).

We were saved into the Kingdom of Christ (Ephesians 2:6-10). From there we immediately seek to enter the Kingdom of God and God's righteousness (Matthew 6:33). A person who has been saved into the Kingdom of Christ, does not have to be saved into the Kingdom of Christ all over again, but if he falls away, he will not get to enter the Kingdom of God, nor the eternal Kingdom of Christ (2 Peter 1:10-11).

In the end, Jesus will send out His angels and they will weed out of "His Kingdom" all who do evil and cause sin (Matthew 13:40-43). Therefore, it is not a matter of losing our salvation, but remaining in and being counted worthy of the eternal Kingdom (Romans 11:22, John 15:6). As 2 Peter 1:4-11 says below, if we do these things, we will never fall and

190

receive a rich welcome into the eternal Kingdom. Instead of saying once saved always saved, we should be saying, once saved, are we remaining?

2 Peter 1:4-11
4 by which have been given to us exceedingly great and precious promises, that through these you may be partakers of the divine nature, having escaped the corruption that is in the world through lust. 5 But also for this very reason, giving all diligence, add to your faith virtue, to virtue knowledge, 6 to knowledge self-control, to self-control perseverance, to perseverance godliness, 7 to godliness brotherly kindness, and to brotherly kindness love. 8 For if these things are yours and abound, you will be neither barren nor unfruitful in the knowledge of our Lord Jesus Christ. 9 For he who lacks these things is shortsighted, even to blindness, and has forgotten that he was cleansed from his old sins. 10 Therefore, brethren, be even more diligent to make your call and election sure, for if you do these things you will never stumble; 11 for so an entrance will be supplied to you abundantly into the everlasting kingdom of our Lord and Savior Jesus Christ. NKJV

2 Peter 1:4-11
4 Through these he has given us his very great and precious promises, so that through them you may participate in the divine nature and escape the corruption in the world caused by evil desires. 5 For this very reason, make every effort to add to your faith goodness; and to goodness, knowledge; 6 and to knowledge, self-control; and to self-control, perseverance; and to perseverance, godliness; 7 and to godliness, brotherly kindness; and to brotherly kindness, love. 8 For if you possess these qualities in increasing measure, they will keep you from being ineffective and unproductive in your knowledge of our Lord Jesus Christ. 9 But if anyone does not have them, he is

nearsighted and blind, and has forgotten that he has been cleansed from his past sins. 10 Therefore, my brothers, be all the more eager to make your calling and election sure. For if you do these things, you will never fall, 11 and you will receive a rich welcome into the eternal kingdom of our Lord and Savior Jesus Christ. NIV

If we do these things we will never stumble (verse 10 above). Why would we want to do these things? Notice in verse 4 above, that we are trying to escape the corruption of the world, by using the promises. We are making "every effort" to do these things according to verse 5 above. Luke 13:24 says, "Strive to enter through the narrow gate, for many will seek to enter but will not be able."

Jesus said that the person who overcomes the world (1 John 4-5) will be given the right to the tree of life (Rev. 2:7), given some of the hidden manna, given a new name (Rev. 2:17), and given authority over the nations (Rev. 2:26). He would be dressed in white and never have his name blotted out of the book of life (Rev. 3:5). He would be made a pillar in the temple of God (Rev. 3:12), unharmed by the second death (Rev. 2:11), and have the right to sit on Jesus' throne (Rev. 3:21). Do you believe Jesus?

What are we doing? We are participating in the spiritual nature through our use of the promises written in our Bible, and we are adding to our faith, goodness, knowledge, self-control, perseverance, godliness, brotherly kindness, and love.

The Thessalonians were considered to be worthy of the Kingdom of God, since their love was abounding, their faith was growing, and they were willing to suffer for what was right (2 Thessalonians 1:3-5). We are also called to live in a manner that is worthy of the Kingdom of God (1 Thessalonians 2:11-12, 2 Thessalonians 2:11).

We were saved into Christ, but when Jesus comes back He is bringing "eternal salvation" to those who obey Him (Hebrews 5:9, 9:28). In this hope we are saved (Romans 8:24-25). Who hopes for what he already has?

Once we are saved into the Kingdom of Christ, it's all about remaining in Christ (John 15:10), abiding in the vine (Romans 11:22), holding to the teachings (1 Corinthians 15:1-2, 2 Thessalonians 2:13-15) in order that Jesus will make His home in us (John 14:21-23), and making the Word of God remain in us to the point of being set free from sin (John 8:31-36, Romans 1:28-32, 1 Peter 1:22-25).

It's about making it into the "eternal" Kingdom of Christ, which will be handed over to God in the end (1 Corinthians 15:24); the Kingdom of God. We can enter it now, or be counted worthy of it here on earth, since it is within us (Luke 17:21), but that doesn't mean that we will remain in it (Luke 13:28).

If you accepted Jesus as Lord a few years ago and your conscience was cleared of past sins, then I am talking to you. Repent and live up to what you have attained (Philippians 3:16). Work out your salvation with fear and trembling (Philippians 2:12). In other words, obey what you have learned, since Jude 1:4 warns us not to use grace as a license to continue in sin.

We stumble because we disobey the message and not because we didn't mean it when we said, "Jesus is Lord" (1 Peter 2:7-8). So, where are we in our faith? Either we are ignorant of the truth (Ephesians 4:17-19), in rebellion against the truth (Hebrews 3:7-19, John 6:60-69), or we are growing in faith, love, and hope; basically allowing the Word of God to work in us (1 Thessalonians 2:13).

FALLING AWAY

If you have cried out to the Lord Jesus, received grace for your past sins, started in the faith, and have since fallen away, then repent of that right away. God the Father will have compassion on you as He did the prodigal son in Luke 15:11-31. However, know that while the prodigal son was away he was dead (cut off), and when he returned he was "alive again" according to Luke 15:24. Many overlook that fact.

When people fall away completely, they do not necessarily stop going to church, singing in the choir, or whatever else. When people fall away, they simply stop repenting of sin.

Hebrews 6:4-8
4 For it is impossible for those who were once enlightened, and have tasted the heavenly gift, and have become partakers of the Holy Spirit, 5 and have tasted the good

word of God and the powers of the age to come, 6 if they
fall away, to renew them again to repentance, since they
crucify again for themselves the Son of God, and put Him
to an open shame. 7 For the earth which drinks in the rain
that often comes upon it, and bears herbs useful for those
by whom it is cultivated, receives blessing from God; 8
but if it bears thorns and briers, it is rejected and near to
being cursed, whose end is to be burned. NKJV

Hebrews 6:4-8
4 It is impossible for those who have once been
enlightened, who have tasted the heavenly gift, who have
shared in the Holy Spirit, 5 who have tasted the goodness
of the word of God and the powers of the coming age, 6 if
they fall away, to be brought back to repentance, because
to their loss they are crucifying the Son of God all over
again and subjecting him to public disgrace. 7 Land that
drinks in the rain often falling on it and that produces
a crop useful to those for whom it is farmed receives
the blessing of God. 8 But land that produces thorns and
thistles is worthless and is in danger of being cursed. In the
end it will be burned. NIV

People who have fallen away do not recognize their sins. They have no conscience of sin, and consequently, they do not repent or ask for forgiveness anymore. When church people fall away, they fall away from repentance.

First, notice that this passage of scripture is referring to those who have shared in the Holy Spirit (verse 4 above). Can that be speaking about anyone other than a Christian?

He says that it is impossible for them to come back to repentance. That means they no longer have any remorse for their sins, but they did at one time. They are in danger of being cursed, and then burned (verse 8 above).

I don't believe that most of us know that we can fall away and be cursed. We need to learn how sin works so that we can control it. We need to follow the teachings straight from our Bible so that we will get accurate knowledge, and separate ourselves from those who speak directly against the truth. It's time to wake up!

An indication that church attending people are drifting away is that they leave the process of being transformed by renewing their minds with the truth. It is far more important to know the truth that sets Christians free from sin than to gather together. Those who do not gather scatter (Luke 11:23), but gathering this day and age is not a guarantee that they will renew their minds. It should be, but it is not.

If you are a new convert, praise God. The most important thing you can do is to read the Word of God out loud from the New Testament where Kingdom teaching is found (Luke 16:16). Read it to the point of retaining it, and allow it to change your mind as you go (Hebrews 4:12). If you believe what you read, you will know the things I have covered in this book. If you can't read, then you need the Bible on tape, or CD where you can hear it in your ears (Romans 10:17).

My name is Alan P. Ballou. I am a servant. If you have questions, or need help with what I have explained in this chapter, please contact me at www.howtostopsinning.com. I serve Christians free of charge.

6. THE WAY

6

THE WAY

⅋⌘

All of us have problem areas in our life that we need to get under control. We're either working on them, or we have learned to use excuses for our shortcomings such as, "That's just the way I am." Basically, what we're saying is that we know we have a problem, but we are not going to change, or we have tried to fix our problem, but we can't. This is the "nobody's perfect" attitude.

It can be overwhelming to try to get every little area of our life right since everything we say and do has consequences whether good or evil (James 2:12-13, Matthew 12:36). Even little sins can gain control over us and hold us for a period of time (Romans 6:17). Therefore, the tendency is to give up trying, but the Christian life is not just a matter of human effort. We need help to live the Christian life. We need the Holy Spirit (John 14:15-18).

Sin brings about destruction and destruction doesn't have to involve drugs or alcohol. We could be led into making a simple mistake which could forfeit our job, our home, our marriage, and so on. Simply by speaking the wrong words we could set up evil days for ourselves in the future (1 Peter 3:10-12). Imagine that.

It is easy to fit in with the world around us and accept this way of life filled with ups and downs, until we become tired of destruction or commit sins that are reported in the local newspaper. At that point, we will be forced to do something about our situation, or drop out of the Christian life altogether.

I would like to say that everything is not our fault, but that's not scriptural. What is scriptural is that God's people are destroyed for lack of knowledge (Hosea 4:6). In other words, the reason we live in destruction is because we don't know what is written in our Bible. We attend church services for years, but we still only know bits and pieces.

Let this sink in. We will live in destruction until we learn whatever it is we are supposed to know because it is written that we will. Therefore, any Christian who steps away from this process will live in destruction.

One of the things many of us do not realize is how much our body can be controlled spiritually. Even if we are continuing in our faith (chapter 2), remaining in Christ (chapter 3), not given over to sin (chapter 5), or under the Law (chapter 4), an evil spirit can still control our body to do what we should not be doing.

Spirits control the body. It could be a man's spirit within himself, an evil spirit, a spirit of disobedience, a spirit of infirmity, a combination of different spirits, or the Holy Spirit. We have no idea how much we have been influenced by spiritual forces over the course of our life, but even that is our fault since we were warned. Once we realize how spirits can control us and then look back over our life, we would have to wonder what part of it did we control, and how much of our life has been under the control of spiritual forces?

As with any story, when we only know part of the story, the blanks are easily filled in. We read one or two stories out of the Bible a month, and fill in the blanks until we learn something else and then we change. It is possible to attend church for years and still only know a few stories.

The very day, week, or month you decide to begin reading the New Testament out loud for yourself, will be the first day, week, or month that you can even possibly understand the Christian life. The power is

198

in the Word itself (Hebrews 4:12, Romans 1:16, 1 Corinthians 1:17-18). Keep reading it until it remains in you (Romans 1:28-32, John 8:31-36, Matthew 13:18-23).

What does the spirit of disobedience make a person do? If you cannot answer that question, you do not understand the Christian life. You might say that it will make a person disobey, but how will it make them disobey? How have you been keeping the spirit of disobedience from controlling you since you have been attending church services? Think about that.

The spirit of disobedience is what has been keeping you busy with what the world is doing so that you will not have time to renew your mind with the truth (Ephesians 2:1-3). You need to know the truth so that it will set you free from sin (John 8:31-36). That is what church needs to be about.

What will a deceiving spirit make a person do? How can you recognize a person controlled by a deceiving spirit? How do you know that you have the Holy Spirit, and how can you know which spirit is controlling you?

Knowledge of the Lord and knowledge of the devil's schemes are the keys to success (Hosea 4:6). Once we know the truth, we will know what to look for and how to prevent it from happening in the first place. Until then, destruction is always one mistake away.

It's time to get help with taking off the old person and putting on the new person. This is how you were taught in this book, and how you come to know Jesus (Ephesians 4:20-24 below).

Ephesians 4:20-24
20 But you have not so learned Christ, 21 if indeed you have heard Him and have been taught by Him, as the truth is in Jesus: 22 that you put off, concerning your former conduct, the old man which grows corrupt according to the deceitful lusts, 23 and be renewed in the spirit of your mind, 24 and that you put on the new man which was created according to God, in true righteousness and holiness. NKJV

Ephesians 4:20-24
20 You, however, did not come to know Christ that way.
21 Surely you heard of him and were taught in him in
accordance with the truth that is in Jesus. 22 You were
taught, with regard to your former way of life, to put off
your old self, which is being corrupted by its deceitful
desires; 23 to be made new in the attitude of your minds;
24 and to put on the new self, created to be like God in
true righteousness and holiness. NIV

It's time to use the promises of God in order to receive what He has promised. It's time to live by faith, to put our faith into practice, and to avoid destruction. It's time for our house to remain standing after the storm hits for a change. It's time for us to purposely position ourselves to experience God's favor rather than always hearing about how others are being blessed.

I want you to be filled with the Holy Spirit (the Helper) by faith and know how to walk in Him so that you can totally avoid the destruction that comes as a result of sin. You may not abuse drugs, alcohol, or food, etc., but you are probably dealing with sins that are not noticeable yet.

The Holy Spirit can change who you are and make you into a new person just as He has done for me. He can guide you into making all the right moves in order that the outcome of every situation you are involved in, will turn out in your favor for the glory of God. Praise God, halleluiah!

SPIRITUAL FORCES

Our struggle is not against flesh and blood, but against the spiritual forces that control our body through our mind for evil (Ephesians 6:10-12). In other words, we don't war against our body, but against what is controlling our body.

Don't get me wrong, since the body of a person does play a role. The spirit of a person can be willing, but his body may be too weak to do what that person wants to do (Matthew 26:41). However, if the Holy Spirit can give life to a dead body, then a living person who is willing to do the will of God shouldn't be a problem (Romans 12:1-2).

The spirit of a man is the part of him that thinks and reasons. It's the part of him that knows; his intellect (1 Corinthians 2:11). Most people have a spirit within them that controls their knowledge, understanding, and consequently their abilities, since the body, without a spirit is dead or lifeless (James 2:26). Nobody would be able to read a book without a spirit.

For the most part, our spirit decides what we will do today based on our wisdom. If we believe it is going to rain, we will think about our umbrella, and possibly take it with us. That's a simple example, but understand that our spirit controls our hands, eyes, feet, and any other body part based on our intellect, knowledge, and understanding. That's assuming our spirit is controlling our body, but sometimes we do things that we would never do "in our right mind."

There are many different kinds of spirits, which can occupy a natural person and take control of his body for one reason or other (Luke 11:24-26). Most of these spirits are known either as angels, which are ministering spirits sent to serve those who will inherit salvation (Hebrews 1:14), and demons (evil spirits), which for the most part are controlled by the devil (Revelation 12:9).

It is common for a person to have multiple spirits within them that control their knowledge, understanding, and consequently their abilities. They either allow these spirits to control them through desires, or the spirits take control of them through certain circumstances or through violated principles.

For example, in Luke 11:14, Jesus cast a demon out of a person that was mute. The demon spirit controlled the person to the point that he or she could not speak at all. Check the verse. Once Jesus cast the demon out, the mute spoke. I'm not saying that everyone who cannot speak has a demon, but I am simply telling you what is written.

Another example is Luke 13:10-16. A woman had a spirit of infirmity for eighteen years, which caused her to be bent over without the ability to rise up. Jesus identified this "spirit of infirmity" as being under Satan's control (verse 16).

In Mark 1:23-25 and Acts 19:15, an evil spirit spoke through a man that he possessed. In Mark 5:1-16, evil spirits caused a man to live in the tombs, without proper clothing, and the spirits enabled the man to have great strength. In Mark 9:17-26, an evil spirit caused a boy to be mute, and seized him at different times, which made him fall to the ground, foam at the mouth, and gnash his teeth. Often the evil spirit would make the boy try to kill himself by fire and water.

The Bible does not say that everyone who has some type of major problem has an evil spirit. Jesus did much more than cast out demons. He also healed the sick (Mark 6:13). Therefore, just because someone is sick, it doesn't mean that it is a demon that is making them sick.

In Mark 7:31-35, Jesus healed a man who had a speech impediment and was deaf. Jesus healed him by placing His fingers in his ears and then He spit and touched the man's tongue. No demon was mentioned.

In John 5:1-15, a man had an infirmity for thirty-eight years due to his sin. In Revelation 2:20-23, a woman and all who committed adultery with her, were in danger of being sick and losing her children because of her sin unless she repented. We can't always say that sin is the cause of every person's illness. In John 9:1-12, a man was born blind, which was not associated with any sin or demon.

An evil spirit doesn't have to be sent by the devil.

1 Samuel 16:14-16
14 But the Spirit of the Lord departed from Saul, and a distressing spirit from the Lord troubled him. 15 And Saul's servants said to him, "Surely, a distressing spirit from God is troubling you. 16 Let our master now command your servants, who are before you, to seek out a man who is a skillful player on the harp. And it shall be that he will play it with his hand when the distressing spirit from God is upon you, and you shall be well." NKJV

1 Samuel 16:14-16
14 Now the Spirit of the Lord had departed from Saul, and an evil spirit from the Lord tormented him. 15 Saul's attendants said to him, "See, an evil spirit from God is tormenting you. 16 Let our lord command his servants here to search for someone who can play the harp. He will play when the evil spirit from God comes upon you, and you will feel better." NIV

If you know the story, then you know that King Saul did not do what he was supposed to do. Therefore, the Lord took His Spirit from him and gave him an evil spirit to torment him. Even Saul's attendants recognized that it was an evil spirit from the Lord that was tormenting him. The remedy was to repent and turn in the right direction.

We might think that was cruel, but if King Saul would have continued in doing what he was told, he would not have been tormented. King David had issues too, but he repented. The Apostle Paul was given a thorn in his flesh "to buffet" him (2 Corinthians 12:7). Regardless of what anyone thinks it was, it was given to him "to buffet" him, or in other words, to keep him humble. We could spend several years researching it and miss that point altogether. If Paul could have been humble without the thorn, he wouldn't have had it to begin with.

Therefore, we can look at this in two different ways, but the bottom line is that the Lord's Word is going to come true no matter what. If we do what we are supposed to do then we will be blessed, but if not, we will receive something we don't want until we change, regardless if we think it is cruel.

As you can tell, demons, or evil spirits can do many different things to a person's body, but spirits can also control the mind of an unsuspecting person. In 1 Kings 22:19-23 below, a lying spirit sent by the Lord, was going to alter the advice given by all of the King's prophets. Imagine that. After reading the verses below, you will understand that the Lord's Word and the Lord's ways will prevail regardless of what man may think.

1 Kings 22:19-23
19 Then Micaiah said, "Therefore hear the word of the Lord: I saw the Lord sitting on His throne, and all the host of heaven standing by, on His right hand and on His left. 20 And the Lord said, 'Who will persuade Ahab to go up, that he may fall at Ramoth Gilead?' So one spoke in this manner, and another spoke in that manner. 21 Then a spirit came forward and stood before the Lord, and said, 'I will persuade him.' 22 The Lord said to him, 'In what way?' So he said, 'I will go out and be a lying spirit in the mouth of all his prophets.' And the Lord said,'You shall persuade

him, and also prevail. Go out and do so.' 23 Therefore look! The Lord has put a lying spirit in the mouth of all these prophets of yours, and the Lord has declared disaster against you." NKJV

1 Kings 22:19-23
19 Micaiah continued, "Therefore hear the word of the Lord: I saw the Lord sitting on his throne with all the host of heaven standing around him on his right and on his left. 20 And the Lord said, 'Who will entice Ahab into attacking Ramoth Gilead and going to his death there?' "One suggested this, and another that. 21 Finally, a spirit came forward, stood before the Lord and said, 'I will entice him.' 22 " 'By what means?' the Lord asked." 'I will go out and be a lying spirit in the mouths of all his prophets,' he said. " 'You will succeed in enticing him,' said the Lord. 'Go and do it.' 23 "So now the Lord has put a lying spirit in the mouths of all these prophets of yours. he Lord has decreed disaster for you." NIV

King Ahab had measures in place to insure good decisions, but if the Lord has decreed something to happen, it will happen regardless of the human measures set in place to prevent it. Therefore, it is far better to heed the Lord's ways than to think that we can get around them.

Think about this. If the Lord has decreed that God's people will experience destruction because they do not know the Word of God, then how can we get around it?

You may attend the best church with the best preacher in the world, but if you do not offer your body as a living sacrifice to God and be transformed by renewing your mind with the truth of God's Word, then destruction is in your near future point, blank, period. They may gather around you, pray for you, lay hands on you, and anoint you with oil seven times, but you will be the reason for your destruction.

Just as the lying spirit mentioned above controlled all of the Kings prophets, one spirit can control a nation. For example, Israel was given a spirit of stupor so that they could not see, or hear the Word of God

(Romans 11:8-10, Isaiah 6:9-10). Therefore, when they read the Bible, they cannot see what they need to see, or hear what they need to hear in order to turn until they accept Jesus Christ (2 Corinthians 3:14-16).

GOOD SPIRITS

Spirits do not have to be evil, or sent to accomplish a particular task, but they can simply be sent for a lifetime of good. For example, Bezalel was filled with the Spirit of God in such a way that he instantly had the knowledge, talent, and the skill to work with gold, silver, and bronze (Exodus 31:3). He was also given the ability to work with wood, stone, and all kinds of craftsmanship. The Spirit of God within Bezalel, could control him or lead him into making articles needed for the building of the tent of meeting.

These are things that can be learned over time, but there is a difference; Bezalel did not learn it through schooling. I'm sure that he could have shown different people how to do different tasks; hammer this, cut that, and saw here. However, just through his God-given ability, he could see what needed to take place in order to have a finished product. That's a God-given talent or gift that was given and not learned, or earned.

In the same way, through the Holy Spirit, we are given abilities, or "gifts of the Spirit." These gifts of the Spirit are given for the benefit of the body of Christ, as He (the Holy Spirit) determines (1 Corinthians 12:4-11). He gives each of us skill, knowledge, and the ability to do something that we are supposed to use to serve each other (1 Peter 4:10, Romans 12:3-8). We are to use our gift in the same way that Bezalel used his.

In the same way, the Lord has given me the ability to speak. I did not learn the things I am teaching you from a man. I have not been to seminary. In fact, I am a high school drop-out, but the Lord has made my weakness His strength in me, so that I cannot boast (2 Corinthians 1:26-31). Freely I have received and freely I will serve.

The Apostle Paul prayed that the Ephesians would be filled with the spirit of wisdom and revelation (Ephesians 1:17). God gave King Solomon wisdom, insight, discernment, and understanding greater than any man before or after him (1 Kings 3:12, 4:30-31). Men from every nation would come to hear King Solomon explain plant life, animals, birds, reptiles, and fish (1 Kings 4:33-34).

Good spirits operate in us just like evil spirits do. We can give them control of our body through our choices, or they can take control in certain circumstances, which usually include violated principles. In order to live the Christian life, we need to avoid the things that give evil spirits the right to control our body, and purposely do the things that give good spirits the right to control us. This is how we are going to allow God's life-giving Spirit to rule our everyday life.

LIFE-GIVING SPIRIT

There is a new and living way by which we may be made perfect and cleansed from a guilty conscience through the blood of Jesus (Hebrews 10:1-25). In this new way, the law of God has been placed in our heart and mind (Hebrews 10:16, Romans 2:15).

Through God's law, we have been taught by God to love one another (1 Thessalonians 4:9). In other words, we have already been taught to obey Jesus (John 13:34-35, 15:12, 17, 1 John 3:23).

To all who receive Jesus as Lord and believe in His name, He gives the right to become children of God (John 1:12), and qualifies them to share in the inheritance of the Saints (Colossians 1:12).

We have the right to become children of God, and children of God allow themselves to be led by the Holy Spirit (Romans 8:14).

Romans 8:14
14 For as many as are led by the Spirit of God, these are sons of God. NKJV

Romans 8:14
14 because those who are led by the Spirit of God are sons of God. NIV

We willingly do the things that allow the Holy Spirit to control us. We want Him to take the lead since we need help to live a sinless life. In this way we are sowing to please the Spirit with the end result being eternal life (Galatians 6:7-10). Know those verses.

Once we receive Jesus as the Lord of our life, which means we have decided to obey Him, He will send us the helper; the Holy Spirit. In this way, we start doing our part and God sends us the help we need in order to live the Christian life in the form of a life-giving Spirit to control bodies.

John 14:15-18
15 "If you love Me, keep My commandments. 16 And I will pray the Father, and He will give you another Helper, that He may abide with you forever — 17 the Spirit of truth, whom the world cannot receive, because it neither sees Him nor knows Him; but you know Him, for He dwells with you and will be in you. 18 I will not leave you orphans; I will come to you. NKJV

John 14:15-18
15 "If you love me, you will obey what I command. 16 And I will ask the Father, and he will give you another Counselor to be with you forever— 17 the Spirit of truth. The world cannot accept him, because it neither sees him nor knows him. But you know him, for he lives with you and will be in you. 18 I will not leave you as orphans; I will come to you. NIV

The Holy Spirit is our helper, our guide, and the teacher of the way or the path we should be traveling (John 16:13, 1 John 2:27). When we step out of line, He will convict us in our spirit; our conscience (John 16:8).

If we allow Him to lead us, we will stay on course, which is to put our old self to death, and put on the new person created to be like God in true righteousness and holiness (Romans 8:12-14, Ephesians 4:20-24). This is our obligation. In other words, this is what we must do as Christians.

Romans 8:12-13
12 Therefore, brethren, we are debtors — not to the flesh, to live according to the flesh. 13 For if you live according to the flesh you will die; but if by the Spirit you put to death the deeds of the body, you will live. NKJV

Romans 8:12-13
12 Therefore, brothers, we have an obligation — but it is not to the sinful nature, to live according to it. 13 For if you live according to the sinful nature, you will die; but if by the Spirit you put to death the misdeeds of the body, you will live. NIV

The person we used to be will no longer control what we do and what we say, but the Holy Spirit will lead us through our conscience (1 Timothy 1:18-19, 3:9).

The Holy Spirit will be "with us" and "in us" (John 14:17 above). Jesus Himself, is the life-giving Spirit (1 Corinthians 15:45, 2 Corinthians 3:17), and He will make His home in us if we obey Him (John 14:21-24).

John 14:21-24
21 He who has My commandments and keeps them, it is he who loves Me. And he who loves Me will be loved by My Father, and I will love him and manifest Myself to him." 22 Judas (not Iscariot) said to Him, "Lord, how is it that You will manifest Yourself to us, and not to the world?" 23 Jesus answered and said to him, "If anyone loves Me, he will keep My word; and My Father will love him, and We will come to him and make Our home with him. 24 He who does not love Me does not keep My words; and the word which you hear is not Mine but the Father's who sent Me. NKJV

John 14:21-24
21 Whoever has my commands and obeys them, he is the one who loves me. He who loves me will be loved by my Father, and I too will love him and show myself to him." 22 Then Judas (not Judas Iscariot) said, "But, Lord, why do you intend to show yourself to us and not to the world?" 23 Jesus replied, "If anyone loves me, he will obey my teaching. My Father will love him, and we will come to him and make our home with him. 24 He who does not love me

will not obey my teaching. These words you hear are not my own; they belong to the Father who sent me. NIV

There are two places the Holy Spirit can be for those who obey Jesus' commands; "with us" and "in us" (John 14:17 above). Jesus Himself will make His home inside us if we obey His teachings (verse 23 above, 1 Corinthians 15:45, Colossians 1:27, Ephesians 3:17, Acts 2:33). Let that sink in.

We all need to take a good look at what is written because being saved and forgiven is not a stopping point. In fact, it's just the beginning. We need the Holy Spirit in order to live the Christian life. We need Him! We can't do it without Him.

We need to be guided into all truth (John 16:13). We need to be reminded of the Word of God as we go about our day so that we will not fall into sin (John 14:26, Psalm 119:11). We need to keep a clear conscience so that we can hear the convictions of the Holy Spirit before we make a mistake, rather than having to repent afterwards (John 16:8, Genesis 20:6, 2 Peter 2:9).

We need the sanctifying work of the Spirit so that we will not be condemned with the world (2 Thessalonians 2:11-15). We need to know all things, even the secret things of God (John 14:26, 1 Corinthians 2:10, 1 John 2:27). We need spiritual gifts and abilities so that we can serve each other (1 Corinthians 12:7, 11, 1 Peter 4:10, Romans 12:6). We need our weaknesses to become His strength within us (Hebrews 11:34, Philippians 4:13, 1 Peter 4:11). We need power (Acts 10:38, Ephesians 1:18-20, 3:20, Colossians 2:9-10, 2 Timothy 1:7, 2 Peter 1:3)!!! Glory, halleluiah!

We need the Holy Spirit to show us what is yet to come (John 16:13). We need Him to help us in our weaknesses and to intercede for us (Romans 8:26-27). We need Him to give life to our body (Romans 8:10-11). We need Him to tell us what to say, so that we don't mess things up (Matthew 10:19-20). We need God's Spirit, the Holy Spirit of promise, the life-giving Spirit, to live in us in order that we may live the Christian life, since without the Spirit we don't belong to Christ (Romans 8:9). We need Him in order to put to death the misdeeds of the body, and to lead us in the way of sons of God (Romans 8:12-14). We need Him to win people for Christ (John 16:8, 6:44, Romans 15:19). We need to please Him in order to have eternal life (Galatians 6:8). We need grace (Ephesians 5:30, Hebrews 10:29)!!! Thank you, Jesus!

If you believe the Gospel, you were sealed with the Holy Spirit (Ephesians 1:13). However, most have not heard the Gospel, except for bits and pieces of it. If you have been reading the New Testament as I have mentioned to you in chapter two, and you believe it, then ask God the Father to give you His Holy Spirit in the name of Jesus.

Those who believe do not remain in darkness (John 12:46). They obey the teachings, and by faith they receive the promise of the Spirit (Galatians 3:14). Those who do not accept or believe the teachings, only follow Jesus up to a point (John 6:60-69). Check the verses.

Nobody who remains under the Laws of Moses will have the Spirit in them, since where the Spirit of the Lord is there is freedom from the Laws of Moses (2 Corinthians 3:7-18). We need freedom, since we cannot make it without it (Romans 4:14-15). If we are led by the Spirit, we are not under the Law (Galatians 5:18).

Therefore, no one who observes the Laws of Moses will be able to stop sinning (Romans 5:20, 7:4-8). We either serve in the new way of the Spirit, or in the old way by the written code (Romans 7:4-6), but not both (Romans 4:14-15). We need the new way. Praise God! The Law is covered in chapter 4 of this book.

I believe that John 14:21-24 above, are among the most important verses in the Bible for those who have been saved. I attended church for years and would always wonder why I made a mess of everything. I was thinking that by attending church I was good and the people who didn't were not. Boy, was I ever a hypocrite.

We can be saved into the Kingdom of Christ, forgiven of our past sins, and still live like the world. Then when we pronounce judgment on the people of this world, what does that make us (Matthew 7:3-5)? We need help to live the Christian life. Help us Lord Jesus! Father fill us with Your life-giving Spirit in the name of Jesus! Amen.

UNITED WITH THE LORD

If we unite ourselves with the Lord in the way mentioned above, we become one with Him in our spirit (1 Corinthians 6:17). The Lord is the Spirit (2 Corinthians 3:17-18). In this way, we can have the mind of Christ (1 Corinthians 2:16); Christ in us (Colossians 1:26-29 above). Imagine that.

If we were purposely trying to be filled with the Spirit of the Lord, we would set our mind on the things above. The Word is Spirit and gives life to the body (John 6:63, Proverbs 4:20-22). We would speak Psalms, and sing spiritual songs and hymns (Ephesians 5:18-19). We would offer our body parts, eyes, hands, legs, ears, and mouth etc., to Him as instruments of righteousness (Romans 6:11-14 below); basically doing the will of God (Romans 12:1-2, 1 Peter 4:19).

Romans 6:11-14
11 Likewise you also, reckon yourselves to be dead indeed to sin, but alive to God in Christ Jesus our Lord. 12 Therefore do not let sin reign in your mortal body, that you should obey it in its lusts. 13 And do not present your members as instruments of unrighteousness to sin, but present yourselves to God as being alive from the dead, and your members as instruments of righteousness to God. 14 For sin shall not have dominion over you, for you are not under law but under grace. NKJV

Romans 6:11-14
11 In the same way, count yourselves dead to sin but alive to God in Christ Jesus. 12 Therefore do not let sin reign in your mortal body so that you obey its evil desires. 13 Do not offer the parts of your body to sin, as instruments of wickedness, but rather offer yourselves to God, as those who have been brought from death to life; and offer the parts of your body to him as instruments of righteousness. 14 For sin shall not be your master, because you are not under law, but under grace. NIV

In other words, we would willingly allow the Holy Spirit to control us for acts of righteousness; doing good (Acts 10:38). Instead of just saying that we are a new creation and that the old is gone (reckon yourselves). The old is gone when the old is gone (Galatians 5:24).

We can purposely force our way into being a new creation by simply doing what Romans 6:11-14 above tells us to do. That would be living for Him who died for us (2 Corinthians 5:15-17). Think about that. Those who will inherit eternal life, please the Spirit, point, blank, period (Galatians 6:7-10).

If the Holy Spirit is in you, controlling your hands, feet, eyes, ears, mouth, and whatever else, what would you be doing (Acts 10:37-38)?

Acts 10:37-38
37 The [same] message which was proclaimed throughout all Judea, starting from Galilee after the baptism preached by John — 38 How God anointed and consecrated Jesus of Nazareth with the [Holy] Spirit and with strength and ability and power; how He went about doing good and, in particular, curing all who were harassed and oppressed by [the power of] the devil, for God was with Him. AMP

Acts 10:37-38
37 You know what has happened throughout Judea, beginning in Galilee after the baptism that John preached— 38 how God anointed Jesus of Nazareth with the Holy Spirit and power, and how he went around doing good and healing all who were under the power of the devil, because God was with him. NIV

I have heard people say that the proof was in the pudding. I really can't use that one, but I can say that wisdom is proven by her actions (Matthew 11:19). God's servants, who have the Holy Spirit in them, are doing good and freeing people from the power of the devil. They are not using what God has given them to rip people off.

Now don't misunderstand me since those who "preach the Gospel" should make their living from the Gospel (1 Corinthians 9:14). That word, "Gospel" is used about ninety times in the New Testament depending on your version of the Bible. First, read all of those verses so that you will know when you hear the Gospel. Then you will be able to recognize those who should make their living from preaching it.

THE LAW OF THE MIND

Spirits that are not allowed to take control of a Christian's body, can still gain control of his body through the law of the mind. The law of the mind is basically a spiritual law that governs the battlefield, which is in a person's mind. Whatever a person desires and then sets his mind to do, that is what has the authority to control him (Romans 8:5-8, 6:15-18); the law of the mind.

One person can have several different spirits within him at the same time, fighting to control his sense of reasoning and ultimately his direction through his mindset and desires (Galatians 5:17, Luke 11:24, Judges 9:23, 1 Samuel 16:14, 1 Kings 22:22-23, Luke 13:10-16). It may take some time for his wisdom or sense of reasoning to allow his body parts to act upon his desires, but once his mind is set on a sinful desire, that will be his general direction.

For example, a drug addict has already decided on Tuesday how he is going to spend his paycheck on Friday. You can go with him to the bank on Friday, and follow him for twenty-four hours straight. However, his general direction was determined on Tuesday afternoon when he realized that he was going to work enough hours to receive a paycheck. That's when he fixed his mind on how he was going to spend it.

He may have bills to pay and a family to feed, but his sense of reasoning has been clouded and he has already rehearsed the excuses he will use to fool you. A spirit has already been placed in the driver's seat of his mind, and he is headed for destruction. At this point, there is no use in even talking about his drug of choice. He wants to stop, but he is not in control of the part of his brain that controls his body. Therefore you cannot reason with him.

When a murderer, rapist, pedophile and the like is searching for their next victim, they have already lost the battle in their mind as far as their direction is concerned. All they need now is opportunity, and for their available wisdom to make them believe that they will get away with it.

If you have one of these problems and you are too afraid to get professional help, please read this book out loud from the beginning to the end. Repent of anything that comes to mind and put into practice the things I have mentioned. If there is something in this book that you do not understand, you can find me on the internet and ask questions. I serve

Christians from all over the world for free. Praise God.

I do not need to know which sins you are involved in. This process will work on any sin for Christians who "want" to stop. If you want to stop, you still have a conscience.

Without Jesus we are all given over to sin's control (Romans 3:9). We were enemies through our mindset (Colossians 1:21). However, Christ condemned sin in the flesh (Romans 8:3). Therefore, those who are "in Christ" are set free from the dominion of sin, but those who are not "in Christ" have their mindset on sin continually (Colossians 1:13). Being "in Christ" is discussed in chapter 3.

If we are "in Christ," our body has to surrender to the mindset and desires of our inner spirit's choosing, but we can still choose sin. Choosing to remain in sin allows us to remain who we are, which means we are unwilling to deny ourselves (Galatians 5:24, Matthew 16:24). Once we choose sin we are then controlled by sin for a period of time (Romans 6:15-22).

After that period of control is over, that is the time that the actual person within can choose righteousness instead of sin, assuming he knows how. Righteousness can control us just like sin can control us (Romans 6:20). Sin's control is discussed in chapter 5, and righteousness is discussed in chapter 3.

Since Jesus died for us, now we are "free in Christ!" Praise God. We have the freedom to choose whom we will serve through the "law of the mind;" mindset and desires (Romans 6:1-23, 8:5-8). Therefore our body has to submit to obedience with the help of the Holy Spirit, if that is how we choose to live (Romans 8:5-8).

We could still be controlled by our sinful nature, but we would have to choose to follow it. However, if we sow to please the Spirit, we will reap eternal life (Galatians 6:8).

Galatians 6:8
8 For he who sows to his flesh will of the flesh reap corruption, but he who sows to the Spirit will of the Spirit reap everlasting life. NKJV

Galatians 6:8
8 The one who sows to please his sinful nature, from that
nature will reap destruction; the one who sows to please
the Spirit, from the Spirit will reap eternal life. NIV

Through the "law of the mind," we continually sow to please one or the other; The Holy Spirit, or our sinful desires. We cannot please both at the same time, since they desire different things, but if we sow to please the Spirit, we will continue to do good (Galatians 6:9-10).

FORSAKE UNRIGHTEOUS THOUGHTS

If you are able to, I want you to stop thinking about anything for the next five minutes. Find a quiet place with no distractions. Try to stop thinking.

Now what do you hear in your thinking? Is your mind still singing the most popular song on the radio? Are your thoughts telling you that you need to send a text that can't wait? Is your mind telling you that you need to check your email or your favorite social network right away? What are you thinking about while you are trying to stop thinking?

Can you sit still for five minutes (Isaiah 30:15)? What's playing in your mind? Is it the latest hip television show, or what tasks need to be done for the upcoming season, holiday, or birthday, etc?

Where are these thoughts coming from? They are coming from your sinful desires, and different spirits that are in you, which are fighting for the control of your mindset. They know that once your mindset and desires are locked on what they are enticing you with, then they will control you for a period of time. It may be a short period of time, but as you learned in the last chapter, the little sins lead to the big ones.

For example, you could have a spirit of fear feeding thoughts of uncertainty in your mind, and until you speak your faith, it will keep on playing its song (Romans 10:6-8, 2 Corinthians 4:13). For the spirit of fear you would speak something like, "Greater is He that is in me than he that is in the world" (1 John 4:4, Proverbs 18:21, 12:18).

However, just like any other sin, if you have participated in things that have given you over to fear, then you have made a home for the spirit of fear. In other words, the time to use 1 John 4:4 was when you first started speaking about the boogie man coming to get you. Now that you have unknowingly made a home for fear, repent of that and then use 1 John 4:4. Always speak in line with the faith and never against it, even in casual conversations (discussed in chapter 2).

Did you hear the things of this world in your thinking? Since childhood, you have lived like the world around you in keeping your mind on the things of this world, and so you could be given over to it. You will need to die to the basic principles of this world in order to be released from it (Colossians 2:20, Galatians 4:9-11).

Colossians 2:20-23
20 Therefore, if you died with Christ from the basic principles of the world, why, as though living in the world, do you subject yourselves to regulations — 21 "Do not touch, do not taste, do not handle," 22 which all concern things which perish with the using — according to the commandments and doctrines of men? 23 These things indeed have an appearance of wisdom in self-imposed religion, false humility, and neglect of the body, but are of no value against the indulgence of the flesh. NKJV

Colossians 2:20-23
20 Since you died with Christ to the basic principles of this world, why, as though you still belonged to it, do you submit to its rules: 21 "Do not handle! Do not taste! Do not touch!"? 22 These are all destined to perish with use, because they are based on human commands and teachings. 23 Such regulations indeed have an appearance of wisdom, with their self-imposed worship, their false humility and their harsh treatment of the body, but they lack any value in restraining sensual indulgence. NIV

The world's ways seem right and seem to help, but they don't change the inside. Only the Holy Spirit can change us from the inside out. The Word of God works inside of those who believe it (1 Thessalonians 2 :13).

A sign that we are controlled by our sinful thoughts is if we cannot make our mind refocus on anything but sinful thoughts. If we cannot change our mindset, then it controls us. If our mindset controls us, then that is the evidence that we have participated in that particular area of sin; slave to sin (Romans 6:16). The solution is to repent of whatever it is and in turn, do the things that please the Spirit.

People, who are given over to a worldly mindset are caught up in what the world is doing through television, radio, cell phones, pagers, computers, tablets, etc. Their thoughts are continually on what the world is doing, and it makes them worry about things that they don't need to worry about.

A person with little faith worries (Matthew 6:25-34). Read the story of Mary and Martha (Luke 10:38-42 below).

Luke 10:38-42
38 Now it happened as they went that He entered a certain village; and a certain woman named Martha welcomed Him into her house. 39 And she had a sister called Mary, who also sat at Jesus' feet and heard His word. 40 But Martha was distracted with much serving, and she approached Him and said, "Lord, do You not care that my sister has left me to serve alone? Therefore tell her to help me." 41 And Jesus answered and said to her, "Martha, Martha, you are worried and troubled about many things. 42 But one thing is needed, and Mary has chosen that good part, which will not be taken away from her." NKJV

Luke 10:38-42
38 As Jesus and his disciples were on their way, he came to a village where a woman named Martha opened her home to him. 39 She had a sister called Mary, who sat at the Lord's feet listening to what he said. 40 But Martha was distracted by all the preparations that had to be made. She came to him and asked, "Lord, don't you care that my sister has left me to do the work by myself? Tell her to help me!" 41 "Martha, Martha," the Lord answered, "you are worried and upset about many things, 42 but only one thing

is needed. Mary has chosen what is better, and it will not be taken away from her." NIV

Martha was busy making preparations that "had to be done." She was worried and upset, but Mary was listening to Jesus' Words. This was considered to be much better, even though things "had" to be done. Faith comes by hearing the Word (Romans 10:17).

Jesus said that what Mary had chosen would not be taken from her (verse 42 above). Imagine that. Those who find their life lose it, but those who lose it for the Lord find it and keep it for eternal life (Matthew 16:24-27, John 12:25-26).

The ways of the world around us keeps us busy with things that "have" to be done, and it's easy to get caught up in whatever the world is busy doing. We need to recognize that for what it is, and keep it in check, so to speak, since we have been programmed to do that since childhood. If we're not careful, there will always be something going on around us to keep our minds set on what the world is doing, instead of accomplishing what the Lord has asked us to do.

Don't worry about holidays, seasons, or anything else the world is doing (Galatians 4:8-11). Don't even worry about tomorrow, since each day has enough trouble of its own. Cast your cares on the Lord, since He cares for you (1 Peter 5:7), and then purposely place your mind on the things above such as verses, Psalms, spiritual songs, etc. (Philippians 4:6-8).

Seek God's Kingdom and His righteousness first place in your life and everything you worry about will be given to you (Matthew 6:33). Ask yourself what type of faith you have and if you have time to grow it (Romans 10:17, 1 Peter 2:2)?

As a Christian, everything is permissible (1 Corinthians 3:12), but when we are mastered by the things of this world it is hatred toward God (James 4:4, Galatians 4:9-11). Once it controls our mindset and desires, we are mastered by it.

Runners run, skiers ski, golfers golf, race car drivers drive, and mechanics repair vehicles. No problem, but when a person is given over to the control of something, his mind is continually focused on whatever it is. Since the law of the mind works whether we know it or not, a man is a slave to whatever overcomes him (2 Peter 2:19).

Therefore, runners run until they are overcome by running in their mind, and then running controls them. We were God's enemies before we accepted Jesus Christ, not only because of our sins, but through our mindset which controlled our behavior (Colossians 1:21, Ephesians 2:3). Our mindset determines our direction, and ultimately our spiritual failure or success, since being filled with the Spirit, and controlled by the Spirit takes a mind, set on the spiritual things (Ephesians 5:18-19, Romans 8:5-8).

Why did God destroy the people of the earth with a flood? It wasn't only because of wickedness, but also because every intent of man's thoughts, were on evil continually (Genesis 6:5). Why did Jesus call Peter, Satan? Peter's mind was set on the things of this world (Matthew 16:23). Who are the enemies of the cross of Christ according to Philippians 3:17-19? Among other things they have their mindset on earthly things. We have to forsake unrighteous thoughts (Isaiah 55:7 below).

Isaiah 55:7
7 Let the wicked forsake his way, And the unrighteous man his thoughts; Let him return to the Lord, And He will have mercy on him; And to our God, For He will abundantly pardon. NKJV

Isaiah 55:7
7 Let the wicked forsake his way and the evil man his thoughts. Let him turn to the Lord, and he will have mercy on him, and to our God, for he will freely pardon. NIV

The Bible calls us to a different mindset, since the new way involves putting to death the misdeeds of the body through the Spirit (Romans 8:12-14). The "law of the Spirit," which is keeping our mind on the things above (Romans 8:5-8), requires us to forsake the thoughts of our sinful nature.

SPIRIT OF DISOBEDIENCE

If you are waiting for the next craze, then it will continue feeding your mind with worldly thoughts (John 3:6), which create desires that will eventually control you. Spirits control the body through the "law of the mind" and if you are focusing on the next "in thing," then the world system keeps you busy through the spirit of disobedience (Ephesians 2:1-3).

We can't have one foot in the world and one in Christ (James 4:4-10). As it is written, "Do not conform to this world" (Romans 12:1-2). We have to stop the world's ways from controlling us in order to live for God.

One thing is very common among worldly Christians. They do not have much time left for God. There is no room for God in the thoughts of the wicked (Psalm 10:4).

Since we have accepted Christ Jesus as Lord, the devil has to fight for our time. Before we accepted Jesus as Lord, we were under the devil's control just like the rest of the world is now through the spirit of disobedience (1 John 5:19, Ephesians 2:1-3 below).

1 John 5:19
19 We know that we are of God, and the whole world lies under the sway of the wicked one. NKJV

1 John 5:19
19 We know that we are children of God, and that the whole world is under the control of the evil one. NIV

The people of this world have no idea that they are being controlled by a spirit. Everything that is written in the Bible is happening just as it is written.

In later times, some people will abandon the faith and follow deceiving spirits and the teachings of demons (1 Timothy 4:1). In the last days, people will turn away from the truth found in the Bible, and turn to myths and man-made stories (2 Timothy 4:3-4). Check the verses because this is happening today. The spirit of disobedience is making unsuspecting people follow the ways of this world (verse 2 below).

Ephesians 2:1-3
1 And you He made alive, who were dead in trespasses and

220

sins, 2 in which you once walked according to the course of this world, according to the prince of the power of the air, the spirit who now works in the sons of disobedience, 3 among whom also we all once conducted ourselves in the lusts of our flesh, fulfilling the desires of the flesh and of the mind, and were by nature children of wrath, just as the others. NKJV

Ephesians 2:1-3
1 As for you, you were dead in your transgressions and sins, 2 in which you used to live when you followed the ways of this world and of the ruler of the kingdom of the air, the spirit who is now at work in those who are disobedient. 3 All of us also lived among them at one time, gratifying the cravings of our sinful nature and following its desires and thoughts. Like the rest, we were by nature objects of wrath. NIV

We used to follow the ways of this world when we didn't have a choice. The spirit of disobedience controlled us by whatever our sinful nature desired (verse 3 above). We thought that we were in control, but we were not.

That tattoo wasn't our inner spirit's desire, since we delight in God's law in our inner being (Romans 7:22), but it was a desire from the spirit of disobedience. That outward adornment, which makes us keep up with the latest fashions and jewelry didn't come from us, since our inner-self has an unfading beauty with a gentle and quiet spirit (1 Peter 3:4). It came through the spirit of disobedience. The spirit of disobedience goes directly against what the Law makes sin and consequently, sin increases (Romans 5:20).

In the end, the people of this world do not have a chance of making it, since they will be judged by the Law (Romans 3:19). The spirit of disobedience makes them disobey the law of God which has been placed in their hearts (Hebrews 10:16).

TRUE WORSHIPERS

God seeks those who will worship Him in their spirit and in truth (John 4:23-24). The Word of God is truth (John 17:17).

John 4:23-24
23 But the hour is coming, and now is, when the true worshipers will worship the Father in spirit and truth; for the Father is seeking such to worship Him. 24 God is Spirit, and those who worship Him must worship in spirit and truth." NKJV

John 4:23-24
23 Yet a time is coming and has now come when the true worshipers will worship the Father in spirit and truth, for they are the kind of worshipers the Father seeks. 24 God is spirit, and his worshipers must worship in spirit and in truth." NIV

God wants us to worship Him in our spirit (in our mind). Basically, God is seeking people who will meditate on His Word at all times. Our "spiritual act of worship," as it is called in Romans 12:1-2, is to offer our body to God as a living sacrifice, which means that we agree to stop conforming to this world, and to renew our mind with the truth (Romans 12:1-2).

This is how we are supposed to worship every day, and not just on Sunday morning. In fact, we could attend church services for twenty years and never worship in the appropriate way. I'm not saying that we should stop attending church services, since it is written that we should not forsake the gathering of the church, but nothing in our new agreement with the Lord requires a temple.

The church is the people (Ephesians 1:22-23) and the body of each church member is a temple (1 Corinthians 3:16). Wherever the church meets is the church; a building, a storefront, a house, a field, etc. Church should not be about "going to church," but learning how to be the church.

The Word of God tells us to keep our mind on the things above (Colossians 3:2, Romans 8:5-8, Philippians 4:8). We are to fix our thoughts

222

on Jesus (Hebrews 3:1). That's an everyday thing rather than a Sunday morning tradition. Manmade traditions can void the Word of God (Matthew 15:6).

Most of the time, my mind is focused on the Word or singing Christian songs. My mind was singing a song from the band "Third Day" as I took a break from writing. I trust in Jesus, my great deliverer... Glory to God! I can't wait for them to return to this area; Hillsong, Jeremy Camp, and Chris Tomlin, also.

These are just the ones I listen to, but there are many talented Christian groups and singers out there. Find the ones that are right for you, but make sure that there are no violations in the lyrics to the songs (1 Thessalonians 5:21). If there are, then it is the same as quoting false doctrines discussed in earlier chapters.

Once we clear our mind of all the worldly stuff, then we can focus on the things above, which is the type of worshiper God is seeking.

WALKING IN THE SPIRIT

Apart from abiding in Jesus we can do nothing (John 15:4-5). However, if we abide (remain) in Jesus by keeping His commands, we will bear much fruit (John 15:5). Our job is to remain in Jesus, by keeping His commands to love one another, and to believe in the name of Jesus (1 John 3:23, John 15:10-17). We cannot love in the way God intended without a clear conscience; clear mind (1 Timothy 1:5).

If we remain in Jesus, the Spirit will control us to bear the fruits of the Spirit; love, joy, peace, patience, kindness, goodness, faithfulness, gentleness, and self-control (Galatians 5:22-23). In the same way, if we remain in sin, our sinful nature will produce sins that lead to death (Galatians 5:19-21).

This means that our behavior will change, if we are governed by the Spirit. The fruits of the Spirit do not produce sin, but exactly the opposite (Galatians 5:17). If we live according to the Spirit we will not carry out the lust of the flesh (Galatians 5:16).

Galatians 5:16-18
16 I say then: Walk in the Spirit, and you shall not fulfill the lust of the flesh. 17 For the flesh lusts against the

223

Spirit, and the Spirit against the flesh; and these are contrary to one another, so that you do not do the things that you wish. 18 But if you are led by the Spirit, you are not under the law. NKJV

Galatians 5:16-18
16 So I say, live by the Spirit, and you will not gratify the desires of the sinful nature. 17 For the sinful nature desires what is contrary to the Spirit, and the Spirit what is contrary to the sinful nature. They are in conflict with each other, so that you do not do what you want. 18 But if you are led by the Spirit, you are not under law. NIV

If we walk in the Spirit we will not sin, since sin starts with a desire or a lust in our thinking (James 1:13-15). If we walk in the Spirit we will not fulfill those desires. The Holy Spirit will control our body in the same way that the spirit of disobedience controlled us in the past. That means that we can't walk in the Spirit and sin at the same time. This also means that we can live and not sin at all as long as we live (walk) by the Spirit (verse 16 above).

Therefore, sinning is evidence of not walking in the Spirit. We cannot claim that we are being led by the Holy Spirit and sin at the same time, because they both desire the opposite (verse 17 above). Imagine that.

Therefore, as sinners, we have one problem; we don't continually walk in the Spirit. We grew up following the ways of this world, and consequently we are accustomed to following them, but we are still without excuse. God's law has been placed in our heart, Christ died for the sins of the whole world (1 John 2:2), the Spirit of God convicts the world of sin (John 16:8), and the grace of God, which has appeared to all men, teaches us to say no to ungodliness (Titus 2:11-15).

With the law of God in our inner being, we could follow the things required of God's law through our thoughts (Romans 1:14-15, Romans 2:26-27). That's the reason the world system keeps us so busy (Isaiah 30:15). We don't have time to think.

We need to take a step back from the world and its ways (James 4:4-10, 1 John 2:15-17), and allow the Holy Spirit to lead us in a different direction (Romans 8:12-14); the new way of the Spirit (Romans 7:6). Walking in the Spirit stops us from committing sins that lead to death, point, blank, period (Galatians 5:16-18 above).

The "law of the Spirit" is simply walking in the Spirit, or keeping our mindset on the things of the Spirit instead of the things of this world, which are opposite one another (Romans 8:5-8, Galatians 5:17). The proof of walking in the Spirit is the absence of sin (Galatians 5:16).

Don't tell me that everybody sins, since a good tree "cannot bear bad fruit" (Matthew 7:18). If everybody continues in sin then we would not be able to make a bad tree good (Matthew 12:33-37). Whoever claims to be "in Him" must walk as He did (1 John 2:6). Check the verses.

MINDSET AND DESIRES

How do we walk according to the Spirit? Walking in the Spirit is simply making a habit of keeping our mindset and desires on the things above, and not on the desires of our flesh (sinful nature).

Romans 8:5-8
5 For those who live according to the flesh set their minds on the things of the flesh, but those who live according to the Spirit, the things of the Spirit. 6 For to be carnally minded is death, but to be spiritually minded is life and peace. 7 Because the carnal mind is enmity against God; for it is not subject to the law of God, nor indeed can be. 8 So then, those who are in the flesh cannot please God. NKJV

Romans 8:5-8
5 Those who live according to the sinful nature have their minds set on what that nature desires; but those who live in accordance with the Spirit have their minds set on what the Spirit desires. 6 The mind of sinful man is death, but the mind controlled by the Spirit is life and peace; 7 the sinful mind is hostile to God. It does not submit to God's law, nor can it do so. 8 Those controlled by the sinful nature cannot please God. NIV

Our mindset and desires determine how we are walking (living). Consequently, our mindset and desires determine if we are going to sin or not, and it positions us to experience life and peace, or hostility and death (Romans 8:5-8 above). With our minds, we serve the law of God, but with the flesh, the law of sin (Romans 7:25).

Those who set their minds on the things above (spiritual things) have life and peace, but those who set their minds on the things of this world have a mind of hostility and death toward God. Most of us do not realize this and never cover the instructions to keep our mind on the things above (Colossians 3:1, Philippians 4:8).

Imagine being hostile toward God and yet praying for God's favor (verse 7 above). Imagine thinking we are waiting on God, when all the time God is waiting on us (2 Peter 1:3-4). The person with his mindset on the desires of his flesh is opposed to the life of God. He cannot obey God's law in his mind, nor please Him (verse 7-8 above). If we do not please God, we will not be able to ask Him for the things we desire (1 John 3:22-23).

Our ability to submit to God's ways is directly connected with our mindset (verse 7 above). Therefore, if we have a worldly mindset, we will not obey God. In fact, a friend of the world becomes an enemy of God (James 4:4).

Not having peace of mind, is an indicator that we need to check our mindset (verse 6 above, Colossians 3:15, Romans 14:19). If our mind is set on sin, then it is time to cast our cares on the Lord (1 Peter 5:7), and then refocus (Philippians 4:6-8). Once we have done our part, as far as remaining in the faith is concerned, then we should leave the rest up to God.

We should be learning these things when we gather. This is the type of teaching we need after we come to the Lord, but the world's ways have slipped into the meetings.

If you are still following the ways of the world around you, which means that you follow the accepted or traditional ways of the people of this world, then you are certainly living by the flesh and not by the Spirit (Galatians 4:9-11). You need to realize that those are the very things that are keeping your mind occupied with the wrong thoughts, and therefore keeping you in death and away from the life of God (James 4:4-10).

James 4:4-10
4 Adulterers and adulteresses! Do you not know that friendship with the world is enmity with God? Whoever therefore wants to be a friend of the world makes himself an enemy of God. 5 Or do you think that the Scripture says in vain, "The Spirit who dwells in us yearns jealously"? 6 But He gives more grace. Therefore He says: "God resists the proud, But gives grace to the humble." 7 Therefore submit to God. Resist the devil and he will flee from you. 8 Draw near to God and He will draw near to you. Cleanse your hands, you sinners; and purify your hearts, you double-minded. 9 Lament and mourn and weep! Let your laughter be turned to mourning and your joy to gloom. 10 Humble yourselves in the sight of the Lord, and He will lift you up. NKJV

James 4:4-10
4 You adulterous people, don't you know that friendship with the world is hatred toward God? Anyone who chooses to be a friend of the world becomes an enemy of God. 5 Or do you think Scripture says without reason that the spirit he caused to live in us envies intensely? 6 But he gives us more grace. That is why Scripture says: "God opposes the proud but gives grace to the humble." 7 Submit yourselves, then, to God. Resist the devil, and he will flee from you. 8 Come near to God and he will come near to you. Wash your hands, you sinners, and purify your hearts, you double-minded. 9 Grieve, mourn and wail. Change your laughter to mourning and your joy to gloom. 10 Humble yourselves before the Lord, and he will lift you up. NIV

Jesus came to destroy the devil's work (1 John 3:8). God didn't save us so that we would keep doing what the world is doing. When we remain in the world after receiving God's Spirit, we become God's enemy. The devil is not going to leave us until we submit to God's ways and resist him (verse 7 above).

That is the only way to destroy the devil's work in us, and it takes time to accomplish. While in this process, God gives more grace to those who humble themselves, and that grace enables them to continue, but He opposes the proud.

The Lord even hates a proud look (Proverbs 6:16-19), and a perverse person is an abomination to the Lord (Proverbs 3:32). To be perverse is to willfully continue in what we know to be wrong. When we continue in the things we know are wrong it goes against our conscience, and keeping a clear conscience is a part of remaining in love (1 Timothy 1:5).

Love comes from a pure heart, good conscience, and sincere faith. Therefore, anything that is against your conscience is sin (Romans 14:23). Always keep a clear conscience before God (1 Peter 3:21, 2 Timothy 1:3).

If you came to the Lord years ago, but still conform to the world's ways of doing things because everybody else is doing it, then you are on the verge of becoming an enemy of God, or hostile toward God (Romans 8:7 above). How many church attending people do you know that are hostile toward God and don't even know it? Use your talent to do something about it.

Now stop and think for about five minutes and ask yourself which direction you are headed in. You can tell by what your mind is set on. A mind controlled by the Spirit is life and peace (verse 6 above). If your mind is singing the latest worldly song and you cannot control it, then you are given over to it. Stop participating in the world's ways, and your mind will eventually be where you can control it again in order to choose God's way (Romans 6:16). In other words, deny yourself.

Tennis players play tennis, and there isn't anything wrong with that. However, if you are given over to tennis or anything else, then it controls you and you cannot get your mind off it. In cases such as these, if you desire to be free and cannot break free, then you need to know how sin controls us (discussed in chapter 5).

Let's fight like Christians

Don't think that reading a story out of the Bible, and listening to a sermon once a week is enough to grow us up spiritually, because it is not. I've heard hundreds of forty-five minute sermons that only contained two verses. At that rate it would take us a few thousand years to know the truth to the point of being set free from sin (John 8:31-36).

The power of God is in the Word of God (Romans 1:16, 1 Corinthians 1:17-18). You shall know the truth, and the truth itself shall set you free; not Alan Ballou or anyone else, but knowing the truth (John 8:31-36). The Word planted in you can save you, in order that you may fight like a Christian (James 1:21).

The last time I checked, the Lord had set a limit on our years here on earth; 120 years (Genesis 6:3). My prayer is that we be given more time than that, but who can speak and have it happen if the Lord has not decreed it (Lamentations 3:37). Therefore, we need to get busy!

Seek first God's Kingdom and His righteousness (Matthew 6:33). That's first place in your life. Desire the sincere milk of the Word so that you may grow up (1 Peter 2:2), and study to show yourself approved (2 Timothy 2:15, 1 Corinthians 11:19).

The Bible says that mature Christians are so skilled in their use of the Word of God, that they can determine what will lead to good and what will lead to evil (Hebrews 5:14). This can only be done through the Word of God living inside us to the point of knowing whether or not something is good or evil, as we hear it. This is how Christians fight (2 Corinthians 10:3-5 below).

2 Corinthians 10:3-5
3 For though we walk in the flesh, we do not war according to the flesh. 4 For the weapons of our warfare are not carnal but mighty in God for pulling down strongholds, 5 casting down arguments and every high thing that exalts itself against the knowledge of God, bringing every thought into captivity to the obedience of Christ. NKJV

2 Corinthians 10:3-5
3 For though we live in the world, we do not wage war as the world does. 4 The weapons we fight with are not the weapons of the world. On the contrary, they have divine power to demolish strongholds. 5 We demolish arguments and every pretension that sets itself up against the knowledge of God, and we take captive every thought to

229

make it obedient to Christ. NIV

In order to walk in the Spirit, we have to learn how to identify and destroy the desires of our fleshly nature with the sword of the Spirit, which is the Word of God (Ephesians 6:17). Anything that comes up in our thinking or that is brought up by conversation should be tested with the knowledge of God living in us (verse 5 above). If what is said is against the Word of God, it should be cast out (demolished).

For example, if the thought enters your thinking that you can be unforgiving then the Word of Christ immediately corrects it, assuming Matthew 6:14-15 is living in you. That's how you fight like a Christian.

Christians are supposed to be taking every thought captive to make their thoughts obedient to Christ by demolishing everything that is against what is written in the Word of God (2 Corinthians 10:3-5 above). However, we have to know the Word of God for ourselves in order to do that. Therefore, even though we cannot be tempted beyond what we can bear, only those who know good from evil fight effectively.

Taking every thought captive is the most important thing a Christian can do against sin because sin starts with a desire in our thinking (James 1:13-15). Our ultimate goal is to walk in the Spirit from now on. Doing so would guarantee that we would never fulfill the desires of our flesh (Galatians 5:16), and this can only be done by our mind being set continually on the things above (Romans 8:5-8). In this way we will defeat the spirit of disobedience.

If we were fighting as instructed in the verses above, how could we possibly come to believe something that was not written in our Bible? We couldn't. The only way we would come to believe something that was directly against scripture is if we did not know what was written in our Bible.

If you are not fighting in that way then you are not walking by the Spirit. You might randomly put your mind on the things above while you are attending a church function, but you are not walking in the Spirit or purposely fighting.

Consequently, you will sin, and then be controlled by that sin for a period of time (Romans 6:15-18). That means you will need to know how to free yourself from being a slave to sin and how to judge yourself.

If not you will be disciplined. If you continue in sin without repenting, then your sinful nature will eventually make you do things that you will be ashamed of (Romans 6:19-22). Those things result in death (Galatians 6:7-10, James 1:13-15). Can you see this process?

Before your sinful nature puts you to death, you will begin to complain about God's discipline (Proverbs 15:9-10, Hebrews 12:2-13, Lamentations 3:39). Before you die, you will lose your way of life, since those who find their life lose it, but those who lose their life in living for the Lord find it (Matthew 16:24-25, John 12:25-26). Sin is very predictable.

Where are you in this process? Are you walking in the Spirit, or have you rejected God's ways? You might say that you didn't know, which means destruction. If you turn (repent), God will see and have mercy on you. Be determined and force your body to follow God's ways today before it is too late.

FILLED WITH THE HOLY SPIRIT

Now there are many spiritual sounding people out there this day and age, and I don't have a problem with that. However, a tree is recognized by its fruit. Apple trees only have apples on them from time to time, but they never produce oranges. The moment they start producing oranges we call them orange trees.

What do we call a cherry tree that produces pears, or a Christian who lives in sins that lead to death? We call them odd and "not Spirit-filled," respectfully. The bottom line is that there is a reason why we are doing whatever it is we are doing, and many times its not something very spiritual. The fruit is evidence of the actions. We can make a tree good, but until it is good, we don't eat the fruit (Matthew 12:33-37).

The Bible tells us not to be in a hurry in laying hands on anyone (1 Timothy 5:22). That can go the other way, too. Before you allow someone, who may not have the Holy Spirit in them, to lay hands on you, simply believe the Gospel and then ask God Himself to fill you with His Spirit (Luke 11:13).

There is nothing in the Bible that says you have to fall to the floor, or even go up to the front to receive the Holy Spirit. Cornelius and his family were filled with the Spirit while listening to Peter speak the Gospel (Acts 10:44-45). He didn't just lead them in a sinner's prayer, but he spoke the truth, they believed it and were filled while listening to him (Acts 10:36-44, Ephesians 1:13).

Beforehand, Cornelius and his family were God-fearing people who helped those in need (Acts 10:1-2). In other words, by faith Cornelius and his family received the Holy Spirit. Their deeds showed that they were following God's law, which was placed in their heart, and as they accepted and believed the truth, they were filled. Having believed the Gospel they were filled with the Spirit (Ephesians 1:13).

This same process is still available today. If you have read this book, then you cannot possibly be against what God has said, since it is filled with scripture. If you believe, then may God the Father fill you with His Holy Spirit in the name of Jesus. Amen. Ask Him to fill you.

Baptizing with the Holy Spirit and fire is something Jesus does (Acts 2:33, Matthew 3:11, Mark 1:8, Luke 3:16). Check it before you speak. I don't know of a place in scripture where man decided to be baptized in the Holy Spirit by his will or in his timing. If you do not hear the rushing wind filling the whole room and see the tongues of fire come down and rest on the person being baptized with the Holy Spirit and fire, as in the disciple's case, then do not call it being baptized in the Holy Spirit.

Many, including the disciples, received the Holy Spirit and were filled with Him before the day of Pentecost (John 20:22), but there is only one incidence in scripture of being baptized in the Holy Spirit (Acts 2:1-3). Therefore, when it happens it will happen just like is it written. Believe what is written and cast out the smooth talk.

Many are filled with the Spirit and speak in unknown tongues (languages) throughout the New Testament, and many do not speak in tongues, but see visions, dream dreams, and prophesy (Acts 2:17-18, 1 Corinthians 14:10). Therefore, tongues is evidence of being filled with the Spirit, but it is not the only evidence of being filled with the Spirit, as some believe. Wind and fire is evidence of being baptized in the Spirit. Check the verses.

DO NOT GO BEYOND WHAT IS WRITTEN

I cannot go beyond what is written in trying to justify my beliefs or my denomination, and neither should anyone else (1 Corinthians 4:6-7). I'm not here to grow a denomination, but the Kingdom of God. Therefore, my desire is to help all people and lead everyone to faith in Jesus Christ.

I'm a servant of the Lord. My denomination is Christian. I believe everything that is written in the Bible. I test everything I hear and you should do the same (1 Thessalonians 5:21). May I never place a denomination or a certain building before my Lord and Savior.

If someone is Spirit-filled then let them show it by not doing anything against the truth (2 Corinthians 13:8). Does the Spirit of truth, Who told us not to go beyond what is written, now send us to go beyond what is written? We only know in part, but the part we know, we can trust (1 Corinthians 13:9). Therefore, speak what is written.

If Jesus tells me to wait at a certain spot, on a certain day, to be baptized in the Holy Spirit, then so be it. Praise God, halleluiah. Until that day, I'm just trying to keep in step with the Holy Spirit and walk in Him for the rest of my life (Galatians 5:24-25).

With Him filling my thoughts and reminding me of what is written, Lord willing I will speak accordingly, and not with human philosophy or distort the truth in order to seem like I am super spiritual when I am not (Acts 20:29-31). I was a burning stick snatched from the fire, and the Lord had mercy on me and gave me words to speak. By setting forth the truth plainly, I set forth a petition to every listener's conscience (2 Corinthians 4:2). If you are a believer, and the Spirit of God rests on you, then test the quality of my words in your clear conscience.

Human wisdom robs the cross of Christ of power (1 Corinthians 1:17-19), and those whom the Lord sends speak according to His Words (John 3:34, Jeremiah 23:22). If I do not speak according to what is written, then I obviously was not sent to speak.

Many teachers run ahead in the spiritual to the extent of losing connection with the Head, Who is Christ (Colossians 2:19), since they do not hold to the doctrine of Jesus or the doctrine that delivers from sin (Romans 6:15-18). If anyone comes to you and does not bring the doctrine of Christ, do not welcome him or greet him (2 John 1:10). Those who do not continue in the teachings of Christ cannot possibly have God (2 John 2:9, John 14:6).

INCONSISTENCIES

Romans 8:9 says that we cannot be in the flesh if the Spirit of God dwells 'in' us, but the Holy Spirit can be in us and with us (John 14:17).

This would explain the inconsistency in our actions while we are learning to walk in the Holy Spirit, or working out our salvation with fear and trembling (Philippians 2:12).

It would not be possible to grieve the Holy Spirit through our poor choices (Ephesians 4:30), if we were totally controlled by Him from the beginning. We would not be able to make Him jealous for our undivided attention when we follow the ways of this world (James 4:1-10), or fall away, insulting the Spirit of grace, if we were not able to choose not to walk in the Spirit (Hebrews 10:29).

These verses indicate that there is not a switch to flip which would make us walk in the Spirit continually from day one. We are told to keep in step with the Spirit (Galatians 5:26), which means that we could lag behind. Therefore, it is our responsibility to continually walk in the Spirit so that we will not sin.

However, make no mistake. The man of God is thoroughly equipped for every good work (2 Timothy 2:15, 1 Timothy 4:15-17). A servant of the Lord gently instructs those who oppose him using the Word of God to correct in the hope that God will grant them repentance (2 Timothy 2:24-26).

By their fruits you will recognize them. Those whom the Lord sends speak His Word and He gives them the Spirit without limits (John 3:34). Therefore, those who speak against the truth, cannot possibly be Spirit-filled.

BE PERFECT

Can we walk in the Spirit for the rest of our life and never sin again? If the Spirit is "in us" we cannot be controlled by our sinful nature (Romans 8:9). Therefore, there is a point where we cannot sin. That would be perfection.

Can we be perfect? Christians who are in the process of being made holy are already perfect in God's sight (Hebrews 10:14).

Hebrews 10:14
14 For by one offering He has perfected forever those who are being sanctified. NKJV

234

Hebrews 10:14
14 because by one sacrifice he has made perfect forever those who are being made holy. NIV

We have been made holy through Jesus' sacrifice (Hebrews 10:10), but we are also called to be holy in all we do (1 Peter 1:14-15, 1 Thessalonians 4:3-4). Therefore, we are made holy and we should also continue in our faith until we walk in holiness.

In other words, now that we are saved, the Gospel calls us to the sanctifying work of the Spirit and belief in the truth (2 Thessalonians 2:13-15, Romans 8:12-14). The blood of Jesus sanctifies us, and at the same time we are "being made holy" as it is written in Hebrews 10:14 above. Therefore, we are holy in God's sight if we continue in our faith (Colossians 1:21-23), and we are being made holy in our conduct by the Holy Spirit, as we put to death the misdeeds of the body, which is our obligation (Romans 8:12-14).

In the same way, we were made perfect through the sacrifice of Jesus, and we are also called to be perfect. As it is written, "Be perfect just as your Heavenly Father is perfect" (Matthew 5:48).

By faith, we will be perfect in God's sight once we are never at fault in what we say (James 3:2). Those who speak in line with the faith and never speak against the faith, are righteous by faith (Romans 10:6-10, 1 Corinthians 2:7, 13). Check the verses. The only way to change the tongue is to change the heart, and the only way to change the heart is to force the Word of God to remain in it (Matthew 12:33-37, 13:18-23). This is discussed in chapter 2).

The Apostle Paul wanted everyone he taught to be perfect. He told the Galatians that he would be in great pain until Christ was formed in them (Galatians 4:19). He told the Thessalonians that he wanted to make perfect whatever was lacking in their faith (1 Thessalonians 3:10), and that he wanted to present them blameless at Christ's coming (1 Thessalonians 5:23).

He warned and taught everyone with a desire that they would eventually be perfect in Christ (Colossians 1:26-29 below).

Colossians 1:26-29
26 the mystery which has been hidden from ages and from
generations, but now has been revealed to His saints. 27 To
them God willed to make known what are the riches of the
glory of this mystery among the Gentiles: which is Christ
in you, the hope of glory. 28 Him we preach, warning every
man and teaching every man in all wisdom, that we may
present every man perfect in Christ Jesus. 29 To this end I
also labor, striving according to His working which works in
me mightily. NKJV

Colossians 1:26-29
26 the mystery that has been kept hidden for ages and
generations, but is now disclosed to the saints. 27 To
them God has chosen to make known among the Gentiles
the glorious riches of this mystery, which is Christ in you,
the hope of glory. 28 We proclaim him, admonishing and
teaching everyone with all wisdom, so that we may present
everyone perfect in Christ. 29 To this end I labor, struggling
with all his energy, which so powerfully works in me. NIV

If the Spirit of Christ is the one controlling us can we be perfect? With Christ Jesus in us our hope is returning to the glory of God (verse 27 above). Would Christ in us promote sin or lead us into sinning (Galatians 2:17)? If the Spirit of Christ was "in" us would we continue in sin (Romans 8:9)? If Christ is in us we cannot be in the flesh (Romans 8:9-11, John 14:21-23).

Everything the Apostle Paul did, including all the signs and wonders that followed him, were done by Christ in Him for the purpose of making the people obedient (Romans 15:18-19). Signs and wonders for any other purpose other than the glory of God are used for the wrong reasons (Matthew 24:24, 2 Thessalonians 2:9-10, John 7:18, Colossians 2:18-19). Check the verses.

The Apostle Paul told the Corinthians that every act of disobedience would receive its due, once their obedience was complete (2 Corinthians 10:6). He warned them that when he returned, God may humble him

236

among them, and that he would mourn over those who had not repented of sins that lead to death (2 Corinthians 12:20-21). In other words, the Apostle Paul was trying to lead everyone into being perfect, but he warned them that there may come a point where God would say enough is enough (Revelation 22:11). I believe that we are very close to that time today (Romans 11:25).

THE BATTLEGROUND

There are two laws in our inner being; "God's law," and the "law of sin" (Romans 7:21-25 below). The "law of sin" continually wars against our mind through our sinful desires.

Romans 7:19-25
19 For the good that I will to do, I do not do; but the evil I will not to do, that I practice. 20 Now if I do what I will not to do, it is no longer I who do it, but sin that dwells in me. 21 I find then a law, that evil is present with me, the one who wills to do good. 22 For I delight in the law of God according to the inward man. 23 But I see another law in my members, warring against the law of my mind, and bringing me into captivity to the law of sin which is in my members. 24 O wretched man that I am! Who will deliver me from this body of death? 25 I thank God through Jesus Christ our Lord! So then, with the mind I myself serve the law of God, but with the flesh the law of sin. NKJV

Romans 7:19-25
19 For what I do is not the good I want to do; no, the evil I do not want to do this I keep on doing. 20 Now if I do what I do not want to do, it is no longer I who do it, but it is sin living in me that does it. 21 So I find this law at work: When I want to do good, evil is right there with me. 22 For in my inner being I delight in God's law; 23 but I see another law at work in the members of my body, waging war against the law of my mind and making me a prisoner of the law of sin at work within my members. 24 What a

wretched man I am! Who will rescue me from this body of death? 25 Thanks be to God through Jesus Christ our Lord! So then, I myself in my mind am a slave to God's law, but in the sinful nature a slave to the law of sin. NIV

With the mind we serve God and with our flesh we serve our sinful nature (verse 25 above). Our mind is trying to force our body to serve God, and at the same time, our sinful nature is trying to kill us through it's desires and the destruction that follows (Galatians 6:7-10).

That's why we force our body to become a slave of righteousness rather than a slave of sin (Romans 6:17-18). When we want to do good, but we do evil instead, the "law of sin" is controlling our body through it's desires.

When you tried to stop thinking earlier in this chapter, it was your sinful nature's desires that kept wanting you to move. It keeps you busy doing what the world is doing. There is nothing wrong with checking your email, but what is the motive, and why can't it wait (1 Corinthians 4:5, Romans 2:16, James 4:1-3, 1 Chronicles 8:9)?

Anything can be used for good and evil, but you may have to take a break from the things that control you in order to stop them. Periodically I will force myself to do without something, if I feel that it has gained control over me. Fasting can be used for this purpose.

This should be used as a wake up call. We have to force ourselves to do good, and the only reason why we would not be able to, is because we are caught up in sin (covered in previous chapters).

Walking in the Spirit rescues us from the "law of sin" (Romans 7:24-8:8), since we sift through our thoughts in order to demolish the suggestions of our sinful nature (2 Corinthians 10:3-5, Romans 8:5-8). We cannot follow whatever enters our thinking, or do what we want until we have tested it against the knowledge of God (Galatians 5:17). In this way, the law of the Spirit, which is keeping our minds on the things that please the Spirit, sets us free from the law of sin (Romans 8:2), which wars in our mind (Romans 7:23, 1 Peter 2:11).

The battleground is in our mind. If we wait until Sunday morning to fight, I'm afraid that we will lose, since the battle doesn't stop until we submit to God's ways and resist the devil (James 4:4-7). We can't do that only once a week. It has to be done everyday.

Think about this. Here is the reason why most people cannot clear their mind. They don't have time for God. What amount of time do you spend focused on godly things per week? Sinful desires make war against your life, and you have to stop them (1 Peter 2:11, Ephesians 4:22-23, Romans 13:14 below). Let that sink in. The fun lasts for a few minutes, but eternity lasts forever.

1 Peter 2:11
11 Beloved, I beg you as sojourners and pilgrims, abstain from fleshly lusts which war against the soul, NKJV

1 Peter 2:11
11 Dear friends, I urge you, as aliens and strangers in the world, to abstain from sinful desires, which war against your soul. NIV

Ephesians 4:22
22 that you put off, concerning your former conduct, the old man which grows corrupt according to the deceitful lusts. NKJV

Ephesians 4:22
22 You were taught, with regard to your former way of life, to put off your old self, which is being corrupted by its deceitful desires. NIV

Romans 13:14
14 But put on the Lord Jesus Christ, and make no provision for the flesh, to fulfill its lusts. NKJV

Romans 13:14
14 Rather, clothe yourselves with the Lord Jesus Christ, and do not think about how to gratify the desires of the sinful nature. NIV

Once a sinful desire is conceived (visualized, imagined, pictured) it gives birth to sin (James 1:15). Therefore, we can sin in our minds. It doesn't have to be physical. We don't have to physically commit murder (Matthew 5:21-22), or adultery in order to sin (Matthew 5:27-30 below).

Matthew 5:27-30
27 "You have heard that it was said to those of old, 'You shall not commit adultery.' 28 But I say to you that whoever looks at a woman to lust for her has already committed adultery with her in his heart. 29 If your right eye causes you to sin, pluck it out and cast it from you; for it is more profitable for you that one of your members perish, than for your whole body to be cast into hell. 30 And if your right hand causes you to sin, cut it off and cast it from you; for it is more profitable for you that one of your members perish, than for your whole body to be cast into hell. NKJV

Matthew 5:27-30
27 "You have heard that it was said, 'Do not commit adultery.' 28 But I tell you that anyone who looks at a woman lustfully has already committed adultery with her in his heart. 29 If your right eye causes you to sin, gouge it out and throw it away. It is better for you to lose one part of your body than for your whole body to be thrown into hell. 30 And if your right hand causes you to sin, cut it off and throw it away. It is better for you to lose one part of your body than for your whole body to go into hell. NIV

By those standards, I would say that many Christians commit adultery several times even before church service is over, and never repent of it. All the spirit of disobedience has to do is to send a worldly Christian to church half-dressed and all who walk according to the flesh will fall, since their mind is set on the flesh (Romans 8:5-8, 2 Corinthians 10:3-5).

Ignorance of the truth is what keeps them in destruction (Hosea 4:6). They have no idea that their eyes can fill their whole body with darkness

(Luke 11:34-36).

All the enemy has to do in order to keep us in defeat is to have one of his disciples send us explicit texts, dirty jokes, or picture messages in order to keep our minds occupied with sin (Ephesians 5:3-7). The Lord knows our thoughts (Psalm 139:4) and we are to forsake them (Isaiah 55:7, Jeremiah 4:14). They defile (pollute) us or make us useless before God (Matthew 15:18-20 below).

Matthew 15:18-20
18 But those things which proceed out of the mouth come from the heart, and they defile a man. 19 For out of the heart proceed evil thoughts, murders, adulteries, fornications, thefts, false witness, blasphemies. 20 These are the things which defile a man, but to eat with unwashed hands does not defile a man." NKJV

Matthew 15:18-20
18 But the things that come out of the mouth come from the heart, and these make a man 'unclean.' 19 For out of the heart come evil thoughts, murder, adultery, sexual immorality, theft, false testimony, slander. 20 These are what make a man 'unclean'; but eating with unwashed hands does not make him 'unclean.'" NIV

Cell phones, televisions, computers, and all sorts of electronic gadgets have increased sin to a point where I do not think this world can last much longer. I'm not saying that technology is evil, but years ago we had to secretly travel somewhere in order to commit the same sins that we openly participate in today. Opportunity itself held sin back, but now it is wide open, even during church services.

I believe that if cell phones were collected this Sunday morning, as the people walked in the door of the church, over half the congregation would have dirty pictures, inappropriate text messages, and the like, on their phone. Lord willing, I am wrong about this, but I really don't think so.

We need to rid ourselves of anything that contaminates our body and mind, which would bring our holiness to completion (2 Corinthians

7:1). We need to throw away anything in our house that is against God, or that hinders us from this process (Hebrews 12:1, James 1:21).

You be the judge of your home. If you cannot control yourself on a computer, don't own one. Anything can be used for good or evil, but some movies, books, pictures, and magazines etc., clearly feed our sinful nature. Get rid of them.

At times I have to sing "Jesus loves me" in order to refocus my mind once it focuses on something that I know is wrong, or after I accidently see something that I am not supposed to see. A friend of mine sings Jesus loves me to the tune of Gilligan's Island, which totally clears away anything that isn't supposed to be there. Try that and see if it works, assuming that you are not a slave to sin (covered in previous chapters).

The spirits of a person are subject to that person (1 Corinthians 14:27, 31, 32), unless they have been given over to sin's control. Therefore, although God's law is in our mind, it is still subject to the law of the mind, which basically says that whatever a man's mind is set on, that is the direction he is headed (Romans 8:5-8). People of this world set their mind on the things of this world (Ephesians 2:1-3), and the people of God the things of God (Romans 8:4-8).

There needs to be a big sign placed in every city that says, "Whatever your mind is set on, that is the direction you are headed in." "It's the law of the mind that works whether you know it or not." "Therefore, the little things you see, read, and hear that fill your mind with desires are not as harmless as they may seem."

Practice fighting in your mind against evil thoughts, and put the Word of God in daily, like it is the most important thing you do, because it is. It doesn't happen overnight, but it works for those who are "in Christ." Absolutely nothing you do can compare to knowing the Lord through His Word (Philippians 3:7-8).

INNER CIRCLE OF RIGHTEOUSNESS

There is an inner circle that few know about today, written in Romans 8:1-4 below, and we should be striving to enter it. I want you to read the following verses over and over a few times, since most people have spoken against them. Then I want you to answer the questions below concerning these scriptures.

Romans 8:1-4
1 There is therefore now no condemnation to those who are in Christ Jesus, who do not walk according to the flesh, but according to the Spirit. 2 For the law of the Spirit of life in Christ Jesus has made me free from the law of sin and death. 3 For what the law could not do in that it was weak through the flesh, God did by sending His own Son in the likeness of sinful flesh, on account of sin: He condemned sin in the flesh, 4 that the righteous requirement of the law might be fulfilled in us who do not walk according to the flesh but according to the Spirit. NKJV

Romans 8:1-4
1 Therefore, there is now no condemnation for those who are in Christ Jesus, 2 because through Christ Jesus the law of the Spirit of life set me free from the law of sin and death. 3 For what the law was powerless to do in that it was weakened by the sinful nature, God did by sending his own Son in the likeness of sinful man to be a sin offering. And so he condemned sin in sinful man, 4 in order that the righteous requirements of the law might be fully met in us, who do not live according to the sinful nature but according to the Spirit. NIV

Why is there no condemnation for those who are "in Christ?" Walking in the Spirit stops us from committing sins that bring about our death. The law of the Spirit is simply to walk in the Spirit, and the law of the Spirit, sets us free from the law of sin and death (you sin you die, Ezekiel chapter 18, Romans 7:5-12).

Therefore, those who do not walk in the Spirit still have condemnation in them. We have to walk in the Spirit in order to be set free from the law of sin and death. Read the verses above again and ask yourself if it is just for those who are "in Christ," or if we have to be "in Christ" and walk according to the Spirit?

Romans 8:1 from the NKJV above has "who do not walk according to the flesh, but according to the Spirit" written, which clearly shows that we can be "in Christ," but still have condemnation in us.

The NIV places this part of that verse at the bottom of the page in the footnotes. However, the word "because" in verse 2 above clearly gives the reason why there is no condemnation for those who are "in Christ;" The law of the Spirit of life sets them free from the law of sin and death. The law of the Spirit is to simply keep our minds set on spiritual things, which is walking in the Spirit.

According to verse 4 above, the righteous requirements of the Law are fully met in whom? Both versions include walking or living according to the Spirit. Therefore, even though it is taken out of verse one in some Bibles, it is still a requirement according to verse 4 and verse 2 in all Bibles.

We have to walk in the Spirit in order to fulfill the righteous requirement of the Laws of Moses. It's how we put to death the misdeeds of the body through the Spirit according to Romans 8:12-14.

We are debtors (obligated) to live according to the Spirit (Romans 8:12-14). That means it is not an option. The sons of God live according to the Spirit, and in doing so they put to death the desires of the flesh (Romans 8:12-14). Those who live according to their sinful desires will die (Romans 6:23, 8:6, 8:12-14,). This way the law of the Spirit sets us free from the law of sin and death (Romans 8:2 above).

When a Spirit-filled Christian desires something sinful, and refuses to put those thoughts to death, it goes against his conscience and it grieves the Holy Spirit. Fighting the good fight of faith, includes holding on to faith and a good conscience toward God (1 Timothy 1:18-19, 3-5).

Therefore, we have an inner circle. Draw a big circle on a piece of paper to help you understand this. Inside that circle draw another circle, and inside that one draw a third circle. Now we have three circles inside one another.

Outside of the large circle write, "Unsaved people." Inside the large circle write, "Saved into the Kingdom of Christ," and inside of the next smallest circle write, "In the Kingdom of God." Everyone within the large circle is saved, but not all of them are in the Kingdom of God, since not all are born of water and Spirit (John 3:5). We have to be born again to be able to see the Kingdom of God (John 3:3). We can be hostile toward God because of our mindset and still be saved (Romans 8:7).

In the inner most circle write, "Walk according to the Spirit." These are the ones who have no condemnation in them, they bear much fruit, and they are pleasing to God. They are living by faith, as described in chapter 2.

This is where all of us want to be in order to receive a rich welcome into the eternal Kingdom (2 Peter 1:10-11). It's not a matter of what we can do at this point, but what we allow the Spirit of Christ to do through us.

Those in the inner circle fulfill the righteous requirements of the Law through faith by walking in the Spirit (Romans 8:4). Please read the verses below, again.

Romans 8:4-8
4 that the righteous requirement of the law might be fulfilled in us who do not walk according to the flesh but according to the Spirit. 5 For those who live according to the flesh set their minds on the things of the flesh, but those who live according to the Spirit, the things of the Spirit. 6 For to be carnally minded is death, but to be spiritually minded is life and peace. 7 Because the carnal mind is enmity against God; for it is not subject to the law of God, nor indeed can be. 8 So then, those who are in the flesh cannot please God. NKJV

Romans 8:4-8
4 in order that the righteous requirements of the law might be fully met in us, who do not live according to the sinful nature but according to the Spirit. 5 Those who live according to the sinful nature have their minds set on what that nature desires; but those who live in accordance with the Spirit have their minds set on what the Spirit desires. 6 The mind of sinful man is death, but the mind controlled by the Spirit is life and peace; 7 the sinful mind is hostile to God. It does not submit to God's law, nor can it do so. 8 Those controlled by the sinful nature cannot please God. NIV

Christians, who have the righteous requirements of the Law fulfilled in them by faith, walk according to the Spirit (verse 4 above), and those who walk according to the Spirit keep their minds on the things above (verses 5-8 above). They are in the inner circle, and have become the righteousness of God (2 Corinthians 5:21).

Every saved person has imputed righteousness (credited to their account), since they believe in the way Abraham believed (Romans 4:22-25). However, the scripture has "not" been fulfilled concerning them (James 2:20-24), which means that they have not passed the testing of their faith for one reason or other. They should be seeking God's Kingdom and His righteousness, which comes by faith, first place in their life, but some people don't know the truth and some reject it (Romans 3:21-26).

This is the same righteousness of God we should be seeking first, which is the same righteousness the Apostle Paul was seeking (Philippians 3:7-9). It comes by faith to those who believe (Romans 3:21-22, James 2:20-26). The action that completes their faith is that they do not walk in darkness (John 12:46). Our faith and actions (deeds in line with faith) work together to complete our faith (James 2:20-26). This is covered in previous chapters.

We can't read Romans 8:1-4 above and say that all Christians have no condemnation in them, since not all Christians walk according to the Spirit. Those who sow to please the Spirit reap eternal life (Galatians 6:8), but not all Christians stop fulfilling the desires of their sinful nature. Not all Christians make every effort to enter through the narrow gate (Luke 13:23-28). Consequently, not all Christians meet the righteous requirements of the Law, but only the righteous make it into the eternal Kingdom of Christ.

It is hard for the righteous to be saved, but only the righteous make it (1 Peter 4:17-19)! Unless our righteousness surpasses that of the Pharisees and the teachers of the Law, we will not enter the Kingdom of Heaven (Matthew 5:20).

There is still a righteous judgment of God coming, but the righteous go free (Romans 4:6-8, Proverbs 10:2). For those who are "in Christ" the Law may be abolished, but God's righteous judgment is still coming (Romans 1:32).

When it comes to eternal salvation, we must obey the Gospel

(Hebrews 5:9, 1 Peter 4:17-19), which means that we have fulfilled the righteous requirement of the Law through faith, rather than by trying to obey all the Laws of Moses (Romans 2:13).

REMAINING IN THE KINGDOM

The Kingdom of Christ will be handed back to God, Who put all things under Christ to begin with, according to 1 Corinthians 15:24-28. Eventually the Kingdom of Christ will be the Kingdom of God, and the eternal Kingdom in Heaven. However, according to the scriptures, some people will be removed from them all.

According to the scriptures, there are some people who will be kicked out of every Kingdom mentioned in the Bible. Not everyone, but some out of all three will be removed.

We know that some in the Kingdom of Christ will make it all the way, since only those who are sinful will be kicked out according to Matthew 13:40-43 below, and even a rich person, who cannot enter the Kingdom of God (Luke 18:23-27), can make it all the way if he is rich in good deeds (1 Timothy 6:17-19). Therefore, some who are only inside the biggest circle, will make it all the way, but certainly there are no losers in the inner circle.

However, those who allow their sinful nature to continue to control them will not enter the eternal Kingdom at the end of the age according to Matthew 13:40-43 below. Jesus gives eternal salvation to those who obey Him (Hebrews 5:9).

Matthew 13:40-43
40 Therefore as the tares are gathered and burned in the fire, so it will be at the end of this age. 41 The Son of Man will send out His angels, and they will gather out of His kingdom all things that offend, and those who practice lawlessness, 42 and will cast them into the furnace of fire. There will be wailing and gnashing of teeth. 43 Then the righteous will shine forth as the sun in the kingdom of their Father. He who has ears to hear, let him hear! NKJV

Matthew 13:40-43
40 "As the weeds are pulled up and burned in the fire, so it will be at the end of the age. 41 The Son of Man will send out his angels, and they will weed out of his kingdom everything that causes sin and all who do evil. 42 They will throw them into the fiery furnace, where there will be weeping and gnashing of teeth. 43 Then the righteous will shine like the sun in the kingdom of their Father. He who has ears, let him hear. NIV

If Christ is in us, then our sinful nature has to go (Galatians 5:24), since Jesus is going to weed out of His Kingdom all who do evil and cause sin (verse 41 above). It's easy to get into the Kingdom of Christ, but we have to allow Christ to change us. We have to deny ourselves in order to live the Christian life (Matthew 16:24-25). There is no doubt about that.

Abraham's faith was sealed through the sign of circumcision (Genesis 17:9-14, Romans 4:11), and so is ours. The sign that we have been circumcised by Christ is the putting off of our sinful nature (Colossians 2:11). In other words, the sign that our righteousness has been sealed is when we stop sinning.

When Jesus was questioned about those who would be saved, He said to strive to enter, or make every effort to enter by the narrow gate (Luke 13). Many will seek to enter, but not be able. How easy is it to accept Jesus as Lord and yet many will seek to enter, but not be able? He is not talking about being saved into the Kingdom of Christ, but entering the eternal Kingdom.

Luke 13:23-28
23 And someone asked Him, Lord, will only a few be saved (rescued, delivered from the penalties of the last judgment, and made partakers of the salvation by Christ)? And He said to them, 24 Strive to enter by the narrow door [force yourselves through it], for many, I tell you, will try to enter and will not be able. 25 When once the Master of the house gets up and closes the door, and you begin to stand outside and to knock at the door [again and again],

saying, Lord, open to us! He will answer you, I do not know where [what household — certainly not Mine] you come from. 26 Then you will begin to say, We ate and drank in Your presence, and You taught in our streets. 27 But He will say, I tell you, I do not know where [what household — certainly not Mine] you come from; depart from Me, all you wrongdoers! 28 There will be weeping and grinding of teeth when you see Abraham and Isaac and Jacob and all the prophets in the kingdom of God, but you yourselves being cast forth (banished, driven away). AMP

Luke 13:23-28
23 Someone asked him, "Lord, are only a few people going to be saved?" He said to them, 24 "Make every effort to enter through the narrow door, because many, I tell you, will try to enter and will not be able to. 25 Once the owner of the house gets up and closes the door, you will stand outside knocking and pleading, 'Sir, open the door for us.' "But he will answer, 'I don't know you or where you come from.' 26 "Then you will say, 'We ate and drank with you, and you taught in our streets.' 27 "But he will reply, 'I don't know you or where you come from. Away from me, all you evildoers!' 28 "There will be weeping there, and gnashing of teeth, when you see Abraham, Isaac and Jacob and all the prophets in the kingdom of God, but you yourselves thrown out. NIV

Notice that Jesus says in verse 28, "and yourselves thrown out;" thrown out of the Kingdom of God! According to those verses, a person can be removed from the Kingdom of God also. Many quote Luke 17:20-21 and say that the Kingdom of God is in us, and praise God for that. However, now that we are in the Kingdom of Christ and the Kingdom of God, we need to make sure that we remain at the end of the age.

Do your personal desires conflict with what Jesus wants to do through you? Sometimes they do, and that is when you are asked to deny yourself. Knowing the scriptures makes denying ourselves a higher priority.

Whoever loses his life for the Lord will save it. Those who live should live for Him who died (2 Corinthians 5:14-15). Now that we are saved, it is all about remaining or continuing in God's kindness (Romans 11:22, John 15:1-6).

Romans 11:22
22 Therefore consider the goodness and severity of God: on those who fell, severity; but toward you, goodness, if you continue in His goodness. Otherwise you also will be cut off. NKJV

Romans 11:22
22 Consider therefore the kindness and sternness of God: sternness to those who fell, but kindness to you, provided that you continue in his kindness. Otherwise, you also will be cut off. NIV

According to Matthew 8:12 (not shown), some of the "sons of the Kingdom' will be cast out of the Kingdom of Heaven. Check it! In Matthew chapter 22 below, a man made it all the way to the wedding feast in the Kingdom of Heaven, but he did not have on wedding clothes (Matthew 22:12). Consequently, he was thrown out into outer darkness (Matthew 22:11-14 below). Fine linen, or white linen stands for the righteous acts of the saints (Revelation 19:8). Check it!

Matthew 22:11-14
11 But when the king came in to view the guests, he looked intently at a man there who had on no wedding garment. 12 And he said, Friend, how did you come in here without putting on the [appropriate] wedding garment? And he was speechless (muzzled, gagged). 13 Then the king said to the attendants, Tie him hand and foot, and throw him into the darkness outside; there will be weeping and grinding of teeth. 14 For many are called (invited and summoned), but few are chosen. AMP

Matthew 22:11-14
11 "But when the king came in to see the guests, he noticed a man there who was not wearing wedding clothes.12 'Friend,' he asked, 'how did you get in here without wedding clothes?' The man was speechless.13 "Then the king told the attendants, 'Tie him hand and foot, and throw him outside, into the darkness, where there will be weeping and gnashing of teeth.' 14 "For many are invited, but few are chosen." NIV

Again, the Bible tells us what the Kingdom of Heaven is like in Matthew chapter 25:14-30. A servant of the Lord did not use the talents that were given to him, but hid them in the ground. When the Lord came to settle accounts, the lazy servant made excuses as to why he did not use what was given to him by the Lord. Therefore, the Lord judged him by his own words, his talents were taken from him, and he was cast into outer darkness (Matthew 25:28-30 below).

Matthew 25:28-30
28 So take the talent away from him and give it to the one who has the ten talents. 29 For to everyone who has will more be given, and he will be furnished richly so that he will have an abundance; but from the one who does not have, even what he does have will be taken away. 30 And throw the good-for-nothing servant into the outer darkness; there will be weeping and grinding of teeth. AMP

Matthew 25:28-30
28 "'Take the talent from him and give it to the one who has the ten talents. 29 For everyone who has will be given more, and he will have an abundance. Whoever does not have, even what he has will be taken from him. 30 And throw that worthless servant outside, into the darkness, where there will be weeping and gnashing of teeth.' NIV

Will these things not come true? They are written, Jesus spoke them

251

and therefore, they cannot fail (Isaiah 55:10).

What we are accomplishing now by walking in the Spirit so that we will bear the fruits of the Spirit, is guaranteeing us a rich welcome into the eternal Kingdom (2 Peter 1:5-11). We are striving to enter through the narrow gate.

BLASPHEMY AGAINST THE SPIRIT

Blasphemy against the Spirit is unforgivable (Matthew 12:31-32 below).

Matthew 12:31-32
31 Therefore I tell you, every sin and blasphemy (every evil, abusive, injurious speaking, or indignity against sacred things) can be forgiven men, but blasphemy against the [Holy] Spirit shall not and cannot be forgiven. 32 And whoever speaks a word against the Son of Man will be forgiven, but whoever speaks against the Spirit, the Holy One, will not be forgiven, either in this world and age or in the world and age to come. AMP

Matthew 12:31-32
31 And so I tell you, every sin and blasphemy will be forgiven men, but the blasphemy against the Spirit will not be forgiven. 32 Anyone who speaks a word against the Son of Man will be forgiven, but anyone who speaks against the Holy Spirit will not be forgiven, either in this age or in the age to come. NIV

Please allow me to warn you to speak only what you know to be true, and not to just say what you assume to be correct. The Bible says that in the last days people will follow deceiving spirits and things taught by demons (1 Timothy 4:1). One sure way not to follow the teachings of deceiving spirits and demons is to only speak what is written.

These are the last days and these deceiving spirits are out there teaching through unsuspecting people. If you can tell the difference between the Word and what people want to hear, then you are safe (2

Timothy 4:1-4). However, if you have not offered your body in holiness to God and renewed your mind with the truth, then you can be deceived (Ephesians 4:13-14).

There are numerous mumbo-jumbo spiritual sayings being tossed around this day and age. If one person says something that sounds good, and gets the crowd going, then the next person quotes him without knowing that he is speaking directly against scripture. Before long it snowballs and everybody is quoting it.

For example, "All our righteous acts are as filthy rags" when it is spoken in such a way as to imply "everyone's righteous acts" and not just those who continue in sin. This false teaching implies that righteous acts have no value. This is discussed in chapter 3.

"Once saved always saved," when it is spoken in such a way as to say that everyone who calls Jesus "Lord" is going to Heaven, or in such a way as to imply that we do not need to seek God's righteousness and Kingdom after we accept Jesus as Lord. Those who call on the name of the Lord are saved, but all who call on Him, must turn away from wickedness (2 Timothy 2:19).

"You are the righteousness of God," spoken without the word "might" when quoting 2 Corinthians 5:21, or spoken in such a way as to omit Galatians 5:5. Both imputed righteous, justification through deeds, and faith (James 2:24) have to be explained when teaching on righteousness. Faith is also a condition of continued justification (Hebrews 10:37-39).

The seal of our righteousness is the putting off of our sinful nature (Colossians 2:11, Romans 4:). Abraham was justified before circumcision (Romans 4:10), and then he received the sign of circumcision, which is the seal of righteousness by faith (Romans 4:11-12). Those who are heirs are righteous through faith (Romans 4:13). This is discussed in chapter 4.

"You have all the faith you will ever need." "Jesus did it all." "You are kept by the power of God unto salvation," and so on. There are too many misinterpretations to mention in this book, but know that they are out there and most of them use words like "we," "us," and "Christians" to imply that a particular promise is meant for everyone. Those are the simplest ones to detect. The others are going to take knowledge (Ephesians 4:13-14) that comes through our sacrifice (Romans 12:1-2, 2 Timothy 2:15, Hebrews 5:11).

Can blaspheming the Word of God be the same as blaspheming the Spirit, since the Spirit is the Word (John 6:63)? Think about that. Do not to go beyond or think beyond what is written (1 Corinthians 4:6-7). Test and verify everything you hear (1 Thessalonians 5:21). This is a safeguard for us in order that we will not blaspheme the Holy Spirit in saying that He is doing something when it could actually be a deceiving spirit instead.

If you have blasphemed the Word of God in ignorance, then ask the Lord to forgive you. The Apostle Paul was forgiven for blasphemy because he did it in ignorance (1 Timothy 1:13).

If you have questions, I am a servant. I can be found on the internet through my website for this book or by simply Google searching my name, Alan P. Ballou. Please read the entire book, since many questions will be answered through it, Lord willing. May the Lord bless you.

http://www.howtostopsinning.com
http://www.howtostopsinning.org

ABOUT THE AUTHOR

Alan Ballou is a servant of the Lord, author, and Bible teacher. He conducts seminars and teaches at church events, small group meetings, homeless shelters, over the internet, and from house to house. He serves Christians, who contact him from all over the world, in matters concerning deliverance and healing, free of charge.

Alan and his wife Lucie work as a team, serving the Lord, and make their home in Inman, South Carolina.

For more information, questions, concerns, or help with stopping sin, please contact Alan or Lucie at HowToStopSinning.com.

www.ingramcontent.com/pod-product-compliance
Lightning Source LLC
LaVergne TN
LVHW011345080426
835511LV00005B/140